"I think there are too many experts. The politicians rely on the so-called forest experts — the foresters, the graduates. People like ourselves, ordinary citizens, can't question forest policy because they say right away, 'Ah! That's a technical problem.' Before you talk about technical matters you have to talk about principles and the fundamental questions of control over the resource."

—*Euclide Chiasson, woodlot owner, Petit-Rocher, N.B.*

Cut and Run

THE ASSAULT ON CANADA'S FORESTS

**JAMIE
SWIFT**

between the lines

© 1983 by Between The Lines

Published by: Between The Lines,
427 Bloor Street West,
Toronto, Ontario

Typeset by: Dumont Press Graphix,
97 Victoria Street North,
Kitchener, Ontario

Printed by: The Alger Press Limited,
Oshawa, Ontario

Book design by Margie Bruun-Meyer
Cover design by Margie Bruun-Meyer and Rosemary Donegan

Between The Lines receives financial assistance
from the Ontario Arts Council and Canada Council.

Canadian Cataloguing in Publication Data:

Swift, Jamie, 1951 -
Cut and run

ISBN 0-919946-30-5 (bound). — ISBN 0-919946-31-3 (pbk.)

1. Forests and forestry — Canada. 2. Forest reserves — Canada.
I. Title.
SD145.S94   634.9′0971   C83-094179-7

Contents

1

Wherein we find that, despite what might appear most bountiful and healthy to the casual eye, the woods are not succeeding as they should. And we are introduced to that formidable science, silviculture.

2

How the Canadian native peoples regarded the forest as a well-spring of creation, to be used but also cherished. And how the Europeans saw the forest as a wild domain to be pushed back and back; or as a profitable empire offering a stream of magnificent sawlogs, neverending.

3

In which some industrious businesspeople, having considered the angles — or perhaps some of them — confirm that money does indeed grow on trees. And how business and government, working together, decided to let the chips fall where they may.

4

Wherein we witness the demise of old style logging, not much mourned by its inheritor, the integrated forest products firm. And how it came about that, once most of the good trees were gone, we decided it was time to conserve — even do a little treeplanting. At the same time, when the cry for renewal goes up, we discover that well-meaning policies — sustained yield, annual allowable cut, tree farm licences — don't necessarily bark up the right tree.

For Jane

A feller-buncher — one modern method of cutting timber for Canada's most important industry.

Preface

OST CANADIANS, if they consider the forest at all, probably regard it as a kind of undifferentiated mass starting somewhere outside the town or city where they live and stretching on and on to a vague location somewhere in the north. If they've travelled any distance by airplane, they may sometimes get the feeling that this country is 90 per cent trees and lakes, and the rest rocks. It's an image that can quickly be reinforced by a drive through the country's forested regions, where the highway appears to be a minor human intrusion into nature's impenetrable wall of green. The wilderness seems more than ample. In a way, it's overpowering, an important contributor to the development of national myths — the inspiration for painters, poets and other cultural iconographers. The retreat for the harried city-dweller fleeing rampant industrialism.

Yet the forest offers human society more than inspiration. It helps to filter the air we breathe and the water we drink. It provides a habitat for wildlife and an anchor for the soil, offers recreational and aesthetic values that are hard to quantify. And of course its trees are used to provide the paper for books like this one, as well as for newspapers, packaging, tissues and towels. Its wood can be used to frame houses, to build furniture, to make hockey sticks and toys.

But the most significant fact about the forest is that it has the potential to keep on providing its aesthetic and material benefits forever. Unlike some other natural resources, such as coal, copper or oil, the forest is renewable. This is something to deliberate upon in an era of resource scarcity, at a time we're told that the world's resources are fast being depleted. Where else can we turn to find both a constant supply of raw material for a vital national industry and a place to enjoy as a refuge from the frenetic pace of urban life? The possibilities are apparently limitless.

Unfortunately, although the opportunities are seemingly limitless, the forest itself is not — even though it has been treated as such for nearly two hundred years. That contradiction is what this book is about. *Cut and Run* explores both the ways the forest has been handled and, more importantly, why there has developed an institutionalized lack of concern for all the benefits it has to offer.

The word "assault" in this book's subtitle was also employed nearly a half-century ago in Canadian historian A.R.M. Lower's analysis of how business had operated since the beginning of the lumber industry.[1] At that time Lower talked about a cut-and-get-out ethic. In *Cut and Run* we see that things have not really changed. Indeed, as technological changes and growing demand have driven forest products companies further into the wilderness, further from centres of consumption, the principal alteration has been in the accelerated pace of forest depletion. The result has been a widely-acknowledged crisis of wood supply for what is arguably Canada's single most important industry. At a major forest congress in Toronto in 1980, sponsored by the Canadian Pulp and Paper Association, Royal Bank of Canada president Rowland Frazee warned: "Years of complacency and shortsightedness are now coming home to roost. Already there are wood shortages in some parts of Canada." Frazee's comments were echoed by Charles Carter, head of the Canadian Pacific-controlled Great Lakes Forest Products, who pointed to a basic fact of life in the Canadian forest products industry — that there are virtually no large tracts of untouched forest remaining in economically-accessible range in this country.[2]

These admittedly self-interested members of the Canadian capitalist establishment are not ones to shout "fire" when no smoke is to be seen on the horizon. Frazee, head of the country's largest bank, concluded that we may soon run out of trees and added: "This may seem incredible to Canadians who live surrounded by one of the world's most massive forest areas." It may indeed be difficult to believe, but by all accounts it is happening.

The tendency to disregard the future benefits of the forest in a shortsighted scramble for present gain is nothing new. In the fourth century B.C. Plato lamented the fate of the forests in the Athenian hinterland: "There are mountains in Attica which can now keep nothing but bees, but which were clothed, not so very long ago, with fine trees producing timber suitable for roofing the largest buildings, and roofs hewn from this timber are still in existence. . . . The annual supply of rainfall was not lost, as it is at present, through being allowed to flow over a denuded surface to the sea."[3]

Capitalist business economics, as it operates in twentieth-century Canada, has a way of treating the forest that in essence differs little from the approach of the ancient Greeks. The costs of degrading the forest are borne by the community at large: Future generations inherit the burden of a depleted resource and the environmental side-effects that come from treating the forest as a free gift of nature. Students of the relationship between economics and ecology have frequently pointed to the manner in which clean air and clean water have been treated as "externalities" by business. That is, these elements of the natural world are furnished free of charge and do not enter corporate bookkeeping systems. The costs of pollution and dissipation of air and water tend to be shouldered by society as a whole. They thus take the form of *social costs*.[4]

Wood fibre from Canada's forests is not exactly taken free of charge by the forest products companies. In most cases, business pays the government for the right to cut wood on Crown land. Government, for its part, attempts to extract as much revenue as it can from the forest, usually without reinvesting in the future of the resource. In this way business and government together have treated the forest as a gift of nature, a source of wood fibre and tax revenue. The social costs incurred remain as debts unpaid. They take the form of denuded timberland unfit for wood production, and of ghost towns — communities with too few trees to supply their mills.

Capitalism operates with a well-ordered system of priorities, chief among which are profitability and perpetual expansion. Government shares these priorities, facilitating wherever possible the cycle of growth. In the case of the forest, its potential for renewal tends to be ignored, lost in the endless spiral of production and accumulation. It is not that these major social institutions are unaware of the implications of proceeding in this fashion. As we will see, the alarm bells have been sounding since before the beginning of this century. It is simply a matter of the future of the forest not entering into the economic equation.

In 1950, well before environmental issues were popularized, K.W. Kapp explained how ecology and economics, pollution and profit, are inextricably linked. In his book, *The Social Costs of Private Enterprise*,* Kapp summed up a basic theme of the present volume. He noted with reference to renewable resources that what he referred to as the "price system" fails because:

> It cannot take account of social benefits and hence fails to avoid or minimize the social costs borne by third persons or society as a whole and it has a tendency to accelerate the rate of use of resources, thereby shifting utilization from the future to the present due to a general tendency to maximize current profits and to minimize current costs. That this may be the road to maximum future costs and minimum future benefits is either tacitly ignored or openly denied by those who put their trust in the price system.[5]

Two years ago a forest industry representative made a statement which, though doubtless causing industry public relations people to cringe, is to be admired for its basic honesty. He confirmed the basic attitude of those who put their faith in the price system: "If we cannot make money, then the forest is not worth anything."[6]

Such a singular view of nature is unlikely to be shared by most Canadians who, if we are to heed prominent advertising images, see the forest in a different light. Advertisers realize how potent forest and wilderness images can be, especially when communicated to city-dwellers. So they mould their imagery accordingly. "Nature" and "natural" have become clichés in the advertising lexicon. A typical commercial in one of the most competitive sales areas, beer marketing, shows a male worker "cutting out" of his weekly drudgery, donning his checked, lumberjack-style shirt and heading off for a weekend's fishing with "the boys". There is the rustic camp, the case of twenty-four, few machines or appliances in sight and a definite aura of roughing it in the bush.

---

*The book was retitled *The Social Costs of Business Enterprise* in 1963 after the author decided that state enterprises in state socialist societies tend to be guided by essentially the same principles governing capitalist enterprise.

Then there was the Bombardier snowmobile TV commercial, which told us how we could become liberated, in touch with the wilds:

> Well, we've still got the country
> We've still got the sunshine
> We've still got the trails and the trees
> Moving, running full
> Got the good times,
> We've still got Ski-Doo.

The following pages attempt to explain how the forest that provides the backdrop for these images has been systematically abused. In doing this, the book's subject-matter ranges from the history of Canadian forest management and exploitation through public policy and the timber resource, technological changes in logging and their effects, forest ecology and the techniques of forest management to finally, and perhaps most importantly, ways in which economic and political forces have determined how the country's forests have been treated.

But, although I've attempted to study forest concerns on a national basis and introduce the reader to the basic issues, what has emerged in the end is neither meant to be an all-inclusive forestry textbook nor a lurid exposé of industrial and government practices. I have not been able to cover equally, for instance, the forest situation in all provinces. What does emerge, I hope, is a general analysis of the politics of forestry in Canada and a discussion of the path we might follow if the present course is to be altered, if the future is not simply to mirror the past.

ALTHOUGH THE PRINCIPAL protagonist in this story is the forest, trees cannot speak for themselves. So the account here is based to a large extent on the words and experiences of some sixty people familiar with the forest and with the institutions most directly affecting this resource. Many of these people are professional foresters, others have lived and worked in close proximity to the forest. Only some of them appear in the book but they all played an invaluable role in its completion, and I thank them for assisting a novice in gaining an understanding of the issues. Ken Hearnden, Ross Silversides and George Marek were especially patient and generous in answering my constant inquiries.

Among others who assisted along the way were Ian Radforth, Peter Gillis and Rod Hay, who all shared their own research on the forest industry. Dorothy Wigmore was a source of new ideas and contacts. Bob MacArthur provided examples of industry self-image. Yolande McArthur, Kim Gallant and John Ford stood out among a number of librarians and archivists — an important group all too frequently omitted from acknowledgments in research projects.

I'd also like to acknowledge the financial assistance of the Explorations Program of the Canada Council.

This book was completed on a modest budget and its very nature dictated a good deal of travel. I owe a special debt of gratitude to those whose generosity and hospitality made this possible. Some even kindly chauffeured me about in varying conditions of weather and terrain. Kevin Whelton, Karen Ochs, Betty Arseneault, Paul Johnston, Brian Tomlinson, Bridget Rivers-Moore, Jack Schuller, Jim Anderson, Madelaine Lane, Cam Beck, Philip Pedini, Michael Young, Shirley Young, Julian Walker, Caroline Walker, Victor Granholme, Kathryn Fournier and Marianne Janowicz: All these people were helpful hosts. For general assistance, good humour and company I particularly wish to thank Rita Moir, Randy Nelsen and Sandra Steinhause.

Finally, it remains to acknowledge the efforts of the workers — both past and present — at the Development Education Centre and Dumont Press Graphix, people who ultimately made the conception and completion of this project possible. Last but certainly not least were the unflagging editorial efforts of Robert Clarke. It is his book as much as it is mine. Any errors or shortcomings are, as they say, my own (and of course Rob's).

J.S.,
December, 1982

1. Forever Green

GEORGE MAREK HOPS OVER the ditch beside the gravel logging road and plunges into the bush. The thick northern Ontario brush and rough undergrowth don't seem to slow him down. Marek is over sixty years old now but the enthusiasm he brings to his job means you have to scurry along just to keep up with him. Ever since he came to work in the boreal forest from his native Czechoslovakia some thirty years ago, he has been doing what he likes to do best: growing trees. Marek is a silviculturalist, a practising tree farmer.

He finally comes to a halt in what is supposed to be a young crop of white spruce trees, a valuable commercial species neatly planted in tidy, straight rows a few years back. But instead of spruce, Marek finds himself surrounded by a jumble of six-foot-tall skinny poplars, which have sprung up in the time since the spruce seedlings were planted. The competing poplar growth has dwarfed the spruce and Marek is more than a little disgusted with this turn of affairs. He has devoted his career as a government-employed professional forester to promoting the spruce and other species meant to furnish the demands of the north's pulp-based economy. The mills won't take much poplar.

"There was a bunch of young foresters from Lakehead University who cleaned the poplar from this site two years ago," recalls Marek.[1] He seizes a specimen of the offending weed and snaps it off with a vengeance. "We were discussing, just like today as we're standing here, when we would have to come back again. Everybody says, 'Well, it'll be alright for the next five or ten years.' Two years later — look! Look at the poplar!"

Marek surveys the stand as a whole and explains how difficult it is to grow trees in what most of us see as a country blanketed in forest. The white spruce may still be growing but it cannot keep up with the poplar. He points out that nature is very fragile, very unpredictable, and complains that foresters simply do not know enough. After thirty years on the job in one place, Marek is quick to point out that he is still learning. Every trip into the forest brings new surprises about recovery, about the effects of spraying, about the resilience of different forms of plant-life. Marek knows that if he had not initiated the cleaning program with the young forestry students two years ago, his plantation would have been hopeless, a write-off.

This is Crown land but Marek is not enthusiastic about the efforts his employer, the provincial Ministry of Natural Resources, has made to tend the forest. "The ministry has lost millions of acres of plantation because nobody looks after them," he points out. "What you see here gives you an idea of the incredible dynamic of forest sites. One day you think it's alright and the next day you have to change your mind as a new element comes in. Sure there's recovery here, but at different speeds on different sites."

To the uninitiated, Marek's forest plantation, a few miles north of the Trans-Canada highway route hugging the north shore of Lake Superior, looks like a hopeless tangle of underbrush. Hardly a "tree farm". But in more than one sense it does resemble a farm, because growing trees and cultivating agricultural crops involve the same principles of "ecological succession" — the replacement, in time, of one distinctive plant or animal community by another. The most apparent difference is the time frame involved. What might happen in a few days in farming occurs over a period of years in the forest. This is most notable when it comes to weeds — or "weed succession". Where farmers have to watch out for weed growth from day to day, foresters watch from year to year. But at the same time, as Marek says, "Foresters are like farmers in that they have to know when and where to manipulate what. And how to do it."

Indeed, the cultivation of forests for the production of wood, known as "silviculture" (from the Latin *sylva*, meaning wood or woodland), is a science in many ways comparable to agriculture. Foresters and farmers are both concerned with the manipulation of a piece of land and all its biological and environmental elements — its "ecosystem" — in order to secure a desired crop. Once the harvest is in, a farmer has to take action to again secure a crop for the following year, akin to a process of ecological succession. So farmers plough and work the land, apply seed and fertilizer, remove competing weed species and irrigate if necessary. Even the harvest itself becomes part of the way farmers manipulate ecological succession. If corn is not taken off the land, within a few years the fields start to revert to weed species and eventually might even turn into woodlands. So farmers work to make sure this doesn't happen, and to promote the growth of a commercially valuable species.

The goal of a tree farmer is similar. The forester responsible for development of the next crop of commercially valuable trees — in Canada, usually conifers such as spruce, pine or Douglas fir — wants to carry out successional manipulation of the ecosystem to produce that crop of trees in as short a time as possible. The parallel with agriculture is apparent. The forester wants to make sure that new seedlings are in the ground soon after the harvest. Competing "weed" species should be repressed. Adequate nutrients should be available in the soil to stimulate rapid growth. The desired trees should be thinned out periodically to prevent the stand from being starved for sunlight and nutrients. Insects and blight should be held in check.

It would seem to be a simple matter: Plant the trees, see that they survive and reap the harvest when the trees are big enough to have some commercial value. Apparently, all should be well in the woods.

But, in the words of George Marek, the task of doing this work and of managing the country's forests is "a full-time job and nobody wants to do it". It is also an important job, crucial to the Canadian economy as a whole because the forests of the country support what is arguably the nation's top industry.

Less than two weeks after George Marek explained his problems about growing trees in the northern forest, the federal government came out with an important discussion paper on forest sector strategy. In reference to Canada's timber supply the paper warned:

> The evidence is unmistakable. The limits are in sight for premium softwood sawlogs in many locations and supplies of larger, higher quality hardwood logs have become very scarce. Pulpwood shortages are emerging in local commu-

nities across the country. Only a fraction of our forests are being managed for sustained production, even today. And in most cases the timber resource is renewable, both promptly and adequately, only if action is taken following harvest or natural calamity.[2]

Evidently, all is not well in the woods.

FORESTRY AND SILVICULTURE are not simple endeavours that lend themselves well to easy solutions. To most of us, forests appear to be a confusing grab bag of thin trees, thick trees, fallen and half-fallen trees and dense underbrush, all of which may, unfortunately, present an obstacle to a pleasant stroll through the woods. Chaos seems to reign in the tangle of growth. It's a different world from that of the orderly arrangements in a farmer's field or a city park. In a Canadian forest, unless we've been particularly zealous Girl Guides or Boy Scouts at one time, most of us would have trouble naming more than a few of the trees we see. In a tropical rainforest, we would have an impossible time of it. There, even an experienced observer would have difficulty, while standing in one spot, pointing out two examples of the same species of tree, so perplexing is the diversity of growth.

But if we stop to consider the forest it becomes clear of course that there is a certain order present, a scheme of things common to the natural forest in Canada or the tropics, to the park and the field. Each living thing in the forest — plant and animal, balsam and budworm — is part of a highly-organized system. Each part of the system helps to provide food and energy to another. So in the Canadian forest small deciduous trees provide browse for deer to feed upon. The foliage of the trees falls to the ground as litter that gradually decomposes and contributes to the development of the soil. Deer and other animals contribute to soil development by death and defecation. The soil, as it is built up, gives earthworms a place to live and becomes the habitat for nitrogen-fixing bacteria — tiny organisms that give vital nourishment to growing plants. Without elements like nitrogen and phosphorus, trees would have nothing from which to build up organic molecules, the essence of their growth: The chemical bonds linking the atoms of each molecule store the required energy.

As the forest matures and the trees grow in size, the amount of energy stored up in these bonds continues to increase, and the forest develops into a kind of vast energy warehouse. All the living things in the forest are part of the system, manufacturing the energy inventory for the warehouse. Of course the trees are not merely static repositories of energy. As part of the interdependent cycle of natural development, they do their bit by dropping litter to the soil, providing browse for deer and so on and so on. . . .

The energy stored in the warehouse is built up over a very long period of time, particularly in those vast northern areas of Canada where trees grow terribly slowly. In many of these areas, conifers have a growing season of three months or even less. Every young Canadian is taught how to tell the age of a tree by counting the annual growth rings. If you look at the stumps of many of the thin trees now being cut for pulpwood in eastern Canada, you can see dozens upon dozens of these annual growth rings, each contributing only a tiny amount to the overall growth of the tree. By contrast, a glance at a cross-section of some of the monster trees cut from ideal growing sites on the coast of British Columbia, where trees have more nourishment and longer growing seasons, reveals much thicker growth rings.

But while yearly tree growth (or, in forestry terms, the annual increment) is often painstakingly slow, the release of the energy stored up in the trees can be rapid. A forest fire quickly leaping from crown to crown in a dry coniferous forest is perhaps the best example of this. In a forest fire, energy is released in a hurry as the organic molecules storing that energy are broken down. After a forest fire the gradual process of transforming the resulting inorganic nutrients back into plants and trees begins again.

Of course, all forests do not burn down. Government and industry are concerned with the commercial value represented by the standing timber and the energy stored in it. And they do everything they can to prevent forest fires. We are all reminded, along with every good Boy Scout or Girl Guide, to do our best to prevent forest fires. After all, forest fires cost money, or at least they represent lost revenues.

The introduction of the chain saw in the 1950s boosted worker produc-tivity and intensified the pressure on the forest resource.

So if forests don't always burn down, what happens to them? Generally one of two things. First, they can be cut down and the energy stored in them can be used by human society for one of dozens of purposes. Perhaps surprisingly, the most common use of wood worldwide is still as fuel: Nearly half of all wood felled is quickly burned in order to capture the energy locked up in it. But, second, if trees aren't felled by humans or burned by fire they will continue to grow and the forest will continue to undergo the process of change known as ecological succession.

The term "ecology" conjures up images of sincere and earnest, often bearded, individuals who regularly appear on television to explain the latest disturbing revelations about chemical pollution choking our lakes or despoiling our air. Yet ecology is the study of the relationships of plants and animals to their surroundings, the environment they inhabit. Forests are thus ecological communities, or ecosystems, containing myriad forms of plant and animal life. Since these forms depend on one another for survival, the forest ecosystem is not static and, like human communities, ecological communities are constantly changing. Those who study and observe these changes are the ecologists, just as sociologists study changing human societies.

Forest ecologists have observed that as forests become older and more "mature", the earlier stages of development characterized by distinct plant and animal communities gradually give way to other different communities. This is the process of ecological succession. For example, northern areas in eastern Canada or areas at high elevation in the west may have thin soils and are likely to be subject to extremes of both temperature and moisture. As a result, early on in the process of ecological succession the only plant growth on what may one day be a forest site will probably be hardy lichens and mosses whose ability to withstand these extremes enables them to cling to rocks and survive. As time passes — and in such cases a lot of time is likely to pass — these small plants develop and die in their own cycles. This may produce a thin layer of organic soil, a repository for the moisture and nutrients vital to the development of later stages of plant and animal life. In time enough of this soil accumulates to allow the more rugged shrubs to survive. The roots of these plants cling to the soil and at the same time their falling leaves litter the ground and decay, helping the soil once more. All this helps to speed up the development of the soil so that, after another period of time, trees with the ability to tolerate the climatic extremes begin to take root. At high elevations in British Columbia, a tree adaptable to such conditions might be the lodgepole pine; in northern Ontario it would be the jack pine.

Once the tree species are established, they slowly grow and eventually, if fire or chain saw does not intervene, some may fall and decay. The energy stored in the fallen trees is slowly released back into the ecosystem as needles, branches and trunk deteriorate and become part of the soil. A forest often reaches the point in its development in which one or two species dominate and a kind of harmony or equilibrium is achieved, with the same species comprising both the upper canopy and the young seedlings on the forest floor. Such stands are called "climax forests" and foresters often refer to them as being "over-mature" or even "decadent". This implies that the annual growth, or the production of more wood fibre, has slowed. Such forest communities can become more vulnerable to fire, and if the stand burns the process of ecological succession reverts to square one and the cycle starts again. Alternately, human intervention may occur, in the form of the commercial timber harvest.

When a forest is harvested, the ecological cycle inevitably resumes. Once the biggest trees dominating a stand have been cut, the site reverts to an earlier stage in its ecological development. At this point nature may be allowed to take its course and proceed through the natural stages of succession. Or human intervention in the form of the harvest can be followed by further intervention designed to ensure the quickest possible growth of another "crop" of trees.

THE COMPARISON BETWEEN silviculture and agriculture doesn't always bear up. There are major differences between the two systems and foremost, as mentioned earlier, is time. In a farming effort, a new crop is usually ready for harvest in a matter of months if appropriate measures are taken to keep down the competing weeds and nourish the plants. But as foresters who have been attempting to nurture the growth of trees know very well, it takes a lifetime for a new crop to be ready. Seventy-five years may easily elapse from the time a fragile spruce seedling takes root until it is ready to be cut for commercial timber. Many of the trees being cut by the forest industry in the 1980s are over one hundred years old. And, if little attention is paid to the forest after the trees are cut, the process can be set back for decades. Sometimes the forest site will not revert to the desired species at all.

This time element is crucial to an understanding of forestry from a political and economic as well as as silvicultural perspective. Farmers can gauge their returns from the harvest on an annual basis, whereas forest operators are forced to think in terms of decades. Dr. Marcel Lortie, a professor of forest management at Laval University, considers this necessity for long-term planning to be one of the principal causes of the current forestry malaise. "People who have power are preoccupied with much more short-term objectives," he observes.[3] Lortie is frequently a keynote speaker when foresters and forest industry officials gather to discuss the problems associated with the neglect of the country's forests. He recalls: "When I was a forestry student there were people who said, 'Let's remove all the forest management from the companies because their objective is one year, their budget year.' We found out later that in government the objective is only four years."

Industry — from the timber barons who stripped the Ottawa Valley of its high quality pine in the nineteenth century to the integrated pulp, paper and lumber companies whose annual reports today inevitably feature reassuring colour photos of fresh green seedlings in the ground — has always taken the attitude of cut and get out. To industry, the wood is simply a supply factor for a distant mill, the corporate profit centre. Managers are accountable to shareholders and the board of directors, financially concerned individuals who are concerned with cash flow, rate of return and net income. The future of the forest eight or ten decades down the line simply isn't part of this equation. In any case, industry always argues, the government owns the timberland so it's up to the politicians and public servants to manage the forest for the future.

As forest landlords, governments in Canada have behaved like many other landlords, treating their property as a source of current revenue. It has always been easy to ignore the future of the forest resource, especially when a bright future necessarily depends on expensive programs of continuous and attentive management. Because government has become increasingly large and centralized, and more remote from an ever-retreating forest frontier, it has been a relatively simple matter to procrastinate and to avoid tackling difficult forestry problems. This is especially true if the symptoms now starting to show up in the form of local wood shortages are not to become acute in the near future. The problem is a bit like cancer, a disease with a long latency period whose basic causes can be ignored until epidemic proportions are reached.

As recently as the late 1970s, both provincial and federal governments were putting back into the forest only five cents for every dollar extracted in revenue. Hardly enough, especially when more of what is spent goes for administration than for active silvicultural programs.[4] For government, it is a depressingly simple matter. Better to use the forest as a source of revenue to fuel other, more short-term programs that have a quicker political payoff. The way disgruntled forest advocates usually put it, a government can get into more hot water by refusing to spend money on highly visible educational and social programs than by cutting back on forestry measures. But, it could be asked, how can the future viability of all government spending be assured when the future of such an important resource is being neglected? The question becomes particularly interesting at a time when governments at all levels seem preoccupied with trying to outdo each other in the practice of spending "restraint".

Another emerging question deals with the efficacy of restraint in spending on the future of such a crucial renewable resource.

The forest resource is the cornerstone of an industry that contributes more to Canada's foreign exchange earnings than agriculture, mining, fishing, oil and gas combined.[5] One dollar in seven, or 15 per cent of all value added in manufacturing, is derived from the forest sector. The country's railways would be far less busy if it weren't for the forest industry, because one carload in five is loaded with materials going to or coming from the plants that process the products of the forests.[6] Canada is the world's leading exporter of newsprint and the United States is its biggest customer. Well over half of all the paper used by American newspapers comes from the Canadian forest. In all, Canadian exports account for two-thirds of the world trade in newsprint. In addition, 300 thousand Canadians are employed directly in the forest products industry and, because this industry has relatively strong backward and forward linkages with the rest of the economy, it has been estimated that the sector as a whole accounts for a million jobs in Canada. In other words, one Canadian worker in ten depends on the forest.[7] Many of those directly employed by the forest industry work in single-industry communities strung out across the country from Port Alberni, B.C., to Cornerbrook, Nfld. When the industry slumps, economic activity in these cities grinds to a halt. Similarly, when the wood supply dwindles, people are forced to move out of

Squaring timber with a broad axe. The square timber trade was one of Canada's first staple exports but much of the wood was left to rot on the floor of the forest.

milltowns where there are few, if any, other employment opportunities.

It is a well-worn cliché. Canada as a nation is a hewer of wood. This has been an indisputable fact for nearly two hundred years. For this period the country has relied heavily on the forests as a renewable resource, but the forests have not been treated in a manner which would sustain their renewability. Trees have not been cut with a view to replacing them with a new crop and the practice of silviculture has been ignored; trees have been extracted like ore from a mine or oil from a well. Even though the forests have the potential to keep supplying our needs in perpetuity, they have been neglected to the point that one of the most heavily-forested countries in the world now faces a wood supply crisis.

Marcel Lortie is quite familiar with the *realpolitik* of forestry in Canada. Formerly the director of Environment Canada for Quebec,* Lortie has seen what it's like to be a forest advocate on the inside of the government. And he has learned the limitations and frustrations of that role. "Back in 1966 I was proposing that the best thing might be to keep forest administration out of the public domain. Bring it into something like a Crown Corporation that wouldn't be subjected to periodic changes in policy, to politics as a matter of fact."[8] Lortie seems a trifle wistful when discussing these ideas and the problems he has had in getting them across. "Ever since then I've been trying to work at it," he says. "But you can't remove so much power from the politicians."

There are others who, like Marcel Lortie, are closely associated with the forest scene in Canada and feel differently about the forest. They tend to see the forest as a valuable resource for the future — not just as a source of wood fibre or revenue but as an important economic, recreational, aesthetic and environmental asset. To this way of thinking, the forest constitutes a vital part of both the *economy* and the science of *ecology*. After all, both words spring from the same Greek root — *oikos*, a word meaning a home to which you can return, a place where you are familiar with the environment.

George Marek is one of the few foresters who shares this perspective on the forest and the trees. Standing in the midst of a boreal forest site where he has been trying hard to regenerate a valuable softwood species, Marek talks about his life's work, with a note of distinct enthusiasm. "I feel for a tree. Not just because it's part of me or part of my work. Because I think that without trees we will not exist for very long. I feel very strongly about it," he says emphatically. "In our system — and I'm a defender of it since I don't think it's any better behind the Iron

---

*Currently lumped in with "Environment", forestry in the federal government has at various times been hooked up administratively with the Mines and Grazing branch of the Department of the Interior, the Department of Fisheries, the Department of Mines and Resources as well as Rural Development and even Agriculture before the widespread concern with matters environmental led to the creation of the Department of the Environment in 1971. Forestry was shunted into this new ministry at that time. Provincially, forest matters have usually been looked after by the same department that is charged with public lands and, perhaps appropriately, mines.

Curtain — there is one big factor built in. The system is never wrong. And our system is built on maximizing exploitation today. The system is going to continue to exploit it right down to the last."[9]

Massive timber rafts floated the pine logs downstream. The Ottawa River served as a commercial highway while the river valley was being stripped of its white pine.

2. Quest for Fibre

$\mathcal{J}$HE FORESTS OF CANADA have always provided a basic underpinning for life here. Before it became common for concerned industrialists to fling about statistics on the importance of the paper and allied sector for the nation's balance of trade position, before the country became a nation, before Europeans began to penetrate and then rearrange the landscape, the forests and its products had already performed a vital, sustaining role for many native societies. The forests gave to Indian peoples — most frequently living in subsistence, pre-feudal economies — their basic means of survival, providing everything from food and shelter to clothing and tools. And it had another important dimension in native life, enriching the cultural and spiritual lives of people who conceived of themselves as being at one with nature and the forests.

The hunting and gathering peoples of northeastern North America had to know as much about the properties and uses of wood as they did about the nature of the other plants and the animals of the forest. Wood not only provided fuel and shelter, it also gave Indians the capability of exploiting the other resources of the forests around them. They fashioned hunting tools such as arrows and spears and they developed the art of bending wood without breaking it, a practice that enabled them to fabricate snowshoes and canoes, toboggans and sleds. Using stone or bone tools, they produced baskets and bowls, mats and moosecalls and wooden wedges for splitting logs.

All this was accomplished without the use of metal implements, introduced only in later years by European traders. Nails were unknown, so the tasks of fastening and securing were often accomplished using string made from the inner bark of trees such as elm and basswood. The bark was peeled from the tree in the spring and the inner bark tied into coils, which was boiled in a solution of wood ash lye. After the bark was dried, the fibres could be separated by rasping them through a hole in a bone or a stone. The fibres were then twisted into a strong and durable twine, useful in construction and in the crafting of a multitude of household articles. Forest products played other roles as well, perhaps less appreciated in modern times: For instance, long before the advent of the disposable diaper (derived, we often forget, from wood pulp), the forest gave native people an abundant supply of a soft, clean alternative in the form of the moss from the forest floor.

On the west coast Indians had one of the wealthiest non-agricultural societies ever known, based on use of the profuse cedar trees and the plentiful salmon, that spawned in the streams of the coastal rainforests. They could preserve food in abundance and had enough time left over to carve wood totems and masks, elaborate representations of the spiritual realm. Salmon roe provided an oily base for paints, and animal (often beaver) teeth could be used to carve the cedar. The expressively carved and painted masks that emerged were used in story-telling and healing ceremonies as ways of reflecting the natural and spiritual worlds that Haida and Tlingit peoples saw as integrated forces. Though they now fetch high prices from art collectors, the masks were not considered to hold wealth or value in themselves. Rather, the right to use them was important.

Native peoples on the west coast also staged elaborate gift-giving ceremonies, or potlatches, where the masks and other goods were redistributed according to social status. The potlatch economy was eventually suppressed by white authorities who were aghast at the very thought of people actually giving away things of value without reference to the market economy.

The European settlers who challenged Canada's original people for possession of the seemingly endless woodlands had a somewhat different conceptual relationship with nature and the forest. What the vast majority of European immigrants from the seventeenth to the nineteenth century had in mind was to set down roots in the soil, to establish farms. For most Europeans, as the products of a feudal and early capitalist society, there was no question of living in and from the forest. In fact the forests, like the native people, were seen by most as something to be conquered, to be driven back. To help them forcibly remove the native people from the lands they wanted to settle, the Europeans had the musket. Against the silent masses of trees they had only the axe and the ox. The trees, the more numerous opponents, would take a long time to conquer.

TO FRENCH AND ENGLISH-SPEAKING settlers, the forest must have seemed an enduring and incomprehensibly vast expanse of wilderness. No one knew exactly how far the foreboding mass stretched. And the last thing these farmers saw in the forest was a renewable source of wealth. Trees were something to remove from the land in order to clear the way for the homestead. Stands of huge butternut, oak, white pine, walnut, maple and even black cherry trees simply represented an obstacle to settlement.

For settlers whose first imperative was sheer survival, the first task was to cut a living space out of the forest. To the settler, the forest's "towering eighty-foot canopy of leaves" was regarded not with wonder but with "a sort of horror".[1] Historian W.H. Graham writes: "To all men of the backwoods the most cheerful sound in the world was that of chopping."[2] They quickly learned to wield an axe with dexterity — although many of them suffered a badly cut foot or leg in the process — and, according to Graham, the most determined of them could clear an acre of "moderate timber" in a week: "This meant felling the trees, lopping off the branches, cutting the wood into manageable lengths and clearing the latter out of the way, by pulling some aside and burning others in heaps. The first cut trees and cleared space were needed for the log cabin, the first real house."[3]

The settlers had to put in a crop as soon as possible, and in Upper Canada this necessity often led them to attack the larger, more unmoveable trees in the form of "girdling": that is, to chop a ring in the bark, thus killing the trees and preventing the development of leaves the following spring. This also meant, unfortunately that when the trees died and dried out they became "iron-hard and difficult to cut down."[4] Dead limbs could also break and fall off, not only constituting a definite hazard to anyone who happened to be underneath at the time, but also providing fuel for forest fire. However, at least in the following spring and summer the first wheat crop could be put in, sown among the stumps and girdled trees.

In spite of the rather antagonistic attitude towards the forest, farmers, like the native peoples before them, did find a multitude of uses for the trees they so busily removed. Besides timber for house and barn, and all-important firewood for the winter, wood was used to fashion necessary tools, barrels, furniture, and to construct fences. Settlers carved shovels out of wood and made nails from dried hardwood pegs. But at the same time there was no danger of these many uses overcoming the excess of timber. So some of the finest natural growth — forests whose succession had for centuries been unmolested by human intervention — was simply burned away in the process of clearing agricultural land. The most the average settler could hope to gain from this endeavour was a few barrels of potash, one of Canada's early export commodities.

Yet even if seen primarily as an obstacle, the forest still had a powerful influence on colonial life and the course of its development. Every farmer was obliged to acquire the skills of a lumberjack, just to clear the land. Before farmers could work a plough, they had to know how to heft a broad axe. Outside the small islands of cultivation, the vast forest domain offered other sources of wealth as well. Once exploration by river and canoe had familiarized the more intrepid colonists with the interior, Canada's first staple trade — the traffic in furs — could flourish. The trade was of course based on the animals of the forest, in particular that most diligent of nature's lumberjacks, the beaver.

From the *habitant* farms of the St. Lawrence valley the fur trade gained the second of its two principal sources of labour, the first being the Indians. The men who became *coureurs du bois* were often settlers in search of gainful employment during the long winter months. Perhaps more often, they were dissatisfied with parish and pasture and so headed out to the more autonomous life of the *pays d'en haut*. In later years the same attraction of life in the bush would draw French Canadian farm lads to the

timber industry, so much so that a century or more of logging in
Quebec and Ontario, not to mention the fortune of many a
timber baron, became based on their labour.

It wasn't until the latter part of the eighteenth century that
the extraction of forest products for export on any large scale got
underway. And the reasons were more geopolitical and military
than technical or financial. Up to that time, settlers could satisfy
the needs of local wood markets by falling timber directly into
river or stream, with little aid from draft animals. Though references to square timber — huge "sticks" of squared-off tree
trunks — appear in French colonial records as early as 1719, it
was the British conquest that brought in a policy which would
eventually give shape to an industry. No sooner had the British
taken over than H.M. Government sent instructions regarding
timber disposal to James Murray, the first English governor of
Quebec. Murray was to set aside townships of 20,000 acres along
the St. Lawrence and to include some land for military purposes
but "more particularly for the Growth and Production of Naval
Timber, if there are any Wood Lands fit for that purpose."[5]

At the time the British had no pressing need for Canadian
timber. Their strategic needs were still adequately supplied from
Russia, Prussia and Poland. In those days Baltic ports like Dan-
zig — now the Gdansk of Solidarity and Lenin Shipyard fame —
were so dominated by British capital that within them communities of British merchants had been established, complete with
Anglican churches. The Baltic was closer to home markets and
its timber was more familiar to British wood buyers than the
unknown Canadian pine. It was war — that "greatest of economic forces"[6] — which provided the boost needed to vault
Britain's North American possessions into the position of primary supplier of timber to the imperial centre.

The beginning of the nineteenth century brought the
Napoleonic wars, and the French leader was eager to sever the
Royal Navy from its supplies of Baltic timber. Having conquered
Prussia, he was in an excellent position to do just that, an action
that forced Britain to turn to Canada. It was an age of wood, and
wood was a key war material. Pine timber was as important for
the military who wanted to dominate the seas as aluminum is
for today's military men who seek control of the air. The white
pine which once abounded in Canada's forests was both light
and strong — the aluminum of its day.

Though Napoleon's military power was short-lived, he still provided the impetus for the rapid growth of the square timber trade in New Brunswick, Quebec and the Ottawa Valley. Between 1808 and 1812 exports of squared pine from Quebec to Britain multiplied by thirteen times.[7] The rapid growth in demand soon attracted businessmen like William Price (of Abitibi-Price fame) from England to Canada, where they established a base at the commercial centre of the trade in Quebec City. Their power was not as transient as that of the French dictator to whom they owed their big break. The commercial interests of Quebec, together with their counterparts on the other side of the Atlantic, soon persuaded the British government to slap a duty on timber entering Britain from northern Europe. At the same time the government was to allow Canadian wood free access to the British market. These colonial preferences assured the future of a thriving industry based on the products of the Canadian forest and also solidified the power of the Quebec timber traders. These interests succeeded in maintaining the duties on northern European timber for the next three decades and, as a result, there was only one year between 1808 and 1858 that imports of Baltic wood surpassed those of Canadian wood. In British ports like Liverpool, "Canada Dock" became a very busy place.[8]

But at first the capitalists who dominated the trade did not extend their power into the bush, and the early days of Canada's first forest-based industry were characterized by the activities of many small operators out where the trees were being cut. There was little or no government regulation, so farmers in need of income could devote the winter to "timber-making". All they had to have was a few strong men, a few strong beasts, supplies for the winter (often advanced on credit from a local merchant) and inclination to devote the winter to work in the woods. There they would fell large pine trees and square them off with a broad-axe right where they landed. This involved tremendous waste. A quarter to a third of a good-sized tree was left on the forest floor; the slabs hewn from its base were often a foot thick. The slightest bit of heart-rot at the centre of a tree would result in it being abandoned altogether. The wasted wood might simply rot; just as easily it could provide fine fuel for a forest fire in the hot days of early summer.

The prevailing ethic was simple. Cut it down and get it out in as great a quantity and as fast as possible. Given the limited horizons of the square timber trade, and even more limited means of those initially involved at the point of production, this attitude is not surprising. These were part-time settlers, part-time woodsmen — people who had to survive the uncertainties of farm life in a pioneer society. Added to these uncertainties were those of the trade. If timber fetched a good price at Quebec one year, more small operators were likely to spend the following year making timber in the hopes of sharing in the good times. This frequently caused oversupply and, the following spring, once the rafts started to back up at the Quebec timber coves, the price would fall and the small timbermakers might not even make enough money to pay off the advances they had received from the merchants. The result was the loss of many a farm to creditors.

In New Brunswick the early period of the trade gave rise to tensions between the settled farming life and the transient existence of the woods worker. Many homesteads — farms that were marginal in the first place — were abandoned or mortgaged after their workers were attracted to the bush. By 1839 Saint John was forced to import 163,00 bushels of potatoes.[9] The Saint John and Miramachi valleys were treated like quarries, their rich veins of pine timber floated to tidewater and exported to Britain. More often than not the money generated by the trade wound up in the pockets of the timber merchants who had set up business at the various New Brunswick ports. Peter Fisher, one of the first historians of New Brunswick, wrote in 1825:

> The persons principally engaged in shipping the timber have been strangers who have taken no interest in the welfare of the country; but have merely occupied a spot to make what they could in the shortest possible time. Some of these have done well, and others have had to quit the trade; but whether they won or lost, the capital of the country has been wasted, and no improvement of any consequence made to compensate for it, or to secure a source of trade to the inhabitants when the lumber shall fail.[10]

The greatest source of square timber for the British market was the Ottawa Valley, where fast-flowing rivers drained 80,000 square miles of virgin timberland. Wood could be rafted to Quebec as soon as spring breakup freed the rivers from ice. The first timber to come out of the area was floated downstream in June of 1806 by those who had cut it, and the man who owned the shipment, Philemon Wright, was on board the raft. A native of New England, Wright had settled at Hull, where he farmed and established a community. The confluence of the Ottawa and Gatineau rivers soon became the centre for a thriving trade in the products of the forest. Many of the country's first big wood-based businesses grew up there. Wright, however, was essentially a "small man" operating with borrowed funds on a season-to-season basis. In his endeavours he was little better off than his fellow settlers who took a chance each year by leaving their farms in the hopes of making some cash money in the bush. Like many other small men Wright eventually succumbed to debt and his business fell into the hands of the trustees.

Everyone knew there was money to be had in square timber and in fact fortunes were made by many operators, big and small, in the river valleys of eastern Canada from the Saint John to the upper reaches of the Ottawa near Lake Temiskaming. But the real money in Canada was being made by those at the centres of power in business: Quebec City and Bytown (Ottawa). The members of Quebec's "Timber Ring" were merchant capitalists whose financial and family ties to English and Scottish businessmen made them the heart of the English establishment in French Canada for several decades. At Bytown another class of businessmen developed, people directly involved with the extraction and transportation of wood from the Ottawa Valley area. The American E.B. Eddy, who arrived in the Ottawa Valley with little in the way of assets, got his start peddling matches door to door. Very quickly the name of Eddy and others such as John Egan and F.H. Bronson, who today have towns and streets named for them, became familiar up and down the Ottawa.

By 1835 timber was being cut 400 miles inland from the confluence of the Ottawa and the St. Lawrence. Twenty-five years later all the timber easily transportable to tidewater had been removed and the upper reaches of the Ottawa were being scoured for pine. As the scale of the industry expanded and the forest receded from areas adjacent to established agricultural communities, firms grew bigger. It became increasingly difficult for part-time bushworkers, part-time farmers, to make a go of it on their own. Each autumn money had to be invested in faraway camps, or shanties, where bigger and bigger crews took the wood out. A return on these investments would not be realized until the wood was sold in Britain a year or more later. Such endeavours called for large, well-capitalized operating units that could take good advantage of economies of scale.

One such company was set up by J.R. Booth, who got his start on the Ottawa and was a dominant figure in the region in the latter part of the nineteenth century. His forest empire was said at one time to be the largest business in the world run by one man. Booth deployed armies of cutters, teamsters, black-smiths and swampers* in a far-flung network of camps. Another enterprise, run by the Hamilton family and based at Hawkes-bury, came to control much of the forest business on the Gatineau River. The Hamiltons eventually got into lumber and then pulp and paper manufacture, finally selling out to what became an arm of the giant International Paper Company of New York.

The nature of the business also changed gradually when British demand for "deals" (rough-sawn chunks of lumber) and American demand for lumber began to complement the square timber trade. This meant that all the trees cut could no longer be hewn to rough export specifications right where they fell. Saw-mills had to be set up, which required capital. This shift in the character and market orientation of the forest industry led to further concentration of control into more powerful industrial hands. Those who had been part of the small gangs of self-employed timbermakers from the farm now became wage labourers in an increasingly-centralized forest business. And the business became more fully integrated: The timber barons ran not only bush camps but also sawmills and plants producing shingles, lath and doors. Some, such as J.R. Booth, even built their own railroads.

By the middle of the century, the frenetic growth of the forest industry had been accompanied by a rush for all available supplies of standing timber. Forests north of Lake Ontario and Lake Erie were soon eradicated as U.S. ports across the lakes got all the timber that Canadians could supply. Previously, trees from Upper Canada had been shipped down to Quebec for the

---

* Swampers were usually less experienced or less skilled lumberjacks who cleared trees from the roads and skid-trails in advance of the main body of lumberjacks.

British market only with the greatest difficulty; rafts had often been broken up by storms on the lakes. American lumber demand helped to solve this problem. On the south side of Lake Ontario, Oswego, New York, became an important point of entry for Canadian lumber. In 1840, 1.9 million feet of Canadian lumber had been off loaded at Oswego. Less than ten years later, in 1849, 44 million feet entered this fort alone. In the following year, the figure increased to 60 million feet.[11] This growth in Canadian imports was occurring in spite of a heavy tariff on sawn lumber and at the same time that American lumbermen were being forced to move west toward Michigan and Wisconsin, states whose rich stands of pine presented an attractive alternative to the forests of the eastern seaboard, which had by this time been "cleaned up".

It was almost as if a gold rush frenzy was gripping the forest frontiers of the Canadas at the time. Demand was good, supplies were apparently limitless and no one, least of all the timber interests atop the trade, seemed to think that the good times would pass. In spite of the inevitable ups and downs of the business cycle, there was an overriding concern with getting on with the business at hand. Lumbermen saw themselves, somewhat nobly, as the economic engine of colonial development, and when a group of five thousand businessmen presented a petition to the British government in 1835, arguing for a retention of the Imperial preference, the prevailing spirit was apparent:

> The lumber trade in its present form promotes emigration by the low rate at which it enables vessels to bring out Passengers, as well as by giving employment immediately on their landing, and holds out great inducements to the formation of settlement in distant parts of the country, by diminishing the expenses of clearing forest lands, and by affording to Farmers a market for their produce at their own door, at a higher price than could be obtained elsewhere.[12]

The very poverty of these "Passengers" made them fall easy prey to the shipowning merchants of the Quebec timber trade. After unloading their pine at British ports, the merchants were only too happy to find a return cargo to fill the otherwise empty holds of their ships. The emigrants, almost always in desperate financial circumstances, had to secure the cheapest passage available. So they were packed tightly into some of the most decrepit vessels afloat, in conditions little better than the slave trade. There were no sanitary facilities, food and water were scarce and in rough weather the holds were sealed tight against the human cargo. Cholera epidemics were common and the possibility of shipwreck was ever-present.[13]

Seen from the top, however, the world was unfolding as it should. Trees were being cut, settlers were busily moving in and growing crops to feed hungry lumberjacks, business couldn't be better. But even setting aside the plight of the immigrants, the picture was not quite the idyll of sweet harmony painted by the leading men of the day. The rush for timber was turning into an uncontrolled scramble. Philemon Wright's grandson must have been looking over his shoulder with some apprehension when he declared, "I have got into a good grove of timber and intend to scoop all the best of it out, previous to any other person having the pick of it."[14]

For one thing, as time passed the cutting away of forest in the Canadas began to reveal not prime farmland but the rocky outcrops of the Canadian Shield. The same situation had already occurred in New Brunswick, where many marginal farmers were forced to abandon their lands after a futile attempt to balance poor agricultural conditions with the uncertainties of life in the bush. At the same time, settlers and lumbermen did not always get along famously. Once wood for export started to be produced from forests in the upper Ottawa Valley, the Muskokas, Kawarthas and Haliburton Highland regions — now Toronto's cottage country hinterland — and the regions between the Ottawa and Georgian Bay, the drive became a race to see who could be the first to grab the best timber. The neat rapport between the settler and the lumberman was simply an illusion, the situation bearing closer resemblance to a modern land-use fight.

The pressure of immigration was continuing as people from the British Isles — those displaced by the traumas of the industrial revolution — continued to pour into Canada. And in both Lower and Upper Canada lumbering interests were irked when settlers moved into good timberland. Quebec's agriculture was stagnating but its population continued to expand. Domestic government policy still favoured agriculture and settlement, even though settlement was being pushed north, beyond the limits of the soil's capability to sustain any crops other than trees and rocks. The mass of the people, for their part, had little choice but to attempt to till the land, as there was little else to support them — besides the lumbering industry, that is.

So settlers would sometimes move into the forest, setting fires in their attempts to clear the land. Such fires would often spread and destroy valuable timber. Other bogus settlers would stake a claim to a piece of land, ostensibly to farm but actually to gain access to the timber. After the timber was cut and sold, the "settlers" would move on to try the same ruse elsewhere. Lumbermen saw this as little better than theft and cringed as potential profits went up in smoke or were usurped by undeserving elements. They wanted to be able to monopolize the timber for themselves, marshalling little armies of *habitant* labourers to travel further and further from their home villages as the cut moved north and west. The drain of French-Canadian youth from the farm displeased the clergy of Quebec. The church thus became a powerful influence in the promotion of various northern settlement schemes, hoping those schemes would remove the threat itinerant lumbering posed to the authority of church and pastoral life. According to one Father Bourassa:

> The first and most immediate effect of the noisy labour of the lumber camps is to remove not the taste, but also the aptitude for the gentle and untroubled occupations of the countryside, whilst the habit of distant journeys, the free and licentious life of the shanty make the order, the regularity of family life boring and too monotonous and render hard and unbearable the return to the paternal yoke. [15]

This continuing tension between lumbering and agriculture exposed the curious position of government. The Crown, after all, controlled the allocation of land, whether for agriculture or for wood production. In the days before it granted a limited measure of autonomy to the colonial elite, the British government had established the germs of a public policy by attempting to regulate the disposal of Crown timber and reserving some trees for the Royal Navy. These early germs had grown and taken shape as the timber trade evolved from a military to a strictly commercial undertaking. By 1826 authorities in the Canadas had realized that the exploitation of the forest could bring in important revenues, so they started to issue licences to cut timber on specific "timber limits" or "timber berths". People cutting wood on Crown land would have to pay a licence fee as well as a duty on the wood actually cut. The principle of government ownership and control over timberland, thus established early on, continues to be applied today in the form of provincial control over Crown land and timber cut on that land.

The development of state control of land went along quite nicely with the overriding preoccupation of government of the day: the encouragement of settlement. For many years the local authorities shared the perspective of the business interests, who based their pleas to the British government on the idea of a healthy symbiotic relationship between settlers and lumbermen. According to them, once a timber limit was played out, a few sturdy sons of the soil could move in and start to work the land. Some timber limits even had to be cleared within a certain time to hurry this process along. Implicit in this policy was the recognition that the forest was a passing thing, an opportunity to make some money before farmers took over the land.

But once it became clear that forest land was not necessarily agricultural land, matters became more complex. Government, as owner of the land, should have been designating it for the various uses to which it seemed most suited: The beginnings of a land-use policy would have been in order. Yet, despite the formal control the Crown exercised over the land, and the fact that early regulations were backed by the force of law, there was little administrative control over lumbering and competing settlements. The government could make sure it collected its dues simply by stationing an agent at a particular point on a river, say at Ottawa. The agent could then levy charges on wood as it was rafted downriver every spring. Back in the bush it was a different story: poaching, trespassing and the generalized plunder of the public estate. Government ownership meant little in the way of control.

By 1849 this problem, coupled with the government's desire for more revenue, prompted the development of a new timber policy. Legislation was drafted with the assistance of several prominent Ottawa Valley lumbermen and a new law was passed. Forest land remained in the hands of the government, enabling it to promote lumbering or settlement, as it wished. Though the timber interests might have been more pleased to see their exclusive right to the land enshrined in law, they were no doubt very pleased with a subsequent amendment to the law that stipulated that holders of timber limits would no longer be required to put cash in advance but would pay a rental fee for the land (a ground rent) only when the timber was sold. This of course liberated their capital for other uses.

As the trade in the products of the forest grew with the development of the U.S. lumber market, so did government revenues from the forest. In an age when income tax would have been regarded as a radical and dangerous measure by the local élites, forest-generated income was an important bulwark to the treasury. Since their businesses were contributing to state revenues, the lumbermen — who frequently found their way into government — gained an important economic and political edge on the settlers.

In the years following Confederation (1867-1906) the Quebec government leased out 51,000 square miles of timberland, for which it received an average of $67.74 per square mile — over $3.25 million. In addition, government collected annual ground rents and stumpage dues* on timber cut from the land. [16] Ontario did as well if not better by the liquidation of its forests. Between 1867 and 1899 the various rents and dues from the forest swelled government coffers by over $29 million. This meant that twenty-eight cents out of every dollar collected by the Crown came directly from the forest resource. [17]

The development of the forest industry as an important revenue source for government was accompanied by a gradual shift in the timber trade. Although Britain continued to import Canadian wood after the reduction of the Imperial Preferences in the 1840s, the United States began to slowly surpass Britain as the most important market for Canadian forest products. From 1849 to 1853 Canadian exports of wood to the United States more than doubled. Then, a brief period of reciprocity from 1854 to 1866, coupled with an explosion in demand in American markets centred at Chicago and New York, stimulated a further boom in the forest-based trade. It was an era of railroad building, of city building. Below the border the frontier of settlement was being pushed westward, and industrial towns were springing up along the way. Each step created demand for more wood, which was accordingly supplied by the forests of Canada's own shifting woods frontier. On the eve of the reciprocity era one

---

* Stumpage is a forestry term for the royalty that the forest owner (the government) collects from the commercial interests cutting trees on the owner's land.

U.S. congressman told his colleagues on Capitol Hill, "The British provinces have an almost inexhaustible supply of pine timber."[18]

Logging spread across Ontario during and after the period of free trade, and the eastern Canadian lumber industry reached its peak in the years following 1870. With business still booming in the Ottawa Valley, J.R. Booth built railroads to the U.S. border and across the Shield to the timberlands of Georgian Bay. In his day, Booth's company produced everything from square timber and deals to planks and pulp. It was the heyday of lumbering on the Ottawa, where some of the country's most famous nineteenth-century lumber barons — Booth, Edwards, Bronson, Gillies — all prospered as they directed their men in "hurlin' down the pine".

In their turn, other parts of Ontario played host to the lumber industry before the guest, having consumed all that was offered in the way of wood, moved on. The Trent watershed and the Lake Simcoe area, the Kawarthas and the Muskokas all had their limited supplies of timber removed in short order. The Georgian Bay watershed, one of the most abundant areas of virgin pine on the continent, was logged over. It had the advantage of being within easy reach of the Chicago market. The cut then swept north to the Lakehead where the pine, though not as abundant as elsewhere, helped to supply prairie markets until the British Columbia industry hit its stride after the turn of the century.

In Quebec, in the second half of the century, wood was still finding a lively market in Britain but exports to the United States were steadily gaining ground. At the same time Montreal had started to supplant Quebec City as the centre of the industry. Montreal had the advantage of being strategically located at the foot of the Ottawa and was a point of shipment for consignments of Quebec and Ontario wood destined by rail and canal for New York. The shift was reinforced by Montreal's ascendancy to the position of financial and railroad centre for all Canada — the country's business capital.

In New Brunswick, much of the good pine had been taken from the forests by 1870s. First it had been shipped, mostly to Britain, in the form of masts in the early period of the transatlantic trade; and later it had gone in the form of square timber and deals. With most of the pine gone, the lumbering industry in

New Brunswick had passed its peak, never to regain its position of prime importance to the provincial economy. Afterwards, the New Brunswick sawmilling industry had to content itself with spruce, widely regarded as a species inferior to the white pine. It wasn't until the later growth of the pulp and paper sector that the New Brunswick forest industry enabled the government of that province to limp into the twentieth century, on the strength of the large stands of spruce and balsam fir passed over in the quest for white pine.

With the decline of the lumber industry many New Brunswickers were forced to follow the shifting fortunes of the trade to other parts of Canada or the United States. In both places they were likely to meet people from Quebec who were also looking for work in the bush, or anywhere else for that matter. Many of the woodcutters who cleaned up the rich pineries of Michigan and Wisconsin had learned their trade in New Brunswick or Quebec.

Some New Brunswickers, however, were not content simply to follow the fast-receding forest frontier westward towards Ontario and the United States. And they were not all choppers of trees. Some entrepreneurs from the east moved right across to British Columbia, where it looked like the gold rush of the 1850s would soon be giving way to an equally feverish timber rush. Sawmills built to service the demand created by the gold rush had their production redirected towards export markets when the gold frenzy fizzled. Gold was apparently a finite resource, but the vast coastal forests seemed to offer unlimited supplies of magnificent sawlogs.

One entrepreneur from New Brunswick, John Hendry, arrived in British Columbia in 1872, bringing the savvy needed to turn the fledgling forest business into big business in a province that had just entered Confederation. Hendry did just that. Realizing the huge potential of the province's rich forest resource, he consolidated the sawmill business by buying up two of the largest mills in Vancouver: the Moodyville Sawmill Company and Hastings Mills. Timberland was cheap in the last of the forest frontiers. Hastings Mills had secured some of what is now downtown Vancouver to supply its wood needs. The cost? A penny per acre per year. It is hardly surprising that other powerful promoters from the east who could sense the end of the lumber boom on their home turf were quick to turn their attention to the west coast as a means of diversifying their operations. James MacLaren, whose family forest empire is now part of the Noranda forest group, made his fortune in Ottawa Valley lumber and moved west. At low cost, the Scottish banker and lumber magnate acquired timber limits in the Fraser Valley and on Vancouver Island, where he found imposing stands of cedar and Douglas fir: some of the best standing timber in the country.

By the late nineteenth century the outlines of the forest as a commercial resource had been roughly sketched. British Columbia had entered the picture as an up and coming supply centre, and government was moving towards regulating the cut, or at least attempting to maximize revenue flowing from the forest. Newfoundland had moved to establish rudimentary forms of control over its timber resource. The government of the colony was alarmed by the regular pillage of the pine on the west coast of the island by New Brunswick loggers in search of "ton timber" (square timber). Raiding parties of these woodsmen helped themselves to the limited reserves of pine. By the end of the century ninety-nine-year leases on Newfoundland timberland were being offered by a government anxious to get away from this type of exploitation and wanting to establish a wood-based industry on a firm footing. The authorities were so keen to attract investors that they waived the traditional right to collect any royalty or stumpage on timber cut on public lands. By the early 1980s, Abitibi-Price was still operating on one of these ninety-nine-year leases, paying 0.3 cents per acre for pulpwood and nothing for stumpage.

MOST OF US THINK of the treeline as something halfway up a mountain or on the edge of the tundra. But as the Canadian forest industry took root, it became apparent that the treeline was a constantly retreating series of outposts where new towns or groups of temporary shanties might appear one day and be gone the next. Financiers, speculators and loggers all followed the shifting forest frontiers. Towns that were once vital centres of the timber trade soon became insignificant in the business. Communities that now owe their existence to forest industries were unknown compass points on incomplete maps before the turn of the century.

Of course, some towns whose early prosperity was based on the timber trade were lucky enough to acquire other, even more highly-visible, means of support. By the time the last raft went through the timber slides at Ottawa in 1908, and after the eclipse of the square timber trade had erased Quebec City's importance as a centre of the forest industry, the growth of government had saved the day. These towns now base their prosperity on activities less tangible than their locations beside broad rivers — rivers once filled with log booms. To be sure, both capitals remain single-industry communities. But Price House, an early stone "skyscraper" and for years Quebec's tallest building, the centre for a 7,700-square-mile woods business that controlled much of the Saguenay like a feudal fiefdom, has been dwarfed by government buildings. The building is now a mere outpost of the private, Toronto-based real estate empire which bought out the firm that bought out the Price company. The E.B. Eddy Company no longer blankets Ottawa with fumes from its mill at Hull, a town now dominated by federal government office towers. In fact, government offices now occupy some of the space that Eddy's riverside factory used to fill. The Eddy forest operations today form part of the Weston grocery colossus.

But at French River, Ontario, there aren't any new blocks of government buildings. There are just a few rusting boilers and some foundations and crumbling walls overgrown by a tangle of bushes on the shore of Georgian Bay. For a few brief years during the 1890s, a two-sawmill town thrived at French River, as long as there was enough pine in the Georgian Bay watershed to keep the saws humming and supply the Chicago market. Once the pine was gone, so was French River. And down the shore of Georgian Bay from French River rests the remains of another once-prosperous milltown, Muskoka Mills, which once drew its pine timber from the watershed of the Muskoka River. In the 1880s the town was a thriving centre with three sawmills employing four hundred workers. But like French River and a score of other small communities based on eastern Canada's retreating treeline, Muskoka Mills disappeared from the map as quickly as it had sprung up, leaving behind a ghost town and a depleted forest.[19]

As Crown control over the forest resource became more firm

Bernhard Fernow, (second from left) the "Father of North American forestry". Here Fernow poses with students during the first field instruction in Canada in 1908.

and brought both government revenues and solid, permanent-looking buildings to Quebec City, Ottawa, Toronto and Fredericton, where decisions about "timber disposal" were being centralized in the hands of various functionaries, the people cutting and milling the trees could just wonder where the next timber mining boom would lead them.

At the same time, the nineteenth century was not without its prophets. There were people who saw through the transient nature of the forest industry and warned that the forest resource was not, as most everyone instinctively believed, infinite. In 1862, even before the end of the square timber trade and the peak of the eastern lumber business, one John Langton told an audience at Quebec to heed a crisis he felt would affect the industry and the future of the town: "We go on practically treating our forests as inexhaustible, and in the face of the yearly-increasing distances, to which the lumberers have to go back from all our main streams, we have as yet taken no steps towards preserving what remains to us."[20]

Another voice in the wilderness was Bernard Fernow, often referred to as "the father of North American forestry". A Prussian immigrant, Fernow was appointed head of forestry for the U.S. Department of Agriculture within ten years of his arrival in the United States in 1876. He later went on to found the first university-based forestry school in the United States at Cornell University and the first in Canada at the University of Toronto. Though at one time a staunch Republican, Fernow was never a favourite in government or business circles. This may perhaps be due to the fact that he was accustomed to speaking out with disarming frankness on forest matters. On one occasion he calculated that from 1867 to 1913, the province of Ontario alone had disposed of 25 billion feet of white pine. He concluded his observation by pointing out, "As yet the forests are viewed solely as a source of current revenue, not as capital, and the rights of the people and of posterity are sacrificed."[21]

A.R.M. LOWER, CANADIAN HISTORIAN and chronicler of the nineteenth-century forest industry, put that same sacrifice into historical perspective: "The sack of the largest and wealthiest medieval cities could have been but a bagatelle compared to the sack of the North American forest and no medieval ravisher could have been more fierce and unscrupulous than the lumberman. His lust of power and wealth have changed the face of the country, built cities and railroads, and created a sort of civilization. . . . If in the process of growth, the forest had to be sacrificed, what matter? No one, after all, except a 'crank' here and there, expected it to be any more than a temporary source of wealth, to give place in due course to the settler."[22]

The warnings would come to be repeated with increasing frequency: but with constant futility. Indeed, they are *still* being repeated by government and industry. But then, as now, government and industry decision-makers believed in an economy of perpetual expansion. There would always be more trees. More settlers could flood in behind the lumberman and if problems arose between the settlers and the loggers, or if the land were found to be barren, there were always the great western plains and beyond them the limitless forests of British Columbia. The forest business meant more government revenue and the money could be used to bankroll railroad promoters and canal builders — all the better to ship out the lumber and grease the skids for settlement. Timber operators like to refer to themselves as "practical men" and it was in their strong hands that the levers of industrial power rested. Who among them did not share the shortsighted yet uninhibited optimism of the day?

A typical boreal forest condition — shallow soils and bed rock. Once cut over, these sites are difficult, if not impossible, to regenerate. The conifers were cut from this site, leaving unwanted deciduous trees.

3. Forests for Sale

THROUGHOUT THE EARLY decades of the twentieth century, it was not unusual for after-dinner speakers — whether at a meeting of a Chamber of Commerce, a business and industry association or a service club — to talk expansively of the *vast, inexhaustible* or even *limitless* forests which blessed the new Dominion. Such evocations, larded with the optimism of the day, could almost certainly be guaranteed to elicit satisfied *hear-hear*'s and considerable clinking of cutlery on glassware from the assembled gentlemen of trade, who were most happy to be reassured that things were well in the woods.

In fact, such optimism was somewhat behind the times. The country's forests were not proving to be an infinite resource. In eastern Canada, even by the end of the previous century, the once seemingly endless supply of the most sought-after tree, white pine, was beginning to peter out. True, the forests of British Columbia seemed to provide lasting opportunities for continued access to abundant reserves of magnificent sawlogs. But the industry was changing.

Large pulp mills now dotted the boreal forests of eastern Canada. A pulp and paper industry was promising industrial prosperity based on northern expanses of spruce trees too small to be turned into lumber. The pulp mills, it was held, represented a fundamental shift from the days of the transient lumber-producing sawmills, which would quickly close down when supplies of timber ran out.* The old industry was mobile

---

*Whereas the industry based on pulp (a reconstituted form of wood fibre crushed and moistened into a soft mass, the basic ingredient of paper products)

and new mills would easily spring up, following the receding frontier of the pine. With the new pulp mills, heavily dependent on expensive and heavy machinery that couldn't easily be moved, huge investments were needed just to get them established; with this large new investment necessarily came a change in attitude.

This level of investment forced operators to think about husbanding the forest resource entrusted to them by the government. Government, for its part by now mindful of the need to protect the resource, began to hire professionally-trained foresters who knew the principles of managing the forests for the perpetual production of wood. The forest-based industries were going into a partnership with government to ensure future forest prosperity.

It began to be unfashionable to talk of an eternal wood supply. Past waste and inefficiency stood in startling contradiction to present shortages of pine and were too obvious for close observers of the forest scene to ignore. After a trip across the country to evaluate the available timber supplies, Bernhard Fernow reported his impressions of Canada's ostensibly unending forest reserves to the Dominion Forestry Branch: "I have become thoroughly satisfied that the timber wealth of Canada has been greatly overrated. There is a vast extent of woodland, but a relatively small amount of forest fit and capable of commercial exploitation of timber. . . . Throughout, Canada is extensively wooded but poorly supplied with timber."[1]

Fernow came to Canada from Germany via the United States. He brought with him a conception of the forest differing radically from earlier North American ways of thinking. North Americans saw the forest as a static entity, an unchanging obstacle to settlement. The European theory of forestry held that the forest was a renewable natural resource. To Europeans, forestry was a scientific and technical field of endeavour and trained foresters could manage the resource so that it would supply wood in perpetuity. This doctrine was something new to North America and Fernow's influence soon spread in the United

---

could use nearly any size tree if the fibre was of the correct specification, the lumber industry had to use trees big enough to produce boards of a desired size. In the early years of the pulp business, that industry was usually quite distinct from the traditional lumber companies; but as time passed, integrated pulp and lumber firms came to dominate the forest products sector.

States, where he was among the first to advocate forestry measures. Fernow's almost reverential attitude toward trees and
wood — "from the cradle to the grave we are surrounded by it"[2]
— inspired him to pursue conservation and reforestation with a
vengeance. His successor as the director of the U.S. Department
of Agriculture's Bureau of Forestry was Gifford Pinchot, a
dynamic young technocrat who, along with President Theodore
Roosevelt, did much to spark the "conservation movement",
which in turn did much to provide the philosophical and political impetus for a new way of looking at resource management in
early twentieth-century North America.

The conservation movement, as it took shape in both the
United States and Canada, clearly saw that forests could not
provide an infinite source of wood supply if past practices continued. The advocates of conservation believed in and called for
centralized industrial management of the forests. If the forests
could be treated like a factory, with maximum control being
exerted by efficient, scientifically-trained technicians, the waste
and chaos of the past could give way to a bright future in which
growth would never be impeded by shortages of supply. This
was a movement whose inspiration sprang from the achievements of the machine age and the industrial revolution. One of
its prophets, W.J. McGee, characterized the movement as
involving "a conscious and purposeful entering into control over
nature, through the natural resources, for the direct benefit of
mankind."[3] No environmentalists, these.

The tone of the conservationist argument — rational and
efficient resource exploitation — did not appear off-key to politicians and forestry industry leaders in Canada around the turn of
the century. When the American Forestry Congress got started
in the 1880s with Fernow as one of its leading militants, its
principal Canadian members were William Little, a lumber merchant, and H.G. Joly,* the former Premier of Quebec. At a time
when government revenues from forest-based industries were
becoming increasingly important and the forest industry was
showing no sign of slowing its growth, those who preached an
optimistic gospel of continued wood supply and businesslike
management were likely to find an attentive audience. And find

---

* Joly's full title — Sir Henri de Lotbinière — bespeaks his seigneurial background.

one they did. The Canadian Forestry Association — "a union of 8,000 Progressive Canadians; Not Affiliated With Any Government or Commercial Interest" — was founded in 1900 with Joly as its first president. By 1906 Prime Minister Wilfrid Laurier had called together all interested parties to a Canadian Forestry Convention.

Such organizations and gatherings attracted not only members of the fledgling community of trained foresters. Forest industry leaders and bankers were also quick to jump on the new forestry bandwagon. The CFA at one time included among its members all 398 branch managers from the Banks of Montreal, Commerce, New Brunswick and British North America as well as the Molson's Bank and the Merchant's Bank. "The lumberman... is not the enemy, but the legitimate lumberman is the very best friend of the forests," Ottawa timber baron and Liberal Senator W.C. Edwards, a leading light among early forestry supporters, told the Forestry Convention in 1906.[4]

Yet it was not simply the appeal of science and rationalism that attracted so many businessmen who, together with politicians, journalists, academics and other urban intellectuals, formed the core of the conservation movement. Certainly, any set of new ideas that appealed to self-interest would appeal to men of commerce. Forestry meant more government regulation of Crown timber and at least some measure of fire protection. To the Ottawa Valley lumbermen who were very active at the centre of the push towards forest conservation, regulation had a strong appeal. They were anxious to have the state restrict access to a pine forest they realized would soon become exhausted. They were frustrated by the incursions of pseudo-settlers and small operators who depleted the resource and at the same time glutted the market and drove down prices through overcutting. They hoped that a planned and rationalized forest regime would go hand in hand with the new forestry credo and assure their large operations the sole right to cut what remained of the pine on the upper reaches of the Ottawa.

But, though the Ottawa timber barons were eager to hitch their wagons to the rising star of conservation, it was already too late for them. The forest action was already shifting northward — in the direction of the spruce forests and their promise of vast stores of pulpwood — and westward to British Columbia, where the lumber business was busily relocating. In these frontier areas the call for regulation and conservation was not heard so frequently. Conservation in Canada was something to which many seemed willing to pay lip service but few appeared willing to do anything about. The Ottawa interests who saw that regulation — government in partnership with business — would benefit them directly were willing to speak out most loudly on the issue. But even their attitude toward the forest was essentially one of *laissez-faire*. If government would only act to keep settler interlopers off their timber limits and help protect the limited reserves against fire, things would be okay. This position was succinctly summed up by Senator Edwards and a fellow lumberman, E.H. Bronson: "The suppression of forest fires . . . is the only way by which future timber supplies in Ontario can be secured; that done and the question of reproduction will very largely look after itself."[5]

The conservation movement in Canada failed to generate the popular enthusiasm it did in the United States, where the energetic Theodore Roosevelt made it one of his preoccupations during two terms in the White House. The Canadian movement did, though, provide a supportive background against which government gradually came to recognize the importance of at least some regulation of the forest resource. Early forest policy usually was concerned firstly with fire protection. But at the beginning of the century separate forest branches of government were established in the principal wood-producing provinces and by the federal government, at that time responsible for forest affairs in the prairie provinces and on the important railway belt in British Columbia.

At the same time the forestry profession gained increased status and came to be recognized as an important field of endeavour. Trained specialists were needed to staff the emerging government departments. Universities set up forestry schools, beginning at the University of Toronto, where a Royal Commission into the university had included staunch forestry advocate B.E. Walker, general manager of the Bank of Commerce. Walker's influence led to the establishment of a faculty of forestry in 1907 with Bernhard Fernow as dean. Fernow had set up the first professional forest school in the United States, at Cornell University in 1898, but he lasted only a few years there. An outspoken individual, the austere Prussian had upset certain interests downstate by advocating selection cutting as a method of forest management in a forest reserve area near Saranack Lake to which prominent New Yorkers were fond of adjourning when Manhattan became too hot in the summer. In 1903 the Governor of New York vetoed the Cornell school's appropriation — which had been unanimously approved by the state legislature — on the grounds that the silvicultural methods advocated by Fernow "had been subjected to grave criticism". Fernow himself made several allegations that the Governor had been influenced by wealthy New York bankers.[6]

The year after Fernow took over at Toronto, New Brunswick set up its own faculty of forestry at the provincial university in Fredericton. The Quebec government had also taken note of the looming importance of forestry. In 1905 the province sent two bright, young scholars, Gustave Piché and Avila Bédard, to the United States and Europe to study the science, which at the time was a novelty — at least in Canada. Piché returned to set up the Quebec Forestry Service and Bédard established the forestry faculty at Laval University.

With all this attention being lavished on the forest, and the increasing acknowledgement of the need for conservation, it might be expected that the governments that controlled the Crown timber, and the industry which cut and processed it, would have turned over a new leaf, as it were. Indeed, some thought that the blind exploitation of the previous century was coming to an end. With prominent business leaders at the helm of the conservation movement and government willing to do at least something in the way of forest administration and regulation, the time seemed ripe for a change. But on the other hand, the country was still apparently well-endowed with timber. Those most enthusiastic about conservation were based on the Ottawa and, though *they* had reason enough to be concerned about immediate supply problems, no such obstacles stood in the way of the entrepreneurs who were busily opening up northern forests for pulpwood logging or exploiting the coastal forests where the lumber business was just taking off.

ON THE WESTERN FRONTIER, people in the timber trade didn't
often talk conservation. They preferred the rollicking rhetoric of
the nineteenth century. It matched the optimism accompanying
the timber boom underway at the time.

M. Allerdale Grainger, the son of a British colonial official,
came to western Canada in search of gold and adventure in the
Klondike. Finding none of the former, the future Chief Forester
of British Columbia soon learned firsthand about the world of
the logging industry with its hard-drinking, rough and tumble
entrepreneurs and rugged individualists. Grainger's novel,
Woodsmen of the West, gives a fine sense of the gold rush atmosphere of the early days of B.C. logging, when nearly any man*
could stake a claim to a square mile of timber and take his
chance on the vagaries of the Vancouver log market. Things
were wide open. Handloggers, sawmilling firms and simple
speculators scurried about the inlets and valleys of the coast, all
trying to grab up the best of the rich timber resources. Douglas
fir and western red cedar were ideal for use as lumber, dwarfing
even the great white pine, mainstay of the eastern lumber industry. And, as with the pine, supplies seemed limitless.

Grainger's first-person narrative describes well the attitudes
of the operators, big and small, with whom he worked and
lived. The small men might resent the huge tracts of forest being
grabbed up by speculators and powerful sawmilling "interests":

> But the woods, to ordinary men, seemed limitless. A logger
> might stake a claim or two over specially tempting timber if
> he intended, some time, to cut logs in that place; but why
> should he take up leases as a speculation? He felt that he
> might just as well lock up a coal mine, speculating on the
> future exhaustion of the world's coal supplies.[7]

B.C. timberland became a hot commodity in spite of the
apparent abundance, or perhaps because of it. And no wonder.
Around the turn of the century, the total cut from provincial
land jumped by over 1,000 per cent in just eighteen years. When
lumbermen from the east had first started to open up B.C. forests, business was still on a pretty small scale. In 1889, 43.9
million board feet had been cut from provincial land. Within

---

* Nearly any man: Grainger quotes what was apparently a common dictum of
the time: "No Chinese or Japanese to be employed in working the timber."

seven years the cut had doubled and by 1901 it had doubled again to 241.3 million feet. The next six years saw an explosive growth in production so that in 1907, 566 million feet of timber were cut from B.C. forests, most of the logs being hauled from the damp woods of the raincoast.[8] The settlement of the prairies provided one market outlet for B.C. wood and the opening of the Panama Canal in 1914 brought another, with new access to the eastern seaboard and Europe.

This production boom provided a new source of revenue for the provincial government. In the midst of the expansion, the government saw an opportunity to cash in even further on the forest. In 1905 it abandoned its old system of granting five-year leases to timber and instituted a system of timber licences. Each new licence was of twenty-one years' duration and each could be bought and sold like any other commodity. What's more, the Conservative government of Richard McBride abolished the previous restriction on the number of licences any single person could hold, thus encouraging speculation. Enterprising individuals with little intention of getting into the timber business bought and held on to land, hoping the price would rise as timber became more valuable. The new policy also paved the way for the concentration of holdings into fewer and fewer hands. In 1910 it was revealed that one person held 375 timber licences of approximately 640 acres each and several other businessmen each held in the neighbourhood of 200 such licences.[9] The result of it all was a terrific flurry of land alienation, which brought the province the revenues it so dearly wanted. In fact, the licence system provided the Crown with more money than the lease system which preceded it, so much so that within two years the government stopped issuing licences.[10]

The large operators must have been well satisfied with the policy of the Crown regarding timber disposal. But, since the forest industry is a long-term proposition and the largest operators were unlikely to use up all their available wood supplies in the short space of twenty-one years, especially given the notorious ebbs and flows of the lumber market, they wanted their access to the timber to be secure over the longer term. In order to persuade the government that the licences should be renewable after twenty-one years, the industry picked up on the rhetoric of the conservation movement. The argument was that, unless tenures were renewable, licence holders would surely high-grade* the timber, getting as much as possible out of the woods in as short a time as possible and consequently depleting the province's valuable timber reserves. This was good political currency. It showed the industry in a favourable light: concerned with the orderly development of what had become B.C.'s most important industry.

However, what the industry was really interested in was the overproduction, market glut and low prices that would result from the unrestrained cutting its leaders knew would accompany non-renewable licences. The lumbermen also knew that bankers who frowned on short-term, non-renewable licences as collateral for loans necessary for mill construction would be more likely to look favourably upon applications from businessmen who held timber licences that could be renewed in virtual perpetuity.

The argument of the lumber industry essentially amounted to blackmail: "Let us have assured, continuous access to wood or we'll cut it all and get out quickly." But their position received sympathetic consideration by the province. The Crown wanted continuous revenue as much as the industry wanted a steady supply of timber. And in any case, the distinction between the representatives of the Crown and the leaders of industry was a fine one indeed.

In 1909 the government of British Columbia appointed a Royal Commission to look into all the questions surrounding its forest policy, among which the renewability of licences loomed large. It was an important inquiry. It not only set the tone for the Forest Act which followed, but also laid the basis for policy in the country's most important forest province for the next thirty-five years. The counsel for the Commission was J.A. Harvey, KC, who, it is acknowledged in the proceedings of the inquiry, "appeared on behalf of the lumbering interests of the province" and later became president of a lumber company.[11] Frederick Fulton, the Chairman of the Commission, was a prominent Conservative member of the assembly, whose Cabinet portfolio was Commissioner of Lands and Works. He was thus conducting an inquiry into the operations of his own depart-

* High-grading is a term often associated with the mining industry. It refers to a practice of removing the richest veins and leaving the lower grades of ore in the ground. In forestry it has the same connotation: taking the best and leaving the rest.

ment. At the hearings of the Commission he was joined by two other Tory commissioners, A.C. Flumerfelt, president of the Hastings Shingle Manufacturing Company, one of the largest in the world, and A.S. Goodeve, Conservative member for Rossland.

In spite of the importance of the Fulton Commission, the principal issue of licence renewability had apparently already been resolved by the government. Without waiting for Fulton to submit his final report, it brought in the renewability provision in 1910, prompting an American lumber operator with large holdings in British Columbia to remark glowingly, "I regard prudent investments in B.C. timber as unsurpassed by any other form of investment."[12] When the Commission did complete its work and the Forest Act of 1912 was drafted by sometime novelist Grainger (who had reportedly got the job as Secretary to the Fulton Commission when the original Secretary took his travel advance and went on a bender), the major forest concerns of the day were apparent.

The act established a Forest Branch to administer the province's key resource and called for new measures to protect the forest from fire. The Royal Commission had heard submissions from numerous industry representatives who expressed concern over fire protection and the importance of maintaining stands of mature timber for the immediate future. As a result, the act created a special fire protection fund. All other monies collected from forest operations in the form of stumpage and royalties were, however, to be ploughed into general revenues.

While Fulton had urged the creation of a special "Forest Sinking Fund", no legislative provisions were made to assure the province long-term supplies of timber through intensive forest management. The prevailing feeling was that, if the forest were protected from fire it would regenerate adequately by itself. It was cheaper to have nature do the job than to have government or the forest industry lay out money for forest management, which would cut into revenues. The do-nothing attitude even extended to the issue of the disposal of logging slash. The residues from logging — branches, tops, broken and rotten trees — not only were an obstacle to future growth. They also posed a serious fire hazard, becoming ideal tinder for forest fires when they dried out. Even though the Fulton Commission had recommended that logging operators be responsible for disposing of their own waste, the industry successfully argued that this would be too expensive. The question was resolved with loggers being obliged to clean up after themselves only if ordered to do so when the Forest Branch considered the fire hazard to be exceptional.

Since the province was primarily concerned with revenue from the forest and showed little regard for regulation, the Forest Branch was chronically short of funds and staff to the extent that government foresters had difficulty carrying out even their limited responsibilities. The government was interested in spending forest-earned dollars on infrastructural works such as roads, bridges and railways, providing entrepreneurs with the physical means to get at the province's resources, whether mineral or timber. In 1900 the B.C. government received $136,000 in forest revenue and by the time the Forest Act had been passed the Crown had pulled in $2.25 million in a single year.[13] But the Forest Branch saw little of this money. It was in the main charged with low profile matters: protecting standing timber from fire, administering the liquidation of that timber and attempting to get a vague idea of how much more was out there.

THOUGH CONSERVATION WAS judiciously used by those charged with administration of the forest, in no way could it be said that the forest in British Columbia, or anywhere else in Canada, was being managed with a view to ensuring future supplies of wood under the "sustained yield management" theory that had become popular early in the century. The longer view was held by a few foresters who, though enjoying some professional status, could only watch with mounting incredulity as their political and industrial masters sacrificed long-term stability for short-term revenues. Twenty-five years after British Columbia brought in its first Forest Act, a piece of legislation hailed at the time as a breakthrough in Canadian forestry, the province's Chief Forester, E.C. Manning, could state without exaggeration: "Forestry, in simple language, means the replacing of old crops. . . . I contend that in that respect forestry in this province has been more of a fancy than a fact. We have been so engaged in collecting revenues and protecting present values in mature timber that a new crop has received insufficient attention through lack of funds and staff."[14]

But, though conservation and sustained yield forest management were not being practised, the ideology of the conservation movement provided the underpinnings for the administrative treatment the forests of Canada received for most of this century. The vast natural reserves of coniferous forest could and would be best harvested and managed by big business in the most rational, orderly and efficient way possible. The conservationist vision, with its abiding faith in the virtues of science and technology — deployed by optimistic entrepreneurs for the benefit of all — could assist in justifying the alienation to large industrial corporations of much of the forest, and particularly the eastern boreal region which offered the promise of pulp. The future of the wood-using industry was bright in the view of those who saw natural resources being developed and renewed under the stable and efficient tutelage of the modern corporation.

Such a perspective was based not only on the rhetoric of the conservation idea, the legitimizing basis for forest administration. It also sprang from the basic changes that were reshaping the eastern Canadian forest industry in the first decades of the century. Trees in the east were now being mashed into pulp rather than sawn into lumber. New species of trees — and particularly the black spruce — previously ignored by makers of square timber and sawyers of lumber, suddenly took on a new importance. With new pulping technologies (paper had for many years been fabricated from old rags) accompanying the growth of literacy, newspapers grew in importance and created a demand for pulp made from long high-strength wood fibre. The growth of consumer spending, stimulated by printed advertising and itself stimulating a demand for paper packaging, also created a demand for pulp. The humble black spruce furnished these requirements very well. Located in northern forests crisscrossed with fast flowing rivers, which provided both cheap log transportation and cheap hydro-electric power to run the mills, the spruce was for the pulp and paper industry what the white pine had been for the square timber and lumber trades — a kind of Cinderella species.

The expanding market opportunities combined with the ideal supplies of raw material helped to create a new industry in

New Brunswick, Quebec and Ontario. It was an industry directed by large joint-stock corporations, unlike the family firms so important in the lumber industry of earlier days. Pulp mills sprouted up all over the east, and towns such as Bathurst, Iroquois Falls and Shawinigan Falls became manufacturing centres. In 1911 and 1913 the U.S. government, under pressure from the powerful newspaper publishers' lobby and particularly the Hearst interests, brought in tariff changes allowing the entry of Canadian newsprint to the U.S. market on a duty-free basis. American forests had been rapidly depleted and could not supply the demands of the expanding U.S. economy for pulp and paper. As a result the value of Canadian exports of pulp and paper rose from $1.8 million in 1900 to $163.1 million in 1920.[15] A brief but intense depression in 1920-21 was the final blow to the eastern sawmilling industry. The forest industry in the east became the pulp and paper business and lumber making was relegated to second place.

The growth of U.S. demand attracted ambitious industrial promoters confident that the boom would continue. Pulp and paper companies went on a wild mill-building spree in the prosperous 1920s, increasing newsprint capacity by 102 per cent between 1924 and 1929.[16] But promoters of the new businesses needed more than solid demand, electricity and the promise of ample wood supplies to get their ambitious plans underway. Because the mills were expensive to build, the business required a lot of capital, and bond underwriters have never liked to issue industrial bonds without getting security. The security necessary for the development of the pulp and paper industry had to be assured access to adequate supplies of pulpwood. With the help of friendly politicians, the paper companies were able to gain a secure grip on the forest through large timber concessions. Naturally, the biggest companies got the biggest concessions, usually on the basis of having promised to build new mills, use more wood and employ more workers.

In New Brunswick in 1896 the ten largest holders of Crown land leases held 40.3 per cent of the total land under lease. By 1926 the same number of large leaseholders had raised their control to 63.1 per cent of the Crown leases. Much of the land went to the International Paper Company, granted fifty-year licences to Crown land on the basis of its commitment to build mills in Dalhousie and on the Miramichi River. The Miramichi mill was never built but the company retained the timberland.[17]

Looking back from the vantage point of the Great Depression, Canada's Chief Forester calculated that in Ontario alone, while 14.3 million acres of pulpwood concessions were held by major corporations in 1921, the same firms held 35.6 million acres in 1930: an increase of 149 per cent. These companies had far more wood than they needed, with twenty-two acres of timberland for every cord of wood cut in 1922 and fifty-six acres per cord cut in 1930: an increase of 155 per cent.[18]

In Quebec the Liberal government of L. A. Taschereau was firmly committed to a strategy of economic growth based on liberal concessions to companies such as International Paper, Price Brothers and Wayagamack. Conservative nationalist elements in Quebec thought that the land should be colonized by Quebec settlers rather than alienated to American and English-Canadian pulp and paper companies. They advocated more control over timber cutting by foreigners and concessions to domestic businesses. The historical tension between settlement and agriculture was still evident in Quebec, where young men from the farm traditionally found work in the bush. Indeed, they had but little choice since it was often the only way to survive. Quebec nationalists watched with growing unease the fast-developing pulp and paper industry becoming increasingly controlled by outsiders. Every fall the French woodcutters would head for the bush: "C'est les gens de Ross-Ritchie qui montent aux chantiers" — the bosses were all English. One nationalist writer describes the widespread feeling towards the domination of forest frontier by *les étrangers*: "All this land was our heritage. Discovered by the French, explored by our ancestors, turned into wealth by the labour of French-Canadians, it remains a rich heritage shut off from us, like a fiefdom in which we can be the poor peasants without the hope of ever being the seigneurs."[19]

But the Liberals had a patronage machine well oiled by concessions to the paper companies and aided by private acts passed through the Legislative Assembly on a regular basis, giving special rights to corporations. Opposition members were quick to point to the outright sale of Anticosti Island to a consortium of paper companies in 1926 as evidence of the resource giveaway. Three years earlier a former Quebec Forest Service employee, Thomas Maher, had denounced the government's forest policy at a colonization convention. He charged that the pulp and paper industry was being allowed to expand too quickly and that the Forest Service was not properly supervising cutting and conditions on the large tracts of land ceded to the companies.[20] Gustave Piché, head of the Forest Service, could do little but place his faith in the large firms, which he considered the only hope for the development of sustained yield forest management. Piché argued that the pulp and paper industry, with its heavy commitments of capital, had to be guaranteed a continuous supply of wood, and pointed to one company he saw as setting an example for the future. "The capital invested in a paper factory is too great to tolerate the supply of raw materials falling. We shall see, therefore, these companies having their forests inventoried and managing them carefully, but also doing reforesting work, as the Laurentide Company has begun to."[21]

IN THE ONTARIO OF THE 1920s, influence-peddling and back-scratching dominated the administration of the province's forests. And the name that best personified government collusion with the industry was that of the sometimes provincial premier, Howard Ferguson.

About Ferguson, a story is told of a train ride westward through the boreal forest of Ontario, toward the end of the decade. The passengers could see around them nothing but dense stands of black spruce and jack pine, the spiky little trees sticking up everywhere like the hair on the back of a wet dog. As they perused the view on this day in 1927, several distinguished travellers on board the observation car fell into discussing the upcoming Conservative leadership race. They were on their way to the Tory national convention in Winnipeg where, as prominent movers and shakers from the back rooms of Toronto politics, they would have a hand in the selection of a man they hoped would lead their party back to power in Ottawa. Naturally enough, the talk turned to the array of potential leadership candidates and the merits of those who aspired to be the next Prime Minister. And, just as predictably, the name of Ontario

Premier Howard Ferguson was raised as a possible choice. One staunch party member must have taken some inspiration from the passing spectacle and was moved to remark, "Ferguson is an able leader, but he still smells too much of the odour of spruce trees to be named the leader of our party."[22]

Evidently, Ferguson's name had about it a whiff of scandal. Back in 1919 Ferguson had been the Minister of Lands, Forests and Mines in the administration of William Hearst. When the Hearst government was dumped in that year by the United Farmers amidst the populist upsurge following World War I, the new administration quickly launched a Royal Commission to look into persistent rumours of shady deals surrounding the administration of the province's forests. The Timber Commission, as it came to be known, soon exposed a tawdry mass of corruption and patronage, implicating Ferguson. In the final year of the Hearst government, Ferguson had, in direct violation of the laws of the province, transferred 1,200 square miles of public timberland to private corporations, without any recourse to public tenders or open competition. What had been common knowledge in forest industry circles became public knowledge — if you wanted access to timber around the Lakehead you had to do business with the "old Tory timber ring" there. This process would inevitably enrich party coffers. One lumberman, J.A. Mathieu, was able to use his position as a member of the Conservative caucus to gain access to timber limits without going through the bothersome and costly procedures laid down in the provincial statutes. For timberland that Ferguson made available to Mathieu, the member's firm, Shevlin-Clarke, paid less than half of the $2 million normally payable to the government.[23]

The fact that Ferguson's party went out of its way to satisfy political friends just prior to election time surprised few close observers of the political scene. Party funds had to come from somewhere and they did not come from disinterested altruists. What was surprising was the political resiliency subsequently exhibited by the Honourable Mr. Ferguson, who became leader of his party and Premier of Ontario before the echoes of scandal even had a chance to die in the halls of the legislature. Ferguson never recanted and vigorously defended his actions. Indeed, once back in power, he continued to favour the largest forest interests.

Ferguson's thinking was simple enough. If the wood

resources of the province were to be developed and to provide jobs, prosperity and government revenue, the forests should be entrusted to the biggest and most able companies around. For the companies to build the mills they needed investment capital. When the Spanish River Pulp and Paper Company and the Abitibi Pulp and Paper Company wanted to expand their northern Ontario operations in the midst of the newsprint boom just after World War I, their cautious Chicago bankers were anxious to know whether or not their customers would be able to secure timber limits from the Ontario government. George Mead of Spanish River and Frank Anson of Abitibi turned to Howard Ferguson, who proved only too happy to oblige. The Minister handed over cutting rights to nearly 7,000 square miles of timberland to the two firms, again without any recourse to the laws of the province, which stipulated competitive bidding for such limits. The bankers were satisfied, as were the paper companies. Unfortunately for them, Ferguson was soon out of office. When called before the Timber Commission to explain his actions he was clear enough about his motivations:

> I worked out that policy along the lines which I think are sound business methods and in the best interests of this province; I have not any hesitation, I am not afraid of these criticisms, because I stand behind these arrangements absolutely anywhere, that these are sound business arrangements made with competent business men with the sole object of developing the forestry interests of the province for the benefit of the people.[24]

If Ferguson had to circumvent certain legal restrictions to ensure that the forest was put in such reliable hands, what matter? Jobs were being created and the wheels of commerce were turning smoothly. The disposal of the timber was regarded as a sound business arrangement, a fact implicitly recognized by Ferguson's foes in the next administration, a joint Farmer/Labour coalition. In the course of that administration and despite objections from the United Farmers' own political organization, the same government that had started the investigation into Ferguson's misconduct turned over pulp limits in northwestern Ontario to E.W. Backus, a Minnesota pulp and lumber operator who was setting up the Great Lakes Paper Company. The only other bids on the timber came from Backus' own partner and his paper broker. In addition, the new United Farmers government made timber promises of its own — similar to the promises Ferguson had been making. It pledged timberland to the Spruce Falls Pulp and Paper Company in a fashion that mirrored the previous government's method of doing business with Abitibi and Spanish River. As a result, when Ferguson came back into power in 1923, he had no trouble justifying the same policy of encouragement and assistance through generous forest concessions for the largest paper companies. As Ferguson explained, "They must have a future assured if they are to interest capital and if our forestry operations are to be carried on in a way that will secure reproduction and perpetuity."[25]

Apparently, Ontario's Ferguson shared with Quebec's Forest Service head Piché an abiding confidence in the ability of the large pulp and paper companies to manage successfully their limits for a new crop of timber. But their confidence sprang more from political and economic than silvicultural considerations. It was a confidence not borne out by subsequent forestry developments or by the way in which logging and forest management were carried out on the lands licensed to the industrial users of wood.

AMONG FORESTERS, and indeed among politicians and company managers, the prevailing wisdom of the day declared that cutover lands could best regenerate themselves and that this natural regeneration would provide a new crop of spruce, the desired species, to replace the previous stands cut for pulpwood. Now, foresters knew then as they know today that natural regeneration, as opposed to artificial regeneration (the planting of the new crop of trees) was a valid method of promoting a new crop. And at the time natural regeneration was almost an article of faith among foresters concerned with silviculture, whether they worked for government or industry. Perhaps the principal reason for the belief in the capacity of the forest to renew itself without human assistance was the fact that natural regeneration is cheap. Since the forests were seen by the state as a source of funds and by the companies as a source of wood fibre for hungry pulp mills, costly efforts at seeding and carefully nurturing new stands of timber were simply unthinkable. Expensive treatments and intensive silviculture: These things were all right in Europe where supplies were tight. But in Canada, where a few large companies held huge tracts of mature pulpwood, often more than they needed for wood but enough to satisfy financiers, there were no shortages looming in the minds of management. Natural regeneration would do very well.

There is certainly some basis for this faith in natural regeneration. On certain sites, if logging is carried out with a view to the promotion of a new growth of timber, the results will be a healthy stand of young trees. But the key here is the absolute necessity of integrating silviculture with logging. For logging is itself a form of forest management, the first in a series of steps which, if carried out in careful accordance with site conditions, will on certain sites result in good regeneration of the trees the forest manager wants. This can mean that little or no human assistance will be needed. For example, clearcutting in checkerboard patterns, shelterwood systems designed to provide seed for cutover land while avoiding blowdown, or selection cutting* can all be applied in some places with good results. But what is important to note here are the qualifications. Forests are complex and highly variable ecological systems. Measures to manipulate ecological succession must be carried out with the specifics of each different site in mind. What works on some sites may not work on others, and cutting systems designed to encourage regeneration must vary accordingly. On many forested areas, natural regeneration as a forest management method will just not work. This is why forestry and silviculture are often said to be as much an art as a science. A cardinal rule forest managers must keep in mind is the fact that everything they do is *site specific.*

---

* In a *shelterwood cutting system,* a substantial number of trees is removed, but enough of the original stand is left to provide shelter and shade for a succeeding generation. This system promotes the growth of an even-aged forest, through a system of regeneration that often involves artificial treatment.

In *selection cutting,* only the mature, overmature and dead trees are removed. This gives the young and near-mature trees more room to grow, and promotes an uneven-aged forest, through natural regeneration.

Clearcutting involves cutting everything in a given area, leaving only the odd commercially-undesirable tree.

A log boom enroute to the mill. Since the early days of the forest industry in Canada the woods have been treated mostly as a source of supply for the mills, rather than as a renewable resource.

For most of this century natural regeneration has been, in forestry terms, the prevailing philosophy. In industrial terms it has been the prevailing expediency. Cutting systems have been designed by woodlands managers of pulp and paper companies with a view to the cost of the wood delivered to the mill yard, not with a view to securing a new crop of trees. There is absolutely no doubt about this, according to foresters who have been employed by the companies. One of the earliest of these foresters was Ellwood Wilson, said to be the first professional forester employed by a pulp and paper firm in Canada. Wilson went to work for the Laurentide Company in 1905, attempting to manage the firm's limits in the St. Maurice watershed in central Quebec. Three years after Wilfrid Laurier's Forestry Convention marked a high point of concern for the future forest, Wilson pointed out the results of the cutting practices of the day. He noted that, while the industry was floating as much spruce pulpwood downstream as it could every spring, balsam fir was beginning to replace the spruce on the cutover sites. Spruce was the key species at the time and no one wanted balsam, except perhaps the spruce budworm, which thrives on it. Wilson reflected, "It seems that such a system of cutting is slowly depreciating the value of the limits. . . . Cutting regulations are in force, but there is no adequate inspection."[26]

The first growth, the virgin timber, was being cut without any long-term considerations. The results are evident today, over seventy years after Wilson noticed the situation. In the east, the spruce budworm is a chronic problem. In addition, if eastern pulpmills continue to use wood at present rates they will inevitably face shortages in the not-so-distant future. In New Brunswick the annual cut of softwood has exceeded sustainable limits by at least 15 per cent in recent years, bringing on "imminent shortages of quality timber".[27] No meeting of government and industry officials concerned with the future of the industry can avoid soul-searching discussions of impending wood supply problems. Seventy years is the approximate rotation age — the time it should take for a new crop of timber to grow and be cut again — for spruce in many parts of the east.

Evidently, Laurier's forestry convention did little or nothing to change the way Canadian forests were being treated. But it did result in the creation of a federal Commission on Conservation. Though the Commission had at its top echelons more than the odd timber magnate, it did provide, for the first time, the opportunity for foresters to carry out in-depth studies of forest conditions in several parts of the country. It was found that in Nova Scotia, where most of the forest land had been allowed to pass into private hands, previously forested areas were suffering the effects of unrestrained, unplanned cutting activity. A survey of the Trent watershed in south-central Ontario revealed that the entire area had been denuded of its white pine and that subsequently settlers had been unable to harvest anything of value, leaving a legacy of abandoned farms and social dislocation.[28] The Chief Forester for the Commission on Conservation, Clyde Leavitt, distinctly saw the crucial factor causing the continuing forest neglect. It was primarily an issue of logging for cheap wood rather than logging for future forests. In a letter to an American paper company official in 1920, Leavitt observed:

> Nothing like enough attention has been given to the question of so regulating the methods of cutting to leave the

> cutover lands in a productive condition. The whole effort
> thus far has been centred upon attempts by woods superin-
> tendants to keep down logging costs and make a satisfac-
> tory showing in comparison with the costs of other com-
> panies and the costs of previous years.[29]

A few months previously Leavitt had issued another warning to the readers of the *Financial Post*. He said that even before the great overexpansion of the twenties, when pulping capacity increased on a yearly basis and newsprint capacity rose from 1,823 thousand tons in 1925 to 4,263 thousand tons in 1935,[30] companies were being forced to go further and further to secure adequate wood supplies for their mills: "The cutover lands they leave behind are, for the most part, not left in a condition that promises the possibility of a second cut within a reasonable length of time."[31] If Leavitt had been wrong about the supply situation, the hand-wringing which has more recently preoc-cupied forest planners in Canada might not have occurred.

What was the reason for this state of affairs? It had been clear enough that the overcutting and waste of the previous century had been an important cause of the demise of the sawmilling industry in the east. The provincial governments were now plac-ing their faith in the ability and willingness of large paper com-panies to do a better job than their lumbering predecessors, hoping the companies would manage the forest well enough to produce wood "in perpetuity". Authorities like those in Quebec, who by the early 1930s had placed 91 per cent of the licensed Crown lands in the hands of the pulp and paper companies, must have had some confidence in these firms.[32]

The paper companies grew in association with the expansion of the demand for newsprint and pulp and as they did so they developed separate woodlands operations to ensure that the raw materials needed to feed the mills would be in reliable sup-ply. The top position in this corporate division would be held by a Woodlands Manager, whose immediate subordinate would be the Woods Superintendant, the person actually in charge of the operation: planning the cut, hiring contractors and generally overseeing the logistics of the timber harvest. Below the Superintendant there might be a trained forester, hired by the company to oversee a forest management plan. These people were involved in a race against time: Bad weather, adverse ter-rain, supply problems and myriad other snags could always delay their efforts to feed the mill for another year. If the piles of pulpwood placed by the stream were not big enough by the time spring breakup came, things could go poorly indeed for the mill's production capacity for the next twelve months. Needless to say, things would also go poorly for the woodlands managers in the event of such a foul-up.

Though technologies have changed radically in the past fifty years, the basic organization of the woodlands operation remains much as it was back in 1927 when John Wilson joined Anglo-Canadian Pulp and Paper Mills Ltd. to work its limits in Quebec. Wilson had received his M.A. in forestry from Oxford University in 1914 and, like most of his young fellow Englishmen, joined the armed forces. After spending three and a half years as a prisoner of war, he spent five years travelling about Central Europe studying techniques developed by foresters there over the course of several centuries. At Anglo-Canadian the knowledge he had gained served him well. Within two years he was the company's Woods Superintendant, having moved up from Assistant Superintendant and Chief Forester. By 1932 he was the Woods Manager, in charge of the entire logging operation. Later in his career Wilson served as chairman of the Woodlands Section of the Canadian Pulp and Paper Association, the industry umbrella group. Speed and efficiency were the hallmarks of a successful forest engineer and Wilson was apparently such a man.

Looking back over his experiences at the heart of the industrial system of log production, Wilson saw that much of the industry was a carry-over from the days of the broad-axe and the sawmill, when "cut and get out" was the rule of thumb for harvesting a crop of standing timber. He saw that the "forestry" point of view was entirely secondary to the "logging" outlook, and pointed out that control over the woods operations of the paper companies was entrusted to "competent loggers who know little and care less about the future of the forest".[33] Wilson's experience was that the Woods Manager would design the organization of his operation with a view to cutting the wood and delivering it to the mill. It was crucial that the logs be available in sufficient quantity and delivered on time. He summed up the way in which the forests were treated:

> This method of obtaining supplies, and the outlook associated with it, has come into being over a number of years,

indeed the ideas, methods and policies which govern the
Supply System of our mills began with the earliest colonists. The fundamental conception of this Supply Policy is
— adequate supplies, ready to hand, from virgin forests,
with no concern whatsoever with the Management of the
forest areas under operation for future supplies.... The
main concern of the owners of the mill is to keep the mill
running at a profit. To do this, wood supplies are essential
— they must be cheap this year, next year, and, if possible,
over the life of the mill. Beyond, the owners of the mill have
no concern whatsoever.[34]

Evidently, the confidence Canadian politicians placed in paper
company owners as custodians of the future forest was somewhat misplaced.

Confronted with any criticism of the way they treated the
forest, company owners would doubtless respond in the way
they still do today. They would point out that their companies
were mere tenants renting the forest land, paying large amounts
in stumpage and royalty charges to the actual owners of the
timberland, the government. Government, of course, displayed
the same outlook as industry when it came to the forest. The
state was interested in industrial expansion, continuity of
exports of semi-finished wood products and a constant flow of
revenue from the forest to the public purse. This was essentially
the same short-term perspective displayed by the paper companies and their owners, whose welfare was also close to the
hearts of politicians. After twenty years of observing this relationship, John Wilson concluded: "It looks as if the parties
interested in our forests are each waiting for the other to do the
necessary. The solution lies in getting together and deciding
what has to be done and who can best do it. Meanwhile, Rome
burns!"[35]

While the economy was expanding, as it was in the years
before the depression of the 1930s, the narrowly-based conception of forest management did allow for the creation of a certain
crude regime of forest regulation. More foresters, hired out of
the newly-established forestry schools, were put to work on fire
and disease protection. Government-employed foresters also
attempted to establish how much wood was actually out there:
No one really knew and even today there is still considerable
debate on the matter. They conducted forest inventories and

rate of growth surveys. But as late as 1929 there was no standard definition of what constituted a cord of wood. Just before the depression all but destroyed forestry in Canada for ten years, a federal-provincial conference was convened in hopes that it could come up with some figures. Its goal: "The attainment of knowledge relating to the area, timber content, growth and use of forests . . . so that the forests of the Dominion may be placed on the basis of sustained yield — that they may be 'cropped' rather than mined as heretofore." The conference concluded that there was indeed no adequate forest inventory and that progress on this front was inadequate due to financial limitations at the provincial level.[36] Apparently, provincial administrations had a financial perspective which reflected the revenue rather than the costs and expenses side of the forest earnings statement and consequently were doing little even in this most basic area.

In fact, just about the only thing government employed foresters could do to work for the future of the forest was to control the size of the trees being cut by enforcing diameter limits. Regulations in most provinces stipulated that trees under a certain "DBH" (diameter at breast height) be left standing to form the basis of a second crop. Diameter limits were a crude form of silviculture, if indeed they could be considered silviculture at all. And, since provincial forestry services were, even before the depression, chronically underfinanced and their personnel overextended, there were problems enforcing even those regulations. It would in most cases be far more likely for a priest than a government forestry official to visit the isolated winter logging camps. In any case, diameter limit control was like the fire protection and other measures that occupied the energies of forest officials when they weren't scaling (measuring) the logs to calculate how much money the industrial tenant owed the government landlord. It was essentially a defensive and reactive mechanism, which did little to ensure adequate reproduction of timber. To accomplish that, natural regeneration was more likely to be prescribed. In any case, since different species on different sites in different parts of the country were being treated in the same production-oriented fashion by the industrial users of wood, any long-term outlook for the forests of the country was by 1929 more of a mirage than a reality.

THE DEPRESSION DID NOT SPARE Canada's forest-based industries, though for a short time it did take the pressure off the forest. The financial crash that affected all industries was combined in the pulp and paper industry with the effects of the overexpansion of capacity which had occurred in the previous decade— an over-expansion promoted by anxious industrialists and encouraged by eager politicians. During that period of expansion, pulp and paper industry executives had borrowed heavily on Canada's forest collateral to finance new mills. They had secured loans, preferred stock issues and bonds to build up their pulpwood empires. When the economy hit the skids, a flurry of mergers and bankruptcies hit the industry. Although demand for pulp and paper products dropped, the debts still had to be serviced, by firms with high fixed costs and rigid financial structures. As a result, over half of the bloated capacity of the newsprint industry went into receivership and east of the Rockies only six firms were left in control of 80 per cent of the mill capacity.[37] A "bankers' committee" was established to encourage governments to force the companies to get together and fix the price of newsprint. Provincial administrations complied, worried that more mill closures in such a large and important industry would be disastrous and further swell the growing number of unemployed. The companies were forced into price "co-operation", much to the chagrin of the American newspapers that bought their products.

While this highly visible and well-publicized drama was unfolding at the various centres of financial and political power, the effects of the big slump on the forest hinterland failed to attract the same attention and interest. Government expenditures on forestry, never very significant, were drastically curtailed. In Ontario the field staff of the Forestry Branch was cut, with 113 employees including five district foresters getting the sack. So many foresters were fired that a group of them got together to petition their association, the Canadian Society of Forest Engineers, to do something to make sure there was some forest management in the province. One CSFE member later recalled, "Though the Depression called for surgical measures, it seemed that panic overrode cool judgement."[38]

There was even concern expressed by some segments of the forest industry over government's willingness, not to say eagerness, to cut forest-related spending. In 1937 J.S. Gillies, a prominent Ottawa Valley lumberman, wrote to the federal Minister of Mines and Resources (responsible for federal forestry) expressing concern over the comparatively small sums being spent on forests in comparison to other natural resources. A subsequent memo from a member of the Dominion Forest Service staff pointed out that Mr. Gillies had been misinformed when he complained that federal forest spending had been a mere $430,000 in 1936. The figure in fact was $314,000. The DFS forest economist went on to calculate federal spending on forestry as a proportion of the value of exports of forest products at 0.17 per cent. The fishery, however, received in federal funds 7.7 per cent of the value of exports of the catch, while the same percentages for agriculture and mining were 3.01 per cent and 2.17 per cent. The disgruntled official then pointed out that, if one per cent of the export value of forest products was spent on forestry, it would be equal to the amount spent on the fishery — an industry whose products had one-seventh the export value of forest products.[39] Apparently there were more votes associated with fishing than with forestry, although during the early 1930s the forest industries were one of the principal mainstays of the Canadian economy. Exports of wood products accounted for $143 million of the $168.9 million in favourable balance of trade between 1931 and 1935.[40]

Funding cuts affected forest branches right across the country, playing havoc with protection, regulation, management and research programs. Those closest to the forest scene saw clearly what was happening but were in no position to take any action. The Director of the Dominion Forest Service, E.H. Finlayson, had despaired when Mackenzie King transferred responsibility for forest and other natural resources from the federal to the three prairie governments back in 1930. (Finlayson was confident that the provinces would ignore forest concerns). In 1934, when he was approaching the end of his career, he wrote:

> Notwithstanding the celerity with which timber supplies were being compromised as a basis for [the] over-

development [of industrial capacity] there has not been
exerted a proportional effort to ensure the safety of the raw
materials upon which the entire industry is foundationed.
Indeed the greater the financial pinch became, the less, pro-
portionately, was done to safeguard the forest. Great effort
was made to ensure the safety of the plants themselves,
when, at the same time, in the forests, upon which these
establishments depend for the material they are designed
to manufacture, the forces for management and protection
were cut to the bone.[41]

For the first time a recurring theme in the history of forest
policy in Canada became apparent to any one of the very limited
number of Canadians keeping tabs on the progressive exhaustion of the country's capacity to reproduce merchantable*
timber. Because this group was so small and relatively powerless
— control over the resource was vested in a handful of
public and private apostles of the creed of mass production —
their concerns could be ignored. Most people at the time were
putting all possible energy into surviving the joblessness and
hard times. They had little time to think about the politics of
resource management. So it was simple enough for government
and industry to ignore considerations of declining future values
— and employment — in the face of present values.

A regeneration study of representative logged-over lands on
Vancouver Island was published in 1938, revealing the success
of the silvicultural strategy of British Columbia's Forest Service.
On the 19,981 acres studied and logged between 1921 and 1938,
only 5.4 per cent were satisfactorily stocked with timber which
would one day be merchantable. The other 94.6 per cent failed to
meet the standard. When areas logged before 1933 were
analyzed, the same results were obtained. And a smaller sample
of 3,204 acres logged prior to 1927 revealed 10 per cent satisfactory stocking.[42] Vancouver Island, with the longest growing season for trees of any area in Canada, also has some of the best
sites, including rich soils and ample moisture. The immense
trees that had flourished on this land before being cut for the
lumber trade were not being replaced by a similar crop, so that
the productivity of the prime growing sites of what was arguably the country's most important industry was being lost.

---

* Merchantable: a buzzword unique to forest talk meaning, roughly, trees economically usable in current industrial processes.

Natural regeneration was not working in the damp coastal valleys because of unregulated logging methods. The British Columbia Forest Service had neither the funds nor the people to enforce detailed cutting guidelines, even if such had existed. Some forest managers, among them E.C. Manning, head of the BCFS, had seen clearly that "artificial" treatments would be necessary if the situation were to be remedied. The top forest manager in what had become Canada's most important forest province even hinted darkly at expensive planting programs which he thought might do more for regeneration than simply allowing nature to take its course. Manning was on his way from Ottawa to Victoria to present his views on the politics of forest management when his plane crashed in the forest near Armstrong, Ont., and he was killed. Though he never delivered his speech, he had intended to warn his audience that those who advocated new forestry methods would have to tread softly for fear of reprisal. In his address, published after his death, Manning argued that presentations illustrating unsatisfactory growing conditions or promoting new ways of alleviating these conditions were likely to be greeted with hostility from certain quarters. Manning wrote: "Where remedies that cost money are involved, finance ministers do not look kindly on such expenditures largely in the interests of a generation not yet represented at the polls. Influential business interests watch any policy that may affect their profits."[43]

Yet if government and forest industry leaders were wary of what they perceived to be excessively costly solutions to the country's chronic forest problems, there was certainly no one else in any position to effect change. Both parties in the deal were likely to avoid doing anything costly, for big investments in forest management do not yield immediate returns — political or financial. Provincial governments were doing little enough to adequately manage the lands they had licensed to the private sector. The Canadian Forestry Association estimated that in 1943 governments at all levels were spending only two-and-a-half cents out of every dollar they received from the primary forest products industries on forest protection and perpetuation.[44]

Thirty-six years later a consultant hired by the Canadian Pulp and Paper Association told that organization's Woodlands Section that provincial and federal spending on forest renewal was only five-and-a-half cents on every dollar collected and referred to the new amount as "a real shocker... not good enough!"[45] The consultant, Les Reed, soon went on to become the Assistant Deputy Minister of the Environment in charge of the Canadian Forestry Service. If Reed was shocked at the pitiful amounts of money being returned by government to the forest in order to assure its future, the head of the economics division of the same Forest Service was equally appalled back in the 1940s at the effort industry was willing to devote to the same task:

> On the licenced lands the state and the licensee should share the responsibility for the perpetuation of the forests. At present the licensees are inclined to shirk their responsibility. The excuse offered is that their tenure being insecure they are not justified in making investments for which they may never secure returns. As a matter of fact, their licences are for the most part renewable in perpetuity though conditions of royalty, rental and regulations are subject to change.[46]

Government interest in change in the treatment of the forest was likely to be confined to moves designed to increase its share of the take. But still, the situation in forestry was not completely static. University and government researchers were expanding knowledge of the country's forest soils, silvicultural potential, protection measures and numerous other aspects of the growing forestry field. Research papers exploring new areas were provoking spirited debate among foresters. The potential for more informed treatment of the forest resource grew. But still, by the end of World War II something as basic as an adequate inventory of the forest resource still did not exist.[47] Without knowledge of how much timber there was, how fast it was growing or being cut or otherwise depleted by fire and pests, and how well it was being utilized it was extremely difficult if not impossible even to begin to manage the forest on a sustained-yield basis. Without this knowledge there could be no calculation of Annual Allowable Cuts (AAC) in specific areas or even entire provinces. The whole idea of sustained yield forest management — ensuring that the resource is in fact renewable — is based on the principle of cutting only an amount of wood equal to the quantity replaced each year by new growth. This is in keeping with a theory of forestry that holds that the forest is like a pool of capital, that in one year you should only extract from the pool an equivalent amount of wood equal to that which the ecosystem replaces through natural growth. Before the turn of the century, and for a good many years after it, this theory failed to take hold. Yet most businessmen know that if you live off your accumulated capital and fail to reinvest earnings, you will soon be in serious trouble. Still, the fact remains that the history of forest exploitation is one of depletion of the forest capital by both government and industry. No thought was given to the use of the forest as a renewable resource, to the use of wood that grew each year — the "interest" generated by the capital — and to the preservation of the forest to ensure the continued production of wood for the future.

But, while knowledge of the forest resource was inadequate, the pressure on timber reserves continued to escalate. The pulp and paper industry, primarily concentrated in the east, had begun to recover before the outbreak of the war. By 1939 production was already up 12.5 per cent from the beginning of the depression.[48] During the war, labour and energy shortages clashed with pressing demands on the forest to provide lumber for the war effort. According to the wartime Dominion Timber Controller, housing construction jumped 75 per cent during the war compared to the previous ten years, stimulating a 40 per cent increase in demand for lumber.[49] The postwar period promised a continuing boom based on the housing needs of the thousands of veterans returning to civilian life. The average production of lumber in the period 1952-54 was 67 per cent higher than for 1926-30 and 89 per cent higher than for 1936-39. But by the early 1950s, Ontario, once the source of so much sawn timber, had become a net importer of lumber. The forest frontier was the interior of British Columbia, where lumber production rose by 440 per cent between 1945 and 1954.[50] B.C. forests supplied about three-fifths of the wood needed for the dramatic increases in postwar lumber consumption.

With the lifting of wartime controls, pulp and paper production took off once again: companies reported record shipments of both newsprint and market pulp. Advertising linage in the United States — the destination of 85 per cent of Canadian exports — rose by 19 per cent over the previous year, promising another period of expansion for eastern Canadian pulp and paper producers.[51] Mills were once again operating at full tilt. This prompted the industry to begin another round of increases in capacity so that in the ten years from 1945 to 1955 production of pulp and paper rose by 71 per cent.[52] Given this expansion, it is all the more remarkable that still, by the early 1950s, more trees were being cut down for lumber than for pulp, thanks to the as yet unexhausted forests of British Columbia.

All of this frantic expansion put more pressure than ever on the forest resource. Wartime overcutting, combined with even greater postwar demands, meant that more wood than ever was being harvested. Once again loggers were forced to follow the receding forest to sites further from mills where trees were smaller and of poorer quality. High-grade wood was simply becoming harder to find. In British Columbia the cut started its move up from the valley bottoms and onto the mountainsides, where the size of the trees declined. The change was reflected in the cost of logs delivered to the mills. In 1928 a B.C. coastal sawmill paid $10.07 for a thousand feet of wood. By 1953 the cost in constant dollars was up to $16.92 — and the logs were smaller and not as good for lumber. The high quality species, especially the much sought Douglas fir, became more expensive as supplies declined. The amounts of stumpage bid by timber buyers at sales conducted by the provincial government rose dramatically. In the period 1931-1940 the average stumpage bid was $2.44 per thousand feet. By 1952 the B.C. Forest Service was receiving bids of up to $10.84 for the same amount of Douglas fir.[53]

The postwar business boom also brought new houses to Canada's growing suburbs and greater flows of newsprint to daily newspapers south of the border, particularly in the key markets of Ohio and Indiana. People close to the industry were faced with the inescapable reality of the decline in timber quality and accessibility accompanying this trend. Wood costs were rising and something had to be done — forest renewal, sustained-yield forest management, production of wood in perpetuity — call it what you will. Meetings were called to bring together government and industry people for consultations over what measures to take.

As early as 1945 the federal forestry officials had brought together the managers responsible for forestry on the limits of virtually every pulp and paper firm in the country. That year, D.R. Cameron, head of the Dominion Forest Service, spoke to assembled industry delegates about his trip to France, where he had hoped to learn about specific silvicultural cutting methods employed to maximize new growth. On the contrary, the French told Cameron that there were in fact no such blanket prescriptions. Rather, cutting methods varied according to soil potential, soil and ground conditions, and species. In short, Cameron reported, the French had learned to design their cutting methods to secure the best possible natural regeneration on a site-specific basis. They "followed Nature and used the best judgement on what should be done in that particular area and if it had to be different from an area a short distance away, that was the way they did it."

But such precise silvicultural procedures weren't often followed in Canada, said one of Cameron's research people, G. Tunstell. The industry position was most often "Sorry, can't do it — costs won't permit it." Tunstell acknowledged that industry was usually concerned only with the costs of the wood delivered to the mill: "Perhaps in order to reduce costs or keep costs down they do sacrifice their future yields for the sake of immediate gains. As I have explained it to some farmers, they wanted to kill the pig when it was half grown."[54]

The importance of the message underlying Tunstell's metaphor may or may not have been lost on the assembled corporate and government forest officials. It's likely that some left the meeting with heightened resolve. But interest in the chronic problems associated with forest renewal has a tendency to vacillate in the same way that the economy follows the rollercoaster course of the business cycle. In periods of economic expansion, such as after World War II, more attention tends to be paid to forestry matters. Postwar prosperity did appear to offer the promise of better things for Canadian forests. There seemed to be a rekindled interest in the stability and endurance of the resource, as the basis for one of Canada's most important industries. But genuine forest management, regrettably, takes on some of the characteristics of an affordable luxury. And luxuries are easy to forgo. This is regrettable because really adequate forest renewal efforts require consistent, long-term commitments, something of a rarity in government policy.

THERE IS A LONG and noble tradition in Canada. When a problem is perceived to be acute, or if there is sufficient public agitation to necessitate something be seen to be done, a Royal Commission is appointed to investigate and recommend remedial measures. Unfortunately, the reports of these Commissions are often ignored, particularly when their recommendations run contrary to prevailing public and private policy currents. But when Royal Commissions recommend measures that mesh nicely with conventional wisdom, their reports are sometimes used a basis for change. When the problems facing the forests of two of the country's principal wood-producing provinces became clear in the 1940s, each province launched a Royal Commission to find out what was to be done.

In British Columbia the best stands of timber in the most accessible areas had been high-graded since the early days of the industry. Few if any provisions for the renewability of those stands were made while at the same time large areas of mature and over-mature timber were ignored. By the 1940s, the opposition in the B.C. legislature was devoting considerable time to criticism of the government for its do-nothing attitude toward the forest. The forest industry was also disgruntled. The explosion in demand for B.C. wood had stimulated business, whetting the industry appetite for bigger mills and the long-term wood supplies necessary for investments in new, larger conversion plants. Existing systems of tenure were inadequate to meet these needs. So the government appointed a judge to explore the problems.

In his final report, published in 1945, the Hon. Gordon Sloan made clear his opinion that the practices of the past could not be allowed to continue without serious consequences: "To permit the owners of Crown-granted lands to log them off and leave them without taking any steps to secure the growth of a new crop is to jeopardize seriously the future development of our logging industry. This, in turn, will lead to unemployment and the decline of communities into ghost towns."[55] Though Sloan was referring in this case to lands owned by private operators, not the province, he could have just as easily been talking of any number of cutover public forest sites in the province.

In fact, ghost towns similar to those left in the wake of the eastern lumber industry already dotted British Columbia. A brief to the Sloan Commission from the government's own Department of Trade and Industry pointed to an alarming number of abandoned communities in the Cranbrook area alone, where rampant, uncontrolled cutting combined with wildfires in the slash had led to wood shortages and the decline of Cranbrook as a major forest centre. But smaller, one-industry towns like Jaffray, Bull River, Wycliffe, Yahk and Lumberton fared even more poorly than their regional supply centre. The mill in Lumberton closed down in 1938 when availability of timber declined. By 1944, of what was once boasted as the biggest sawmill in the B.C. interior, only the decayed foundations and piles of rubbish remained. The mill had been in operation only fifteen years and its demise forced the town's 250 residents to abandon their homes, leaving little trace of their short-lived presence. "The disappearance of Lumberton was to Cranbrook what the disappearance of New Westminster would be to Vancouver," concluded the authors of the government's brief.[56]

After a lengthy series of hearings in which he was peppered with such alarming tales, Sloan delivered his landmark report in 1945, recommending a sustained yield policy for the forests of British Columbia. The hope was that putting the forest industry on a new resource footing would give it some sort of stability and protection while assuring a future for towns like Lumberton. To obtain a perpetual supply of timber, Sloan figured the best thing to do would be to divide the timberland into both private and public working circles, each to be managed on a sustained yield basis. The government thought the idea was a fine one and quickly changed the law to create two distinct types of tenure, eventually known as Tree Farm Licences (TFLs) and Public Sustained Yield Units (PSYUs), the very names evoking images of permanence and perpetuity in the minds of concerned citizens. Timber management on the TFLs would be carried out by the licensees under Forest Service supervision while the Forest Service itself would look after things on the PSYUs. For the first time the forests of British Columbia were formally recognized as renewable resources and a specific policy was outlined to treat them as such.

Companies granted individual units of land under the TFLs (first called the forest management licences) became responsible for logging on the basis of sustained yield principles, reforestation programs, forest inventories and allowable cut calculations. The companies were to prepare management plans for their new tenures, and get those plans approved by B.C. Forest Service foresters. The idea was to give companies such solid security of tenure and to subject them to such close regulation that they would embark on serious programs of forest renewal, which in turn would ensure long-term timber supply and community stability in an industry not noted for those features.

But these reforms did not go to the root of the problem. Government was anxious to maintain its ultimate control over the resource without having to lay out money to manage the TFLs. What's more, the new policy gave the Minister of Forests absolute control over the granting of licences, the amount of land each licence would cover and which firms would be blessed with the best timber. The government could still adjust royalty arrangements to bring in more money from the forest when it needed the revenue. It was under no obligation to put money from the forest back into renewing the resource. Yet such financial guarantees were crucial to keeping the promise of perpetual timber. The door was left open to continued timber mining because the Forest Service was not guaranteed sufficient funds to do an adequate job of policing the activities of Tree Farm Licence-holders or managing regeneration efforts on PSYUs. But the complete ministerial discretion contained in the new sustained yield policy pleased the politicians who were ever mindful of opportunities for extracting funds from companies anxious to secure timber licences.

The forest industry also liked Sloan's recommendations and the policy that came from them. The initial TFLs were granted in perpetuity, this provision later being amended to twenty-one years with renewability. Once a company got a TFL, its renewal was virtually guaranteed. No government was likely to cancel or refuse to renew a TFL if a company mismanaged the forest: The company would simply respond with warnings about possible mill closures and job reductions. So enthusiastic was the industry about the TFLs that it deluged the government with applications. By the time Sloan was again hired to report on the province's forests in 1956, twenty-three TFLs had been awarded, covering some of the best timberland in the province. Most went to big, integrated forest-products firms, such as MacMillan-Bloedel and Crown Zellerbach, much to the dismay of the small logging and sawmilling businesses who were getting very edgy about their access to timber and their ability to compete with the big companies the government was favouring. But the PSYUs turned out to be a versatile tool the government could use to allocate timber to operators both large and small. This flexibility was important as a way of placating the independents when it was felt necessary. Once again, the Minister made the crucial decisions about the allocation of the PSYUs.

So Sloan provided a framework within which the government confirmed its control over the resource and developed mechanisms for the regulation of the forest. Whether or not anything was actually done to improve forest conditions and management practices was left largely up in the air. It was obvious that the Forest Service would come to play a crucial role as both direct and indirect supervisor of efforts aimed at securing adequate restocking of "used" land. While no specifics of what the user and owner were obliged to do were laid down at the time, the government's order of priorities was made clear. As the most recent in the series of B.C. Royal Commissions on forests concluded (with a delicate sense of understatement) when it looked back at the result: "The arrangements for exacting the Crown's financial interest in timber have become steadily more rigorous and sensitive. The regulation of licensees, in terms of their harvesting practices, forestry activities and resource use has also gradually increased."[57]

While the B.C. government was busily enshrining the key recommendations of the Sloan Commission into legislation, a Royal Commission in Ontario was also looking into causes of and possible solutions to the continuous and progressive deterioration of that province's forests. Timber there was being degraded both in terms of quantity and quality. The Commission, headed by Major-General Howard Kennedy, warned that unless major steps were taken, the preference of the pulp mills for spruce would do to that species what the appetite of sawmills had done to the former pine forests of eastern Canada.[58] To remedy the forest malaise Kennedy, like Sloan, proposed the implementation of a sustained yield policy. But any similarity between the two commissions ended there. The only way to make the forest resource last, Kennedy felt, was to embark on a major reversal of existing policy.

Major-General Kennedy had just finished a stint as Quartermaster-General of the Canadian army during World War II, responsible for keeping the military effort running smoothly by providing adequate supplies of food, ammunition and equipment to the troops. Before that he had worked in the forest industry as an engineer and forester. This work experience provided the essential direction for his approach to the forest, an approach that Kennedy himself maintained was not visionary but simply practical common sense. "To those who are well-satisfied with forestry matters as they are, it may come as a shock," Kennedy reported. "After an exhaustive study of prevailing conditions, I am convinced it is necessary to protect a probable majority of operators against their own folly in wasting forest resources which are the lifeblood of their industries."[59]

Kennedy's 1947 report concluded that all existing timber licences should be *taken away* from the pulp and paper companies for at least ten years in order to establish a totally new regime governing timber disposal and forest management. In the interim, he proposed, the government would guarantee existing mills a continuous supply of wood. The old system would then be replaced; the forests would be redistributed on a watershed basis* among a number of new operating companies responsible for cutting and managing the forest. Each of these new forest companies would be entirely independent from the mills and would be run by a board of directors including representatives of the government as well as the wood-using industries in the area. The operating companies would have as their principal task the delivery of a reliable supply of the cheapest wood possible *after* considering the best possible forest practices. Timber would be cut with a view to silviculture, the actual harvest being directed by foresters who, Kennedy hoped, "would protect against jeopardizing future forest conditions for the sake of present dividends."[60]

---

* At the time of Kennedy's report, roads had yet to penetrate the northern forest and logs were still being floated downriver to the mills. This being the case, it seemed logical to divide the cutting areas according to the way the rivers drained the timberland, thus "on a watershed basis".

Why the differences with Sloan? The B.C. commissioner's ideas had paved the way for a policy designed to increase the control that a small number of increasingly large, centralized forest products firms had over the forests of British Columbia — precisely the opposite of what Kennedy was proposing.

Sloan was a lawyer, a judge, a political appointee who was regularly employed by various B.C. governments to conduct Royal Commissions into various touchy affairs and eventually became Chief Justice of the B.C. Supreme Court. He had little direct or practical knowledge of forests or forestry. Kennedy had spent fifteen years before the war working for E.B. Eddy Ltd., eventually becoming Woods Manager for the firm. He was the former manager of the Quebec Forest Industries Association and after the war had been the vice-president in charge of woods operation for the Ontario Paper Company and the Quebec North Shore Paper company. In a bit of rhetorical flourish one magazine dubbed him "Canada's top lumberjack". By all accounts Kennedy, a former amateur wrestler among all these other things, was a bit of a renegade.

Kennedy knew corporate woods operations and the way the system actually functioned. And he knew it from the inside, a perspective Sloan could never share. More importantly, though, Kennedy was willing to swim against the flow, to oppose prevailing government and industry inclinations. He saw clearly the fundamental elements of forest folly. He knew that the only time the corporate financial, sales and mill executives were seen anywhere near the woods was on periodic fishing and hunting junkets. These were the men who set the quotas for the mills and actually ran the show. Production itself was left up to woods bosses. "Organization, financing and planning have been directed toward the production of raw materials and the processing, manufacture and sale of finished products," said Kennedy. "On the other hand, the renewal of the forest resources, the lifeblood of the enterprises concerned, has been largely left to chance."[61] Kennedy also felt that, from the government side, there had never really existed any general line of policy beyond the overriding concern with revenue. It was apparent that companies received their limits because of influence or luck. Kennedy even pointed out that the collection of some of the revenues was faulty, that the government's own timber scalers were dependent on logging operators for their food and lodging.

Should scalers follow the government rules too closely, Kennedy noted, their lives could be made most unpleasant. The system seemed designed for abuse.

Unhappily for Kennedy and the province's forests, the Conservative government ignored the Royal Commission's findings and recommendations. This fact is not surprising, given Kennedy's contemptuous opinion of executives "who normally know little or nothing of the inescapable effects of unsound forest practices and are mainly concerned with immediate costs."[62] Anyone who felt, as Kennedy did, that the forest had to be "emancipated" from control by such people would very likely have their notions of forest management spurned by those in control at the provincial level. Indeed, Kennedy's report was held back for more than three months after it had been submitted. The government was obviously reluctant to defend the report's recommendations for government control over forest companies. It might have feared that the report would provide the opportunity for others to take up the demand for complete state control over the industry. When the report was eventually released, there was a short chorus of alarm; several newspapers insisted that it not be shelved. The *Ottawa Journal* was adamant. "This is probably the most important document yet issued on the great wood industries of the province and their destinies in the years to come. 'Timber mining' must stop." The *Napanee Beaver* added, "If [this report] does anything to prevent the riotous waste of our forest resources, we are all for it."[63] But Kennedy's report was quietly shelved. Its principal ideas for policy reform were brushed aside — never to be seriously considered. Business was good, the forest industry was expanding, sales were up.

Ontario now suffers from local timber shortages, as do British Columbia and many other parts of the country. These threaten to increase. Yet back in the forties and fifties there seemed to be more timber on the other side of every ridge, sufficient to ignore the small voices of warning. In 1947, L.R. Andrews of the B.C. Lumber Manufacturers Association urged all governments in the British Empire to *abandon* sustained yield plans for ten years in order to alleviate lumber shortages.[64] Five years later a group of visitors asked the woods manager at Howard Kennedy's former firm, Quebec North Shore, what the company would do when there were no more trees left. "That time will never come," the woods manager replied with a smile.[65]

4. On the Threshold?

ORDON GIBSON IS A MEMBER of an endangered species in the Canadian forest industry. He is a pioneer logger whose successful family business was based on "hands-on management" and a hard-working, hard-nosed approach to the business of getting the logs out of the bush. The self-styled "Bull of the Woods" has been a merchant, a sailor and a politician as well as a logging boss. Gibson and his three brothers ran logging operations up and down the west coast of Vancouver Island for sixty years, starting out by felling cedar trees forty-five feet in circumference directly into Clayoquot Sound. The Gibson family eventually sold out to a powerful international forest corporation based in Denmark.

This Horatio Alger of Canadian logging brought what might be called an old fashioned approach to the modern forest industry: a perspective closer to that of an old Ottawa Valley timber baron than a modern forest industry executive. "Logging will always be done best where the owner puts on his caulk boots* and goes where he's logging," Gibson once stated. "How can we expect efficient logging with the owner in New York — someone who can't tell a hemlock from a cedar?"[1]

Gibson's story, told in his rambling autobiography, reads like an ode to the virtues of honest, hard work and rugged individualism, a sharp contrast to the new era he saw coming in, when the multinational forest firm and the notion of sustained yield forest management were taking firm root.[2] Gibson, the no-nonsense, do-it-yourself logging operator, had no use for

* Caulk boots (pronounced cork) are the spiked boots worn by B.C. loggers in order to stay upright working on the wet, fallen timber of the coastal region.

the new ways of the forest business which characterized the sixties and seventies.

In 1960, while still a sprightly fifty-six years of age, Gordon Gibson sat down with C.D. Orchard, who had just retired as B.C.'s Chief Forester, to discuss the state of the woods and the changes both men had seen in their long careers.[3] As head of the B.C. Forest Service (BCFS), Orchard had been the civil servant chiefly responsible for administering the transformation of provincial forest policy in the wake of the report of the first Sloan Commission. It had been Orchard's job to initiate the system of forest management licences, the basis of the new-look postwar policy of intensive forestry in Canada's premier forest jurisdiction.

The former B.C. Chief Forester was understandably miffed when confronted with Gibson's adamant rejection of a concept that Orchard himself regarded as sacrosanct: the idea that forests cut down had to be replaced through the active intervention of forest managers. Orchard asked Gibson what they were here for, if not to grow trees? "To cut down the ones we've got, make a living out of them and maybe make a fortune," replied Gibson. "The trees are no more important than the pleasure they give the human race out of using them. That's all trees are for."

Clearly, the logging operator and the forester could scarcely see eye to eye when it came to a discussion of the way the forest should be treated. Orchard was well aware that the province's overwhelming dependence on the forest industry would continue into the twenty-first century. He asked incredulously, "Aren't you preaching now that we have no responsibility to posterity?"

Gibson was forthright. "Absolutely none at all. . . . We have to cut trees. The more we cut, the better it is."

The irascible businessman, who knew the timber trade from the end of a cross-cut saw on Clayoquot Sound to the halls of the legislature down the coast at Victoria, maintained that the risk of running out of timber was the same as any other business risk. As for the government's modern-day policy of managing the forest to assure a sustained yield in the future, he said: "I'm not much of a believer in a country as big as B.C., talking yet about planting, thinning or pruning. It's too costly. . . . I don't think we can afford it."

Now, no executive of any forest products firm in Canada today would ever think seriously about expressing such an attitude towards the forest. According to conventional corporate wisdom, active forest management is a must, and both government and industry must bow down together before the altar of sustained yield. To affirm anything else — and especially to echo Gibson's sentiments concerning forest management — would probably propel any government or corporate forestry official into career oblivion. Most Canadians familiar with forest matters, particularly in a forest-dependent province like British Columbia, recognize the crucial need for care of a resource that has vaulted so many communities to prosperity. So the top executives of the largest forest firms are hurrying to disassociate themselves from the "cut and get out" attitudes of the past.

Noranda Mines controls more of the Canadian forest products industry than any other firm. Among its several forest products affiliates is MacMillan-Bloedel, the country's biggest forest company and a dominant firm in British Columbia. The views of Adam Zimmerman, the president of Noranda, stand in sharp contrast to Gibson's. Zimmerman believes that government and industry have to commit themselves now to long-term forest management. In his view, because 17 per cent of Canada's total exports are exports of forest products, that makes the forest the country's most important natural resource.[4] "We are over the threshold. We are no longer pioneers stomping into the woods to extract our God-given bounty," states Zimmerman. "We must go to it and augment the natural production of trees. . . . Delay will be the next thing to a natural disaster."[5]

This is the type of urgent admonition uttered regularly in recent times by the highly-placed men who control Canada's forest industry from their lofty office towers. There seems to be an unwritten code that translates the longstanding industry concern over wood supply into a newfound anxiety that, yes, unless we do something now, we'll soon run out of timber.

Bill Pauli is the type of production-oriented manager who in days gone by could have been expected to discount worries about long-term wood supply or impending shortages. From his highrise office just across Toronto's Bay Street from the executive suite where Zimmerman runs Noranda, Pauli does not convey the image of a high-flying corporate executive busily buying up companies like MacMillan-Bloedel and administering a

A "utilization problem". The poplar in the background is rejected wood. The forest products industry continues to waste valuable wood.

worldwide resource conglomerate. Pauli is a top woodlands manager for Abitibi-Price but, unlike Zimmerman, he worked his way up through the forestry end of the business, spending years in remote logging communities coping with the day-to-day problems of getting the wood to the mill.

In the past, Pauli did not engage in handwringing over lack of timber and saw little need for forest management. But now he agrees with people such as Zimmerman who say that the time has come to get serious about regeneration. He is confident that Ontario's new policy of handing over forest management responsibilities to corporate licensees is a good one and will quite neatly take care of the wood supply problem. Pauli is convinced that industry and government have turned over a new leaf, that with the new system whereby government pays the companies for silvicultural work, things will be just fine. "The management of the forest will take place so we won't run out of wood. There will be lots of wood. As a matter of fact we'll increase the volume of wood way down the line. But if it's not done — there's trouble."[6]

If such sentiments are so widespread, why should a timber operator like Gibson turn his back on forest management, this modern article of faith? Surely, one would think, Gibson's roots and direct experience at the heart of the forest business should have led him to see the task of forest management as crucial. The answer lies in Gibson's direct experience with the politics and policy directions of forestry in British Columbia.

IT WAS THE INAUGURATION of the Tree Farm Licence system — the new tenure system introduced in the 1945 Sloan Report and heralded as the move that was going to institute the principle of sustained yield in the province — that so irked Gordon Gibson. This was the policy regime that was being implemented during C.D. Orchard's term as head of the B.C. Forest Service and it upset Gibson to the degree where any sympathy he might ever have had for the careful husbanding of the forest resource evaporated.

The problem was that for Gibson the new forest policy meant the death of the small logging operator. Huge tracts of timberland were locked up by large companies deemed by the Minister to be worthy of tree farm licences. Gibson felt that the little fish — like his own family business — were being swallowed up by the large industrial sharks and that the necessity for forest management was just being used to legitimize the process.

"The people of B.C. were led to believe... that our forests were in danger," Gibson later recalled. "It was on this false premise that the timber of British Columbia was delivered into the hands of the few companies who are now in control of our resources and who are in a position to make vast fortunes out of a heritage that rightly belongs to everyone."[7]

Once the new licensing system came in, Gibson turned his attention to the political arena, where he hoped he could more effectively combat this tendency toward the concentration of control of the forests into a few powerful hands. He knew it was impossible for his family to fight on the terrain of direct competition with the majors. Once the new policy was in place, "The next thing we knew we had tree farm licences all around us. Our days were numbered.... An independent logging company such as ours would be forced out of business because it could not secure sufficient timber cutting rights to maintain its camps and make a profit."[8]

In 1953, in the midst of the first flurry of tree farm licence signings, Gibson was elected Liberal MLA for the Vancouver Island riding of Lillooet. He hoped to use his position in the Legislature to make things hot for the new Social Credit government of W.A.C. Bennett. Gibson, like many insiders in the B.C. forest business, had for several years been suspicious about just how the timber licences were being awarded. There had been rumours of corruption and scandal and many industry observers believed that the government of the day was getting the benefit of hefty campaign contributions from forest companies grateful for their TFLs.

In 1954 Gibson visited the Socred Minister of Lands and Forests, Robert "Honest Bob" Sommers, to air his concern over the granting of a TFL to British Columbia Forest Products (BCFP). This company, formed not long before on the initiative of E.P. Taylor, was an amalgamation of a number of old firms that had mills but were short of timber supplies. Desperately needing wood for its mills, BCFP had exerted influence in Victoria, where it succeeded — against the advice of Chief Forester Orchard — in getting an agreement to transfer the entire Public Working Circle in Clayoquot to a new BCFP tree farm licence. The move alarmed small operators in the area, who lost access to valuable stands of Crown timber as a result of the new arrangement. But it must have pleased Taylor and the other BCFP shareholders, for within days of the licence being awarded, the firm's share price had more than doubled from $7 to $15 and the shareholders were left with a potential profit of $24 million.[9]

When Gibson queried Sommers about the affair he was told to mind his own business. The next day, Premier Bennett personally offered the feisty logging operator the same advice, prompting Gibson to adjourn to the legislative chamber where he made an inflammatory speech alleging that "money talks" in getting public timberland in the province. Gibson predicted that someone would wind up in jail if these things continued.[10] What happened immediately, however, was Gibson's expulsion from the House and a demand from the Socred Attorney-General, Robert Bonner, that the Liberal MLA retract his allegations. Gibson refused and later explained the government's hard line against him: "To my mind it was like calling a man a 'bastard' when he doesn't know who his father is. He's apt to be a bit touchy."[11]

Gibson resigned his seat in anger. When he contested it again in the subsequent by-election he was defeated in a flurry of Socred baby-kissing and road building. But the pot continued to simmer. In late 1955 the second Sloan Commission heard charges that bribes had been paid in the awarding of forest management licences. Both Attorney-General Bonner — who in 1982 was still one of the most powerful men in the province as head of B.C. Hydro — and Premier Bennett — whose son went on to be Premier — already knew of evidence against Forest Minister Sommers from an RCMP report thay had received dealing with the allegations. But it took the top Socreds two years to do anything about the matter and it was not until 1958 that Sommers was sentenced to five years in jail for receiving cash, bonds and rugs in exchange for "considerations".

Gibson subsequently told Orchard his feelings about the results of the case: "The men who made the $24 million were friends and associates of E.P. Taylor, in that particular graft. . . . The very people, and I claim there's fifty of them in B.C., who paid the bribes, did the conniving, bought the whiskey and changed Sommers' character, are more guilty than he is and should be in jail at the present time."[12] No one from BCFP was ever convicted in the case.

Small wonder, then, that Gibson associated the notion of sustained yield management with concentration of control over the forest by a few large, powerful corporate concerns. On the other hand, C.D. Orchard, in keeping with many forest policy administrators in Canada today, believed the path toward perpetuation of the resource lay through placing the responsibility for the job in the hands of the small number of corporations that have emerged as the dominant forces in the Canadian forest industry: the BCFPs, the MacMillan-Bloedels, the Abitibi-Prices. The days of the small, independent logging operator are over, according to this line of reasoning.

Men like Gibson might think that the old-style logging boss out in the woods with his caulk boots was good enough for the job. And they might resent the looming power of the corporations. But, as Orchard told Gibson, it is not the government's fault that economic units are becoming larger and more centralized. Government is just responding: attaching its forest management initiatives to this growing power. "Supposing your little man had been a grocer instead of a logger. He couldn't compete against the big chain stores. What I'm driving at, Gordon, is that it isn't the action of the government that's causing the change, but it's the general movement of economics North America-wide. And even worldwide. . . . It's something you and I and the government can't control. There is just no use our kicking against the bricks. It's in the packing business, it's in the fishing business and it's in the grocery business, too."[13] Given the inevitability of corporate concentration, the argument seems to say, why not hook forest renewal to the rising star of the integrated forest products corporation?

In British Columbia, where just such a policy was adopted (albeit amidst the furor over the Sommers scandal) after the recommendations of the first Sloan report of 1945, concentration of control over the forest industry and the forest resource has been a continuing trend. In that province the public relations minions of the forest products corporations never tire of pointing out that fifty cents out of every dollar flows from the forest. With a provincial economy so dependent on a single resource,

Royal Commissions on forestry are regular occurrences. The most recent such Commission, completed in 1976 by Peter Pearse, provided ample evidence that concentration in the industry had increased since Gibson helped unearth the web of connections between BCFP and the Socred cabinet.[14]

For instance, in 1940, before the new policy of tree farm licences and sustained yield was adopted, 52 per cent of the four million acres under Timber Licence were held by fifty-eight firms. In 1954, more than half the acreage was in the hands of just four licensees. By 1965 four major corporations held two-thirds of this acreage and eight controlled 82 per cent.[15] Pearse's report showed that by 1975 six companies held 73 per cent of the committed annual cut in the coastal region; in the interior the six top companies had over 40 per cent of the committed annual cut locked up.[16] Pearse also pointed out, "The introduction of the tree farm licence system provided an opportunity for those holding Crown-granted forest land and old temporary tenures to add to these holdings substantial tracts of additional Crown land." His report concluded that, since the 1950s, "Control over timber rights has become increasingly concentrated in the hands of a few large corporations in spite of the dramatic growth of the forest industry in the last twenty years."[17]

Two years after Pearse completed his mammoth study of the forest industry, the Socred government brought in a new forest act incorporating some of his recommendations. The government's new policy offered greater incentives to forest management, higher annual cuts if company regeneration efforts pointed to higher future yields and replaced the old twenty-one-year TFLs with twenty-five-year tenures. But by that time the ten biggest forest firms in the province as a whole (both coastal and interior) controlled 60 per cent of the annual allowable cut. Pearse noted that the Socred changes failed to address his concerns about the dominance of a few corporations. "Some of my recommendations were seen to be in conflict with established interests, and indeed it was in this case that the government seemed most reluctant to accept my conclusions," he reflected. "The tenure system promises to lock up most of the timber among established firms which can be expected to consolidate holdings and positions through takeovers."[18]

Less than two years after Pearse made this prediction, some of the largest of the few dominant forest firms in Canada had been gobbled up in a spate of corporate acquisitions. Control of more and more of Canada's forest resource passed into the hands of financiers and corporate managers who inhabit the highrise-office world of Noranda's Adam Zimmerman and who are, to say the least, rather removed from the concerns of the forest. In 1981 Zimmerman himself orchestrated his firm's $626.5 million takeover of MacMillan-Bloedel, the number one firm in the industry. This catapulted Noranda into top position of control over the forest industry. Even before the MacMillan-Bloedel takeover, Noranda already held Northwood Pulp (B.C. Interior), Fraser Inc. (New Brunswick) and the Maclaren Company (Ottawa Valley).*

However, 1981 did not close with Noranda firmly in control. Four months after it had acquired control of MacMillan-Bloedel, Noranda was itself swallowed up by Brascan, the one-time Brazilian utility operator, now a vehicle for the holdings of Edgar and Peter Bronfman. Brascan had previously acquired control of Scott Paper, North America's largest purveyor of toilet paper.**

Just weeks before Noranda bought MacMillan-Bloedel, Abitibi-Price had been bought out by the secretive Reichmann family of Toronto through their real estate arm, Olympia and York. The cost was estimated to be $670 million. Abitibi-Price was itself the product of a 1974-75 takeover of Price, the old Quebec-based forest empire, by Abitibi, the newsprint giant with extensive holdings in Newfoundland, Ontario and Manitoba.

Indeed, even before the summer of 1981 had given way to fall, two more big takeovers had startled observers of the Canadian forest products industry. In mid-July Canadian Pacific

* In 1981 Noranda, through Maclaren, also bought 27 per cent of Quebec's family-owned Normick-Perron, the largest manufacturer of softwood lumber east of the Rockies.
**An interesting footnote to the Noranda/MacMillan-Bloedel/Brascan connection came to light after the takeover dust settled in late 1981. As part of a deal worked out between Noranda's Zimmerman and the B.C. Socred government, which assured Noranda of provincial go-ahead in its MacBlo takeover bid, Noranda agreed to sell off its 28 per cent interest in BCFP. This allayed Socred "worries" about excessive concentration in the industry. Noranda's BCFP shares were duly sold to the Alberta Energy Corp. Noranda got $215 million for a block of shares it had bought for $30 million ten years previously, realizing a tidy profit on the deal. However, once Brascan acquired Noranda, the same colossus again held a powerful hand in British Columbia, by virtue of Brascan's newly-acquired Scott Paper, *itself* a major shareholder of BCFP.

Enterprises paid $1.1 billion for the Canadian assets of the International Paper Company of New York. Canadian International Paper, the American newsprint giant's Canadian subsidiary, had for many years been one of the principal forest products firms in Quebec and New Brunswick. Canadian Pacific, in 1981 the largest publicly-traded industrial corporation in Canada, was already well-represented in the forest products business through its control of Great Lakes Forest Products of Thunder Bay: number eight in the Canadian industry.

Within three months of the CIP takeover the government of Quebec had used its civil service pension fund to buy control of the Quebec-based Domtar, which at that time ranked second only to MacMillan-Bloedel among Canadian forest companies. Clearly, B.C.'s Royal Commissioner had been right about the tendency to more concentrated control of this industrial sector. Within the space of seven short months, four of the top five firms in the industry had changed hands along with several other major producers. In several cases the companies doing the buying were already well-established forest corporations.

To some it might seem that such changes in control at the upper levels mean very little for the forest itself. It might also occur to some skeptics that priorities were somewhat misdirected and that the $2.5 billion spent on the acquisitions was money unproductively exchanged — that such a huge sum might have been more logically funnelled into new initiatives in forest management, a costly but chronically underfinanced activity. But then again, the argument could be made that the forest is better off being used by the most powerful industrial organizations, that the corporations represent efficiency and astute management in the lean, dynamic private sector.

IN THE MODERN AGE of Canadian forestry, the men at the top of the government and corporate bureaucracies controlling the forest are eager to point out that they have made a clean break with the past. There is a new optimism abroad about the health of the future forest. One of the best weathervanes for the state of official attitudes toward forestry in Canada is Les Reed, a former consultant who moved into a key slot as an Assistant Deputy Minister in charge of forestry for Environment Canada. Reed, a slim, young-looking man with a quick grasp of forest problems, was perhaps more than anyone else responsible for sounding a timber supply alarm in the 1970s, when he authored several reports pointing to an impending forest disaster unless something was done and done quickly.[19]

Les Reed's principal report indicated that provincial figures on total wood reserves give a false impression: that there is a comfortable cushion in the amount of wood the country has in its forest warehouse. In 1978 there was an apparent physical reserve of 69.6 million cubic metres of softwood, but of this total 36.4 million cubic metres — more than half — were deemed inaccessible. Furthermore, the economically-inaccessible supplies of softwood trees were for the most part made up of species and sizes unfit for existing processing plants. As Reed pointed out, even in the case of accessible forests, when government forest owners calculated inventories they used data that tended to overestimate the amount of wood on the ground. Alarmed by this discrepancy between what is thought to exist and what in fact is available in the forest, Reed quoted a Swedish forester's assessment of Canadian forest inventories: "The plain fact is that the owner does not even know what the forests contain, or can produce. . . . Canada has one of the lowest levels of forest inventory in the developed world."[20]

Reed's research exposed the deplorable state of forest management in Canada and told Canadians that their most important resource had been both over-exploited and under-utilized.* His studies point to a sorry record of reinvestment of money into the forest. In fact, the "Reed nickel" has become a catchphrase used by people worried about the fact that government puts little of the revenues it collects from the forest back into the forest. One study by Reed's consulting group found that the federal government pays only two cents for forest renewal out

---

* This apparent contradiction is explained by the fact that, though harvesting pressure has steadily increased without a corresponding jump in regeneration efforts, the forest resource as a whole remains under-utilized. That is, small logs deemed unprofitable are left to rot on the forest floor, low-volume stands are ignored, wood not appropriate for mill conversion is left in the bush, good timber more difficult to cut than other more useable, more profitable stands is ignored and those species not yet convertible into finished products by current technology are also ignored.[21]

Bob Ploss, a British Columbia treeplanter, makes his way through a cut-over area. Silvicultural work could provide employment for tens of thousands of Canadians today, as well as assuring wood supplies for tomorrow.

of every dollar it collects in forest revenue, while the provinces on average put nine cents back into the forest, for an average of five and a half cents. Reed also pointed out that, of the money which *is* spent, only 21 per cent goes back into stand renewal and tending.[22] In 1978 Reed estimated that a basic, intensive regime, which would treat *only* the areas cut over every year and ignore the massive backlog of not satisfactorily restocked (NSR) land, would cost about $200 million annually. This figure does *not* even include administration and overhead. Still, it is quite a jump compared to the $50-60 million per year actually spent in the late 1970s on regeneration, an amount which *did* include overhead costs.[23] And the basic $200 million per year is less than a fifth of the amount Canadian Pacific had to shell out to buy Canadian International Paper.

Yet in spite of this history of neglect and a record of government-industry relationships characterized more frequently by corruption swirling around officials like Howard Ferguson and Robert Sommers than by a serious commitment to rational forest management, Reed and many others at the top of Canada's forest hierarchy remain optimistic. Reed is confident that because there are no new forest frontiers over the next hill, Canadians will have to make the best of the resources that are left. And he thinks the country is on the right road. Reed knows the task will be difficult and he is used to talking to journalists visiting his Canadian Forest Service office about the magnitude of the problem. He listens carefully to questions and tends to respond with easy, quotable platitudes: "We like to bite chocolate bullets — not real ones." Or: "If it's hard to do, then we should do it. That's the problem these days. Nobody will learn to play the violin because it's too hard. It's easy to learn to play guitar."[24]

Behind the homilies Reed exhibits a personal commitment to the difficult job of getting the federal government, provinces and industry to do something serious about the major problems he has underlined. He knows that we do not inherit the forest resource from our forebears. Since it is renewable, we in fact borrow it from our children. But, with our line of credit being stretched very thin, Reed says time is running out for forestry in Canada. He believes the 1980s are the decade of forest renewal. And he is confident that, at the very least, the corner has been turned. "The provinces have made a quantum leap in the past three years in policy and planning and putting up money for forestry. The industry has made a leap out of the dark ages.... The professional foresters, for the first time in their history, are beginning to articulate forest management."[25]

Being optimistic is part of Reed's job, a vital means of convincing reluctant holders of industry and government pursestrings that now is the time for sustained effort. He talks of a new political commitment to long-term planning, of industry people being transformed into believers in forest renewal through the introduction of new tenure arrangements and legislation. He says, "The private sector is coming around in quick fashion. Five years ago they wouldn't have given you the time of day. They would have thrown you out of the office, said you were stupid, been insulting. Not anymore."[26]

Some of Reed's friends in high corporate places are also optimistic about the future. Unlike the old logging boss Gordon Gibson, but like the high-level corporate leader Adam Zimmerman, they regard forest management as a key to future industrial prosperity. One such corporate forestry advocate is Gerry Burch, vice-president in charge of forestry for British Columbia Forest Products.* In the days since BCFP was implicated in the bribery scandal over the granting of a tree farm licence, the company has made efforts to improve its public image and executives like Burch are eager to explain the corporate attitude to forest management. In his office several dozen stories above Vancouver harbour's winter fog and drizzle, Burch, a frank and friendly man, projects an unassuming, sincere image. He talks with enthusiasm about forestry matters.

"B.C. is really on the threshold of a fantastic development... as long as we can get the landowners to continually, over a long period of time, support the financial outlay necessary to keep the goose laying the golden egg," says Burch.[27] He explains that, from the company's perspective, it's up to the government landlord to provide much of the money needed to carry out silvicultural work on cutover sites. He likes the province's new forest act: It gives big firms like his own security of tenure; it enables them therefore to go to the banks and use

---

* Very few forest products companies have someone at the vice-president level who is responsible for forestry on company limits. The usual pattern is to have a vice-president in charge of wood and operations and logging, who is incidentally responsible for forestry measures.

assured access to public timber as collateral to back the private borrowing that will finance construction of big pulpmills and sawmills. Not only that, but the solid tenure gives companies holding tree farm licences access to an assured supply of wood fibre for those mills. In Burch's view, "Next to [Crown-granted private land] the tree farm licence is the best tenure you can get. Bill Young [British Columbia's Chief Forester] will tell you the TFL is the best tenure in the province. But, politically, they have to be very careful how many they parcel out because these tenures are forever."[28]

Burch's assessment of the political sensitivity of the TFL issue is accurate enough, for the provincial government came under heavy fire from various quarters when the Forest Act was passed in 1978. Gordon Gibson, then leader of the provincial Liberals, told the Legislature that the policy showed the government was against competition and that the small operator would suffer as a result of the new act. "The big fellows think they've got the government pretty well where they want them," was Gibson's assessment of the state of the public forest/private industry nexus in British Columbia.[29] The public sense of the issue is brought home when one hears veteran Vancouver Island loggers refer to large areas of public timberland as "MacMillan-Bloedel country" or "Crown Zellerbach country".[30]

But Burch argues that the tree farm licence system has provided the best forest management on public lands in the country and even perhaps in the world. He believes that up to the time when C.D. Orchard went before the first Sloan Commission to argue for long-term security of tenure for private firms on public land, there was no way to get either government or industry to do anything serious about forest renewal. With security of tenure, there was incentive to take future forest yields into account, because both parties to the new licences had a clearer idea about the shape of things to come. At the same time Burch acknowledges that there is no money to be made in the *logging* end of things: "A big company like ours does not pay too much attention to uneconomic stands or species. We have lots of camps that lose money but we need the fibre to make money on the next stage."[31]

The point here is that forest-based companies, no matter how secure their tenures, look at the forest as a cost factor in their accounting equations. Like other costs, forest work is something to be minimized, whether in the logging phase or in the later stages of forest management. Forest management measures, unlike logging, do not furnish immediate supplies of wood fibre, and Gerry Burch would be the first to confirm that it is up to the government to provide the core of the funding needed to make those measures financially feasible. Like Les Reed, Burch is optimistic, believing that at last the various levels of government are getting together with industry to do whatever is necessary to guarantee supplies of fibre: fifty, seventy or ninety years from now.

In theory, once silviculture becomes as commonplace as agriculture and all cutover timberland is immediately treated to promote growth of desired species, the "allowable cut effect" takes over. The concept is quite simple. According to the theory of sustained yield forestry, operators cut only that amount of wood which can be replaced by new growth every year; they do not withdraw any of the forest "capital" but use only the annual "interest".* Once reforestation boosts the amount of interest the forest will yield in the future, you can proceed to make early withdrawals based on those future yields.

Both Reed and Burch are hopeful that the allowable cut effect will guarantee a sunny future for the Canadian forest industry. Such hopes are based on a belief that today's investments in forestry measures will provide such solid guarantees of expanded yields in the future that, even in the interim, the annual allowable cut on company limits can be expanded. According to Burch, "It's almost too good to be true. It's the shape of the pie — it's this big now and you increase the size of the pie with the increase in cut. You get more manufacturing plants, more employment and more intensive forestry. So you make the pie bigger yet. And this keeps on. It almost sounds like a perpetual motion machine — which it is!"[32]

Bill Young, Gerry Burch's opposite number — Young heads up the provincial Forest Service just as Burch directs the forestry efforts of BCFP — shares the same optimism. From where Young sits in the Forest Service offices on Victoria's Government Street, across Georgia Strait from the corporate headquarters in downtown Vancouver, the forest's future seems firmly in control. Young's office is attractively panelled in knotty boards. As

*See also chapter three, page 80.

he knows, if the finishing work had been done sixty or seventy years ago, the wood panelling might have had no knots at all: In those days they didn't bother with knotty parts of a tree. In fact, any part of the tree above the lowermost branches stood a good chance of being left in the damp coastal woods to rot. That is a type of waste that now sends chills up the spines of foresters like Young and Burch.

Young, head of the largest, most important government forest service in Canada, uses phrases like "the green-eyed Arabs of B.C." when he talks about the province's future forest prosperity.[33] But at the same time he tempers his optimism with the knowledge that, in the end, the levels of forest management his people can undertake are directly dependent on the levels of funding his political masters are willing to commit. The dark-haired, heavy-set administrator takes pains to emphasize that not enough is being done: "We'll have troubles in the future if present levels of forest management stay as they are — and God help us if they do."

There is good reason for his caution. Anyone familiar with the operations of government is also familiar with the volatile nature of its spending programs, in particular the way they respond to the political peccadillos of cabinet ministers and the ups and downs of a roller-coaster economy. Forestry expenditures provide as little in the way of immediate political payoffs as they do in immediate supplies of wood fibre. This is the dilemma faced by every government forester in Canada: the lack of secure, sustained funding for programs that are by their very nature dependent on consistency of support. There is little sense building up large nurseries to produce millions and millions of young spruce and fir seedlings if planting and tending programs several years down the line are plagued by uncertainty of financial support.

As head of the B.C. Forest Service, Bill Young is well aware of the fact that government programs compete with one another in visibility and immediate return, that each program is evaluated according to how much bang will reverberate for each political buck. Familiar catchwords — spending restraint, belt-tightening — are tossed about as politicians seek to impress the public with their frugal habits. When elections loom, spending programs often take on a peculiarly partisan character. "I don't know what should be high profile — closing down part of a hospital or destroying seedlings in a nursery," Young reflects.[34]

A look at the yearly revenues and expenditures of Young's Forest Service shows that both have risen constantly and dramatically since the end of World War II. This was a period of rapid expansion of the forest industry and the inauguration of the provincial sustained yield policy. It was also a period when government expenditures as a whole jumped, heavily supported by income from the forest industry. In 1947-48, when the first tree farm licences were being negotiated, the Forest Service took in $7.26 million and spent $2.88 million on all its programs. By 1979-80 the BCFS had revenues of $571.25 million and expenditures of $166.14 million.[35] The differences in the figures are remarkable not only because of the sheer increases in the dollar figures. It is equally startling that in the earlier fiscal year, when C.D. Orchard was first pushing the idea of sustained yield, expenditures on forestry and administration were 39.7 per cent of revenues while in the more recent period, when sustained yield was an article of faith, forest-related spending was just 29 per cent of revenues.

This is not to infer that these proportions have been declining steadily. Far from it. A comparison of two different fiscal years in the same period shows the opposite. In 1948-49, British Columbia spent 45.1 per cent of its direct forest receipts on its Forest Service while in 1980-81 it poured 74 per cent of direct revenues back into Bill Young's administrative backyard.[36]* The point is that the amount available to the Forest Service fluctuates wildly in relation to the direct income from the sector, reflecting the troughs and peaks of the economy and similar ebbs and flows of government commitment to forestry. In some years the BCFS has spent more on forestry than it has earned in direct revenue. Sometimes spending slips to a mere quarter of income. It is just very difficult to predict what will happen in the future, what the reinvestments in forest renewal will be. It seems the only certainty will remain uncertainty.

---

* It is important to note that the Forest Service's direct revenues in no way reflect the complete picture of government revenues flowing from the forest sector. Corporate and personal income tax, sales tax and other taxes generated directly by the forest industry combine with all the indirect economic spinoffs from forest-based industrial activity to provide government with many more millions being pumped into provincial coffers from the forest resource.

IN SPITE OF HIS FISCAL HEADACHES, Bill Young is glad that policymakers from two other key forest jurisdictions — Ontario and New Brunswick — have taken a close look at B.C. tenure and forest management policies before drawing up their own new provincial policies. And he is equally proud of the Forest Service's mammoth replanting program. No sooner has a visitor to Young's office been seated than a large cardboard graph is displayed illustrating the progress being made in this direction. Though the chart seems to be getting a little frayed from such use, it does show an erratic but steady rise in the number of seedlings planted in the province since the early 1950s. Young notes that at the low point in 1956 his organization planted 3 million young trees. By 1980 the Forest Service had managed to get 75 million seedlings into the forest soil of the mountainsides and valley bottoms of the province. Not only that, but Young hopes to double the 1980 figure to 150 million trees by 1985.[37]

The treeplanting effort is the necessary cornerstone of B.C.'s forest management program. Natural regeneration is a hopeless dream given the clearcut logging techniques preferred by the logging operators. The massive clearcut areas often comprise entire valleys: One can stand on a logging road carved into a hillside and see nothing in the way of standing timber except perhaps for a narrow "leave strip" alongside a stream. The clearcutting removes or destroys much of the natural seed source. As a result, foresters turn to a regime of intensive artificial regeneration in order to put the land back into production as soon as possible. This practice shortcircuits the process of natural succession, so that the desired species, such as Douglas fir or lodgepole pine, get a headstart over competing growth. The entire undertaking can cut years and even decades off rotation periods, and treeplanting is a vital step in this.* While scarification** followed

* Other steps *can* include spacing (or thinning) the trees to give them access to sunlight and more nutrients and water, fertilizing the new stands, spraying competing vegetation with herbicides or cutting it away manually, spraying the forest to kill predatory insects and protecting the forest from fire.

** Scarification refers to the technique of churning up the forest floor to expose the mineral soil, where young seedlings can take root. It is often carried out by dragging chains and other rough, heavy objects behind a bulldozer.

by natural or artificial seeding is a common practice in eastern Canada, planting of young, nursery-bred seedlings is the rule of thumb in British Columbia.

Treeplanting is an expensive, labour-intensive undertaking. Engineers and inventors, who have experienced trouble enough developing logging equipment, have had even more difficulties in designing treeplanting machines. But the reasons are similar. Forest terrain is rough, unpredictable and frequently hostile to delicate mechanisms. The problem is accentuated when the machine must do a job like planting a fragile seedling with enough care that it will grow: a trickier proposition than the more coarse tasks of shearing and hauling mature trees. Machines have trouble differentiating rocks from soil whereas people do not; as a result trees are still most often planted by people.

Bob Ploss, one of those people, has worked as a treeplanter for ten years, following the planting season from its start on Vancouver Island in March to its conclusion in northeastern British Columbia and northern Alberta in late July. Ploss is tall and his build reflects the demanding nature of the work. It is a job he likes because he can earn a year's income in the space of six months, planting seedlings on a piecework basis for up to $200 a day. For the rest of the year Ploss can travel, work on building his house and spend time with his family — including doing his regular volunteer shift with the children at the Slocan Park Community Daycare Centre. Unlike most Canadians, he has the luxury of being able to quit his job every year.

But the job is not easy. It involves scrambling up and down steep slopes in the rain, bending over to plant the trees while carrying a backpack filled with a heavy load of seedlings, living for weeks on end in tents, exposed to the elements: Winds of seventy miles an hour are not uncommon on the coast. The cutover areas tend to be covered either with black, charred wood and soot left over from slashburning or with an obstacle course of logging debris. "It's no picnic," Ploss says. "I get up in the morning and I'm sort of dry but I know by 8:30 I'm going to be soaked and I'm going to be wet all day. You don't even try to stay dry — you just try to stay warm."[38] Still, according to Ploss, money is not the only incentive in the treeplanting business: "It's a bit of a rush to see the eagles flying and the otters diving." It is on the shoulders of people like Ploss that the forest

Pulpwood being unloaded at the mill. According to the federal government, "Pulpwood shortages are emerging in local communities across the country. Only a fraction of our forests are being managed for sustained production."

renewal hopes of the men at the top levels of forest administration — men like Les Reed, Gerry Burch and Bill Young — rest.
Literally.

Ploss thinks the big treeplanting programs are extremely
important, not only as his primary source of income but for the
future well-being of his children. He agrees that the programs
are well-intentioned. But he is rather wary of the optimistic view
of forestry that comes down from on high. As someone who has
walked over as much cutover forest land in various regions as
anyone else in British Columbia, he thinks that the Forest Service is having a lot of trouble just keeping up with the amount of
land that is cut over every year. It is enough of a task and a
challenge to plant these recently-logged areas. As a result, he
notes, very little is being done on the huge areas of backlog,
"not satisfactorily restocked" (NSR) land that accumulated in the
many years when the Forest Service did little in the way of
artificial regeneration. The reason? Money.

According to Ploss, the B.C. government is only committed
to forest management "if it doesn't cost them anything" and "if
they don't have to raise tax money" to spend on it. Those are big
if's, he says: "Once the stumpage* drops off, then if we're going
to maintain these large treeplanting projects, they'll have to take
the money out of general revenue — which means squeezing
the taxpayer harder. And no political party wants to do that,
especially with elections coming."[39]

In 1978 the cost of regenerating *a single hectare* of forest land
in the B.C. coastal region, to make it produce an increased yield
and thus produce the treasured allowable cut effect, was calculated at nearly $500. This estimate came from a team of consul-
tants headed by Les Reed, one of the principal boosters of the
allowable cut effect, and included only planting and spacing
costs. The team made no allowance for fertilization or any other
treatment.[40] Such costs are bound to rise as people like Bob
Ploss continue to expect decent wages for their heavy exertions.
Ploss is a founding member of a fledgling union of treeplanters,
the Pacific Reforestation Workers' Association, a group skeptical

---

* Under Section 88 of the Forest Act, the B.C. government pays for regeneration
by having the companies do the work and allowing them to deduct the cost from
the stumpage fees they pay the government for the rights to cut the timber. In
this way the government pays for the planting by forgoing revenues. The system is known as "stumpage offset".

of the long-term commitment that government and industry now profess. Using the slogan "Don't steal from our children", the PRWA has been pushing the government to do more forestry work.

Ploss has had mixed experiences in taking the concerns of the treeplanting co-op to the Forest Service. While he is quick to acknowledge the solid efforts of committed government and industry foresters, he sees some structural obstacles to good forest management. One of them is the apparent double standard the forest service uses in dealing with the different ends of the forest business.

One of the problems is waste. Every recent government report on forest problems in Canada points to the obvious fact that we must now adopt a "close utilization" approach to the forest resource. This means that less wood should be wasted, more used. Ploss, who in addition to planting trees, has worked setting chokers* on "logging shows", sees that wood is wasted as a matter of course. "There's the easy stuff that you can throw your chokers on and drag out and make your five truckloads or whatever you're trying to make. But if you have to start climbing back over there to get just that one log that's down over the way — it's just not worth it for the guys on the crew."

Loggers, like most workers, are responsible to a supervisor or foreman, who must produce a certain amount of wood to satisfy the demands of his own superiors back in the office. At the end of the day the foreman looks at the number of logs the crew has delivered to the sorting yard. He doesn't look at the number of logs left on the ground. "If the production's there the guys get good feedback," Ploss notes. "If the mess is left behind, nobody gets shit. It doesn't reflect badly on anybody. The foreman has his production and the crew has theirs. In one week they have put out twenty-five loads. That's good. If they left another twenty-five loads lying in the bush, well — there's another block of timber waiting to attack over there."[41]

Ploss explains that when he is planting seedlings in areas where logging waste has not been burned off, he spends most of the day climbing over wood in the form of large logs. He has to

---

* Chokers are the short secondary cables attached to a main cable, or "mainline", which extends out from a central winching point. In order to drag the logs away, the chokers are wrapped around them, pulled tight, and the logs are then hauled in to the landing to be loaded onto trucks.

wear spiked caulk boots just to stay on his feet. If he wanted, he could spend most of the working day without walking on the ground, because there is so much waste wood littered about to walk on. The Forest Service has the job of monitoring wasted wood: logs hung up on obstacles, too far from the mainline, broken or otherwise damaged; or large, abandoned tops and branches. According to the system, companies are paid to check their own waste. Ploss thinks this system is biased in favour of the companies and can lead to inaccurate waste assessment.·

At the same time he finds it ironic that the Forest Service is so zealous in auditing the performance of the people who plant the trees. The veteran planter tells of the time a Forest Service employee brought a protractor out to the job to check the angle of lean on the newly-planted trees. He knows of occasions when planting crews have had to threaten to abandon entire contract jobs because of overexuberant monitoring by the Forest Service. In one case Ploss and a group of other experienced planters did quit because too many of the trees they had planted were being rejected. Because planters are only paid for the trees they plant to the satisfaction of the Forest Service, it would have been absurdly costly to continue.

Ploss explains why the double standard in the enforcement of the forest rules exists. "It's the same reason the government cuts the welfare people. If [Forest Service people] come down hard on MacMillan-Bloedel they get transferred to Fort St. Remote.* If they come down hard on the Poopdike Treeplanting Co-op, everybody thinks that they're being hardnosed and tough. Don't let those hippies get away with anything."[42]

Although he likely has more direct experience in the business of reforestation work than 99.9 per cent of Canadians, and although he has a solid understanding of the ecological relationships in forestry, Ploss is not an acknowledged "expert" in the field. And in forestry, as in most other specialized fields, we are used to looking to the experts to provide us with an accurate picture of what is really happening. So, the story goes, why believe Ploss when senior government and industry experts tell us that we are finally at the dawn of a new age in forestry?

Gerry Burch points to three big conferences — one in Quebec City in 1977, another in Toronto in 1980 and a third in

*The reference is to Fort St. John or Fort St. James, relatively isolated hinterland communities in northern British Columbia.

Banff in 1981 — as milestones in increasing Canadian awareness of looming timber shortages and the necessity of doing something about them. Les Reed agrees that the Quebec City and Toronto conferences drilled home the message to politicians and corporate managers: "You finally got them to listen to the facts."[43]

Canada's largest bank, the Royal, was even moved to publish an alarmist newsletter in the wake of the National Forest Regeneration Conference in Quebec City, pointing out that the forest industry is Canada's most important source of employment and that 20 per cent of the timberland cut each year does not and will not regenerate adequately. The country's leading financial institution concluded that the problem is simply that not enough is being done about reforestation. It underlined the need for a deliberate commitment by government, industry and the public at large to salvage the future of the country's most important resource.[44]

"TOMORROW'S FOREST... TODAY'S CHALLENGE" was the fitting name for the 1977 conference sponsored by the Canadian Forestry Association in Quebec City, a place that was once one of the country's principal centres of the timber trade. Gerry Burch chaired the meeting along with Marcel Lortie, the Laval University forest management professor. One of the keynote speakers, a person asked to sum things up, was John Walters, a professor of forestry at the University of British Columbia, director of the university's research forest. For years Walters has been wrestling with problems of forest renewal and spending countless hours attempting to develop the ideal treeplanting machine. At the conference Walters was rather harsh in his remarks, lamenting the paltry effort at forest management in the country. He cited B.C.'s 1976 expenditures on reforestation: Only one-half of 1 per cent of the provincial government's total expenditures went to provide for the future health of an industry making nearly 60 per cent of all the provincial exports combined. At the same time, Walters reminded his audience of experts and nonexperts, British Columbia was spending more on forestry than any other provincial government.[45]

Walters went on to attack the various levels of government for not having *any* accurate data on supplies of timber. He asked, "How empty is the larder?... No one knows." He described this fuzzy perception of available wood as the result of "apathetic administration and gross mismanagement" and defined the history of forestry as "a century of depression and despair".[46] As for the optimistic future, Walters cited the hopes of the Ontario government, which expected to be logging 65 per cent more by 2020. A false hope, according to Walters, who said no increase would be possible, due to the lack of forest management.[47]

Not all the experts, then, agree with the optimism of forest planners in top decision-making positions. Ken Hearnden is another acknowledged expert. He worked for the Abitibi Company for twenty-three years as a divisional forester in the Lakehead region, served a term as President of the Canadian Institute of Forestry, and chaired the School of Forestry at Lakehead University in Thunder Bay, where he has also taught forest management for fifteen years. Hearnden believes that nothing meaningful will be done about forest management until we run out of forests. He looks back over the history of European forestry, where timber famines proved necessary to provoke intensive silvicultural practices. Hearnden also reflects on his visits to Italy and Yugoslavia, countries whose barren, rocky slopes were once occupied by productive forests before logging and grazing denuded them of plants and soils.[48]

Ken Hearnden is one of the more analytical foresters on the scene in Canada, one of the few who has gone beyond hand-wringing over lack of care of the resource or cynicism about inaction to consider the causes of this lassitude. He is not enthusiastic about Ontario's future forest management regime and disagrees with the flush of optimism in some quarters about the new Forest Management Agreements (FMAs) between provincial governments and the major forest products companies. The FMAs take a leaf from the B.C. book and like the tree farm licences turn vast acreages of forest over to the companies to be managed on a sustained yield basis, to produce wood "in perpetuity". As in British Columbia, the Ontario government has agreed to pick up the tab for the necessary silvicultural treatments. Les Reed, for one, is convinced that this is the way to go: "Ontario is covering the province with FMAs and it's a very strict regime. . . . You look at those FMAs and you find that the commitment is so heavy that it frightens the government people."[49]

But a brief glance at one such FMA, a contract signed between the Ontario Ministry of Natural Resources and the E.B. Eddy Company, shows that the government is not quite so firmly committed as Reed believes. Like every other Ontario FMA, the E.B. Eddy contract contains a key clause (Section 32.1) stating, "The obligations of the Minister to pay moneys under this agreement are each subject to the condition precedent that moneys are appropriated therefore by the Legislature of the Province of Ontario."[50] This means that, in spite of the reassurances by both government and industry, there is *no* legal obligation on the part of the government to pay forest corporations like Eddy or Abitibi-Price to do the job. If the money is not forthcoming from the Legislature (that is, the Conservative government whose forty-year administration has done so much to plunge the province's forests into crisis) the companies are not obliged to proceed with silvicultural work on their own. The corporations have in the past shown no inclination whatsoever to shoulder the forestry burden by themselves. As they so regularly state, they are simply forest tenants: The government landlord is responsible for maintenance costs.

Hearnden points out the weaknesses in this approach, noting that today's enthusiasm for forest renewal could turn into tomorrow's apathy. "The House is apparently willing to vote the money to support (the FMAs). But who knows? In four or five years we may find there's some other serious matter occupying their attention, calling for provincial funds. And they may decide they have to reduce the allocation for silviculture. . . . That's the concern that many of us have — there's no assurance the thing will be sustained."[51]

Forestry is not a one-shot, high-profile affair like Ontario Place, B.C. Place or Expo '67. Hearnden's years of attempting to practise forest management on Abitibi's limits and teaching student foresters have taught him that you cannot simply establish thousands of acres of jack pine or black spruce stands, then move on to another cutover to do the same in the hopes of returning in sixty or eighty years to harvest a new crop. "All those plantations will need tending and care and management right through their lives. . . . Everybody's enthusiastic about regeneration but that's only a small part of the real task of managing a forest. Years after, repeated effort is needed — tending, spacing, assuring that they're properly-spaced to maximize growth rates."[52]

As for the forest products corporations, the multibillion dollar giants slated to do the silvicultural work on expanded, secure timber limits, Hearnden's experience tell him that their priorities rest not with the future of the resource but with writing off current investments in plant and equipment. Once again the theme of mill as profit centre and forest as supply centre emerges. "In spite of all the happy utterances about sustained yield and 'We're here in perpetuity' and so on, really that is the main concern — is there enough wood for us to write off this investment?" This is Hearnden's assessment of the order of priorities inside the big companies.[53]

Such stumbling blocks to living up to the rhetoric are institutional, inseparable from the rest of the fabric of production as it is organized and executed by the major firms that have come to dominate both the industry and the forest itself. Things have not really changed since J.O. Wilson reflected on his own experiences as a woodlands manager for the Anglo-Canadian Pulp and Paper Mills Ltd. in the 1930s and criticized the priorities of the corporations. Bill Pauli, assistant general manager of woodlands for Abitibi-Price's largest division, calls woodlands managers "country cousins". He confirms, "Second class citizen is the word. It's always been that way. The top people in the company are the mill people." The woodlands people do not like this set-up, he says, but "It's a fact that [wood] is just another raw material in the mill, whose real function is making paper. If they could buy their wood without ever having to produce it in the woodlands, I'm sure they would. I'm talking now about the entire industry."[54]

In his own wry fashion, thoughtful yet saddened to be resigned to the reality of the situation, Ken Hearnden sums up what it all means for the principle of sustained yield, the theory that is supposed to guide all forestry initiatives. The tall, white-haired forester has come to believe that most woodlands people are only interested in wood supply in the short term, perhaps seeing no further than the date of their retirement. "I once said at a professional meeting that perhaps the best way to recognize how allowable annual cuts are calculated by any company is to divide the volume of wood growing on the limit by the number of years until retirement of the woods manager. Beneath all the bullshit that's the way people are really thinking."[55]

This type of short-term thinking has dominated Canadian forest practices since the earliest days of the square timber trade. With the rise of the lumber and pulp industries, the changes were in the end-products coming from the mills — factories that got bigger and more efficient as time passed and more powerful firms assumed control of the industry. The philosophy of perpetual expansion based on immediate priorities led to the creation of ghost towns like French River, Ontario and Lumberton, B.C. When the rights of future generations to some resource wealth are ignored, the economic and social decline is first felt and most keenly appreciated not in the corporate office towers and government blocks where the decisions regarding timber disposal are made. Rather, it is the people who live in the remote communities, where logging and milling are mainstays of local economies, who must bear the burden of the misdirected priorities of the men in the southern metropoles.

One such place is Terrace, a northwestern B.C. city largely dependent upon the forest industry. From the earliest days when sternwheelers plied the Skeena River, people found work cutting cordwood to pile on the river banks. The era of river transportation soon passed with the construction of the Grand Trunk Pacific Railway. But the new line needed ties, so there was still work to be had cutting them. The railway connected the northwestern part of the province to outside markets for the red cedar poles and sawn lumber cut from the rich forests flourishing in the region's valley bottoms and on the mountain slopes. Within a few years ten sawmills were doing business in Terrace and though the booms and busts of the resource economy took their toll, wood products continued to be shipped eastward by rail and, often, westward to Asia from the port of Prince Rupert.

In the early days, a time of an unregulated but selective timber harvest, independent loggers did most of the cutting. But new government policies helped to transform the industry and the era of the independent logging operator was short-lived. The new provincial regulations were based on the government's desire for more revenues from the forest. And the province wanted to place control of the resource in the hands of the large economic units, the corporations it regarded as more "rational" and better able to implement the new credo of sustained yield forestry. A tree farm licence was granted to the Cellulose Corporation of America,* putting an effective end to the dominance of the logging industry by the independents. This was TFL #1, the first such licence issued in British Columbia.

With the Cellulose Corporation's licence came new logging techniques, clearcutting in particular. Large volumes of wood fibre were needed to supply CanCel's mills during the boom periods of the fifties and sixties. By 1982 loggers in the Terrace area had to travel for up to two hours to get to work as the resource receded further and further. There became a widespread feeling in the community, underlined by mill closures and declining employment, that the end was near for the locally-based forest industry.[56] "People here are becoming quite aware of the fact that there isn't that much timber left," says Betty Kofoed, a Terrace resident. "If they cut very, very carefully and take the poorer stuff there might be twenty years left. If they continue to cut as they do now, there mightn't even be ten years left."[57]

Betty Kofoed and her husband George have taken a close look at the development of the logging industry in their community, where George's father cut timber in the early days and used some of it to build the house where George grew up. Their outlook is based on their own experiences and particularly on George's twenty-five years of working as a logger. George subsequently took a job monitoring the effects of logging on fish-bearing streams for the federal government. The Kofoeds are not "official experts".

George explains that when CanCel first started logging after it got its tree farm licence in the late 1940s, it took the easy timber, the trees along the valley bottoms. In the company's rush for a quick return on investment it mashed sawlogs into pulp because that's where the best market for wood fibre was to be found. But the forests of the northwestern interior are not like those of the B.C. raincoast where Gordon Gibson spent his years as a logging boss. There are heavy snows in the winter, especially at higher levels up the mountainsides. Since CanCel

---

* Later Canadian Cellulose (CanCel), now an arm of B.C. Timber, a unit of the British Columbia Resources Investment Corporation.

had already cut the timber in the valleys of rivers like the Kit-sumkalum and the Lakelse, and since the market for woodpulp was still strong, it sent its falling crews up onto the higher slopes to cut timber. The end result of having men with chain saws standing on top of deep snow to fall trees was, of course, very high stumps, in some cases up to twelve feet tall. Not only does the enormous waste become apparent when spring arrives but also, the wasted wood is the best in the tree for lumber; it is the clearest and most free of knots.

"They could still sell the product, so it didn't matter how deep the snow was and how high the stumps were," recalls Kofoed. "You logged, you went to work. I wore snowshoes. Now we have a depressed economy, they are suddenly concerned about how deep the snow is."[58]

The B.C. Forest Service controls logging and in theory assesses heavy stumpage penalties as a deterrent against logging practices that do not adhere to the principles of close utilization. In this case, however, the penalties were waived. When asked why it did this, the BCFS explained weakly that less top-wood was wasted by breakage in winter-falling due to the cushioning effect of the snow when the trees were falled.[59] The Forest Service chose to ignore the fact that not only is the wood at the base of the tree of better quality than topwood but also the waste involved — when the stumps left are taller than people — is enormous.

The Kofoeds acknowledge that the BCFS forest managers are now thicker on the ground than they used to be, checking logging practices and attempting to develop accurate forest inventories. For if you want to implement sustained yield forestry it is vitally important to find out how much wood is out there and so establish allowable annual cuts. But in George's opinion the foresters are a little late in the Terrace region, so they're assessing what they haven't got. "When the ship has just run out of freeboard and the ocean is just starting to run over the side, then they start plugging the holes," he concludes.[60]

Jack Walters, a widely-respected research forester whose criticisms of forest practices and forest policy have been rather pointed, extends Kofoed's metaphor. "I don't think we know where we're going," he observes, looking out over the rainswept experimental forest just outside Vancouver. Walters is somewhat resigned in his appraisal of the forest future: "It's a great big ship with nobody on the bridge. Or if they're on the bridge they're playing cards. Or the ship has no rudder."[61]

Most of the official optimism about a dramatic new commitment to forest preservation comes out of the vast, centralized bureaucracies that have over the years assumed increasing control over the resource. It is not that such optimism is based on a faulty conception of the basic need to stop making withdrawals from the limited forest "capital" without making appropriate deposits of money and effort. The problem is that such optimistic views ignore both the historical record and current developments. The forest is still essentially a supply of general revenues for government and wood fibre for industry. It seems that skepticism about big government and big business is generalized in Canada. This is reflected in the specifics of how people in forest-based communities, remote from the distant institutions that control the forest resource, feel about the way the woods are being used. Many people with long and varied experience dealing directly with actual resource extraction wonder how the long-term commitment necessary for adequate forest renewal can neatly dovetail with the short-term priorities of distant planners.

The men at the top of the forest hierarchy in Canada may well be sincere in their belief that things have finally turned around. They have the power to make important choices. But the danger is that the corporate executives will accept too quickly Henry Ford's definition of history as being just so much "bunk". And in their eagerness to reassure the rest of us that there is at last a firm *resolve* to put an end to the era of thoughtless exploitation, they may be disregarding the historical and systematic reasons for the current crunch. Those reasons have everything to do with the inherent inability of capitalist enterprise to think beyond its own balance-sheet, little to do with deep-seeded habits. As one veteran forester remarked about the apparent new resolve, "Everything is a facade. It's just like an alcoholic who swears he's going to beat it — and he does, until five o'clock rolls around."[62]

Horse logging. Until the 1950s, horses were used throughout Eastern Canada to haul logs from the bush.

5. The Cutting Edge

ROM THE TIME commercial logging in eastern Canada came into its own with the rise of the square timber trade at the beginning of the nineteenth century, right up to the 1950s, the extraction of wood from the forest depended largely on muscle power, both human and animal. To some extent the source of either kind of power was the farm. French-speaking farmers from Quebec and northern Ontario, for instance, drifted into the forest every fall to cut wood for the seasonal operations of the pulp and paper companies. Men whose families had the misfortune to plant themselves on inhospitable northern homesteads, where soils only reluctantly yielded meagre crops of root vegetables and fodder for a few horses and cattle, found the woodcutting skills they had learned from their fathers to be one of the few marketable commodities they had to sell.

Yet the New Brunswick farmers who worked the pulp limits of Quebec's north shore and the Quebeckers who migrated westward as far as the Lakehead brought with them more than a deft hand for felling a spruce tree and an eye for good timber. They also knew how to handle a team of horses, an ability crucial to the logging operators. Bush teamsters would sit atop a sleigh piled high with four-foot bolts of pulpwood, driving their animals along narrow forest skid trails covered with a surface of glare ice. Descending a steep slope was particularly treacherous, for if the load got away and overtook the galloping team, the resulting chaos could easily crush both man and beast under a torrent of potential woodpulp. The skills of the farm extended not only to cutting wood and driving teams. The care and grooming of horses and the tending of harness and horseshoe were important jobs in the forest products industry.

In eastern Canada, in the days of the horse, the axe and the bucksaw, the forest was dotted with winter logging camps. It didn't matter whether the camps were run directly by the large pulp and paper companies or by subcontractors employed by the forest firms to cut on company limits. The stable and the forge, the teamster and the blacksmith were basic requirements for the delivery of wood to the mills. Since wood is a particularly cumbersome, heavy commodity, hauling it from the forest in the huge volumes the mills required meant that a lot of man- and horsepower had to be deployed every winter. As the demand for wood continued its unrelenting growth, so too did the demand for brawn to move it along its way.

Until the years immediately following World War II, the forest and the farm continued to be bound together by this logic of production. But less than thirty years later the old logging camp had disappeared from the boreal forest. In its place came the large, centralized woodlands garages of the pulp and paper companies, installations that had more resemblance to military compounds than to the rough wood shanties and stables they replaced. Today's woodlands garage is surrounded by a large, chainlink fence topped with barbed wire. You could play a night baseball game under the floodlights if it weren't for the rows of logging trucks, feller-bunchers and skidders lined up like tanks in the yard. The teamsters and the blacksmiths have been replaced by diesel, electrical and hydraulic mechanics who work in large, metal-sided sheds similar to airplane hangars. Smells of manure, hay and leather, shouts to the horses and the clang of hammer on anvil have given way to acrid welding fumes and the odour of solvents, grease and oil. The high-pitched whine of the power tools makes you feel like you're in a factory, not a logging camp. The uniform colours of the logging machines matches the colour of the corporate flag flying beside the maple leaf outside the main shed. The machine age has entered the woods.

But what is curious is not that the horse and buggy era was edged out of the logging industry, but that it took so long to happen. Other modern industries — electrical, automotive, metallurgical — had by the early 1950s not only passed through the age of mechanization, but were also on the verge of automation. The assembly line and "scientific management" had long been established techniques in most industrial production. Even the mining industry, which shared remote locations with the logging operations, had put down the pick and shovel in favour of machine-powered methods of extraction.

Not so in the bush. As Alexander Koroleff, a forester and logging expert with the Canadian Pulp and Paper Association (CPPA), noted as early as 1941, although he shaved with an electric razor, trees were still being felled by hand. And he added: "While today even baby carriages are on ball bearings, logs in many regions are skidded*... by animals with such methods as appear to be most difficult; by dragging them completely or partly dragging them on inefficient and clumsy carriers."[1]

This apparent paradox is all the more telling given the enthusiasm that top managers of large wood-using firms had for technological innovations on their mill sites — as opposed to in the bush. At the mill, improvements in methods of pulping and sawing wood offered both more efficiency and higher profits. But the same large firms both controlled most of the country's forest land and directed operations in the bush as well as at the mill. And in the bush, changes in wood-gathering technology did not proceed at the same pace as changes in wood processing.

Why were eastern logging operations so late to mechanize? The answer rests on a number of complex economic, environmental and technological factors, some of which are closely related to the organization and structure of the forest industry — and the forest itself. For one thing, decisions around important capital expenditures in the industry were made by executives who had little interest in the forest except as a remote source of supply of fibre to the mills. As long as the wood fibre was cheap and ready to hand, it really made very little difference to these men how it got to the mill. When traditional manpower and horsepower seemed as cheap and abundant as the trees being hauled out, there was no apparent need for time and motion studies of loggers by efficiency experts, or for new

* Skidding, in the parlance of the logging business, means dragging or hauling logs from the stump to a roadside stream or "landing" where they are loaded onto some means of transportation for the journey to the mill. Modern landings are often locations for delimbing, sectioning and chipping machines.

machinery. For that matter, new methods of logging were considered in the same light as new ideas about forest management and silviculture — expensive undertakings that could offer no short-term payoff. When a shortage of woods labour had developed around the end of World War I, the CPPA established its Woodlands Section to look into mechanization, but a return to normal market conditions and stand-pat management attitudes stifled any moves towards change in logging techniques. That irrepressible lumberman and forestry spokesman, Senator W.C. Edwards, who thought that there was no real need for forest management, was also skeptical of new-fangled notions about logging: "Give me two French Canadians in preference to any machine you can introduce," he told the Woodlands Section.[2]

By the end of the next World War, things had changed. The changes, however, were not in the market for paper products and lumber: Sales boomed in the postwar period and logging activity accelerated. The principal change was in the market for labour, with the steady urbanization of Canadian society. With the increasing mechanization of farms, rural populations went into decline. Former farm workers were lured into factory jobs in the cities, where sprawling suburbs reached out towards the countryside. The period was one in general of economic expansion and increased employment opportunities. The trend was accompanied by an upswing in labour organization: Large industrial unions began to make their mark on the workplace.

These shifts had serious implications for the forest industry in the east. The horses that had hauled the logs "from stump to dump" were more scarce: The equine population decreased at a rate of 10 per cent per year after the war.[3] Even more serious for woods managers was the decline in the number of workers available to cut the wood and drive the teams. This was partly the result of the decline in farm labour, the traditional source of supply of woods workers. But as well, many of the men left started to wonder whether it was logical to haul wood about the bush in the freezing depths of northern winter. Logging camp conditions were arduous, indeed primitive. Dozens of men were crammed into dimly-lit, foul-smelling shanties cluttered with snow-soaked clothing and invaded by sweat. Sanitary conditions were rudimentary. Workers had virtually no opportunity to bathe, even after weeks of heavy work.

Using conventional, unmechanized logging techniques —

the "cut and pile" system — the workers would fell and delimb trees with saws and axes, divide each trunk into neat four-foot "sticks" of pulpwood, and finally pile the day's production next to the skid road. In the late 1940s, one manager, J.O. Wilson, calculated that, to move *a single cord* of wood to the mill involved lifting twelve tons of wood by hand. Wilson, a man with long experience on pulp limits in Quebec, labelled the system of work "inhuman" in comparison to labour conditions in other industries of the day.[4] Another manager, from the Quebec North Shore Company, called the French Canadians who did this work "the backbone of our pulpwood industry . . . a happy, hardworking class of men who have borne the hard slugging in lumber and pulpwood camps for years". He found it remarkable that the workers didn't complain, despite what he labelled the "deplorable conditions" under which loggers lived and worked in his own company.[5]

Though some may not have complained, others initiated successful organizing drives leading to union certification for many loggers, particularly in northern Ontario. Still other loggers in the east simply voted with their feet, either abandoning logging altogether or becoming very choosy about where they would or would not work. Because the labour market for loggers had become a seller's market, it became increasingly easy simply to tell the boss to take the job and shove it when camp conditions, food or the timber did not measure up. This had the result of making logging operators very edgy: A reliable supply of wood to the mills was completely dependent upon a reliable supply of woods labour to the camps. That supply, for decades quite ample due to the availability of large numbers of farm boys and Scandinavian and other European immigrants, was far from stable by 1950.

The shortage of available workers, combined with union gains, helped to drive up the cost of woods labour. Loggers started to gain a sense of their own power as a collective group. They started to negotiate not only higher wages but also conditions of work, cutting into management control over details such as skidding distances, road location, and which stands of wood were to be cut by which workers. These developments also combined to increase the cost of getting wood to the mill, much to the chagrin of mill managers.

But, just as important, these major changes finally forced

pulp and paper companies to pay serious attention to what was happening in the woods. Management's first reaction was predictable enough, in a way comparable to its reaction to a shortage of trees. The companies simply tried to increase the supply of the commodity in question by hollering to the government to lend a hand. When it was a matter of wood supply, the strategy had usually worked. When the industry had dropped hints of mill layoffs or deferred mill expansion plans and raised concerns about wood shortages, government usually responded with bigger timber limits. When labour shortages developed, the industry had taken a similar tack. During World War II the government had supplied German prisoners of war to fill the gap in labour supplies. When shortages persisted and became even more acute after the war, the industry pressured government to organize special immigration programs to meet the shortfall in the supply of loggers. The eastern pulp companies were particularly keen to get access to the labour pool represented by the thousands of Displaced Persons (DPs) who had nowhere to go in the aftermath of the war in Europe.

A confidential 1947 letter from Alexander Koroleff of the CPPA to the federal government's Dominion Forester put the industry's case. Koroleff was busily pushing the development of mechanical logging within the industry but felt the government should lend a hand to make sure the wood would in fact be cut: "The possibility of increasing the supply of woods labour by controlled and selected immigration of suitable subjects from Great Britain and the Scandinavian and European countries should be carefully investigated."[6]

Though the government did comply with industry requests for more immigrant loggers, this did nothing to stem the flow of regular bushworkers out of the forest and into more attractive jobs. Immigrants and French Canadian farmers were no longer in reliable and adequate supply to meet the explosion in postwar demand for logs. Fewer and fewer workers using traditional techniques of production would simply cut less and less wood. Ultimately, new ways of getting wood had to be developed. And that meant machines. By 1948 the Woodlands Section of the CPPA, under the able leadership of Alexander Koroleff, established committees to study woods mechanization. The industry was finally getting serious about technological change in timber cutting and hauling.

IRONICALLY, THE PRINCIPAL technological innovation came from outside the Canadian pulpwood logging industry and would have made its appearance whether the companies were serious about change or not. In the 1950s the chain saw, now a familiar tool to every Canadian cottager, hit the bush with all the inevitability of a machine that is too useful not to catch on.

The idea of using a machine to do the time-consuming and repetitive work of actually cutting down trees had been around for nearly a century. In 1858 one Harvey Brown of New York was issued with the first patent for a chain saw, which was described as an "endless sectional sawing mechanism".[7] In the decades following, numerous ideas were floated and prototypes tested but with little practical success. The monstrous saws that emerged were both too heavy and unwieldy to be effective in difficult terrain or among dense stands of trees and underbrush. But by 1925 a German, Andreas Stihl, had come up with a 140-pound, two-person power saw. Within ten years the machine was refined so that by 1936 the H.A. Stihl Company was marketing a 46-pound power saw. After war interrupted the progress of innovation and marketing, Stihl's saws found themselves without protection of patent, and North American companies began to produce similar machines using the German design. The war stimulated the development of lighter metal alloys and light, air-cooled engines and by the late 1940s further refinements had been introduced. One American inventor, intrigued by the efficient woodcutting ability of the timber beetle, took his inspiration from nature and the grub beetle's jaw and developed a new, more effective cutting chain.[8]

Even though the early saws were cumbersome and heavy, loggers started to use them because they could do the job so quickly. The new demand in turn prompted further improvements in design, so that the chain saw became a constantly-improving machine.

Jake Hildebrand, who cut timber for over thirty years in the Ear Falls-Red Lake area of northwestern Ontario, used his first chain saw in 1952: the big, awkward Precision model, which Hildebrand describes as "pitiful". The machine, says Hildebrand, "weighed about 60 pounds. It was quite a thing for us at the time because nobody knew any better. In some cases it was better than the Swede saw — you could produce more and limb easier. Everybody was for it."[9] The first chain saws that Terry Slaney of Parksville, B.C., remembers from his forty years' experience as a logger were 130-pound monsters that required two workers to manipulate. Now he and his fellow loggers accept the high-powered, light chain saws — "fairly wicked machines," says Slaney — just as their fathers took for granted the cross-cut saw and the axe.[10]

The chain saw caught on fast because it was a relatively simple machine that could not only do the job quickly and efficiently, but also had little "down time" when it was unavailable due to mechanical problems. It made loggers' work more lucrative. In many cases their wages were tied to productivity through a piece-rate system, so it paid to buy their own saws, necessitating little prompting on this point from the industry. With the ease and economics of it, the virtually overnight shift to mechanical felling of trees was carried out to a great extent by the workers themselves. By 1960 there were virtually no muscle-powered saws left in the Canadian forest. In Newfoundland, for instance, within five years after power saws were introduced into the pulpwood logging industry in 1954, the machines accounted for 87 per cent of all production.[11] In British Columbia the new saws allowed workers to cut trees with a high content of pitch, trees that might have been ignored in the days of the hand saw due to the necessity of constantly oiling the saw to prevent sticking. As early as 1952, the Woodlands Section of the CPPA was reporting productivity increases of 15 to 20 per cent as a result of the introduction of chain saws.[12]

The power saw in fact performed no new functions in the bush. It simply did the same job that workers had previously done with hand tools. But it did its work at such a fast, steady pace that skidding operations using horses could no longer keep up. A substitute for the horse was needed, something to do the job faster. The earliest solutions attempted to introduce mechanical skidders to the woods. These were basically rigid-framed vehicles that frustrated equipment developers and loggers alike. The machines needed a large turning radius and had extreme difficulty manoeuvring under difficult forest conditions. Inventors soon came up with a different machine, the mechanical wheeled skidder, still to be found in the yards of equipment dealers from Prince George to Grand Falls.

The mechanical wheeled skidder, adaptable to most Canadian forest conditions (except for terrain such as the steep-slope logging of British Columbia) does the same job as a horse: It pulls logs out of the bush. The machine's articulated steering enables it to bend in the middle, even more so than a horse. The most up-to-date skidders, with their four-wheel drive, can manoeuvre efficiently in the most difficult natural conditions, rolling over large rocks, stumps and piles of slash, turning on a short radius, getting out of tight spots. And the skidder can pull a much heavier load than a horse. Its engines, ranging up to 185-horsepower, are combined with powerful winches that can reel in steel cables attached to a half-a-dozen large, tree-length logs. The introduction of mechanized skidding changed much of Canadian logging from a "shortwood" system in which all wood was cut into short lengths at the stump to a "tree length" system in which the entire trunk is dragged to a roadside landing for sectioning and transportation to the mill.

The new machines were the answer to the prayers of the logging boss. Within about a dozen years after power saws were first introduced, the internal combustion engine had replaced brute strength in both the cutting and hauling of trees. In 1959, three articulated skidders were sold in Canada. By 1971, almost ten thousand machines found a home in logging operations big and small.[13] The rhythmic sound of the buck saw and the yell of the teamster in the woods were replaced by the high-pitched whine of the chain saw and the ear-numbing roar of the skidder's diesel engine. Many a logging horse was consigned to the glue factory.

This first phase in the mechanization of logging might not have fundamentally altered the old system of sawing down trees, cutting them up and dragging them from the woods. But it did result in dramatic increases in productivity within a very short time. In 1964, even before skidders made their biggest impact, E.E. Grainger, a manager for the Abitibi company, told a logging industry seminar about the advantages of the new system. In the 1951-52 season, Grainger reported, the workers on the Abitibi limits had taken 1.19 days of labour to produce and deliver a cord of pulpwood. Ten years later, changes in technique had whittled the labour requirement down by 46 per cent, to 0.64 days. In 1951-52 Abitibi was using almost 2,000 workers to produce every 100,000 cords of wood. By 1961-62 the company needed only 603 people to do the same job: a drop of 69 per cent.[14] Management was well on its way to ironing out its problems with labour supply.

The changes in cutting and hauling wood to the roadside were accompanied by new methods of getting wood to the mill. More forest roads were built, and large logging trucks gained access to even the most remote forests, a development sealing the fate of the springtime river drive, one of the most colourful, romantic and dangerous aspects of the glory days of logging. Since the earliest days of the square timber trade logging had been a seasonal occupation, beginning with the fall journey to the camps and culminating with the spring river drive. After the drive loggers would either drift back into agricultural or construction jobs or spend the summer waiting for the logging camps to reopen. Workers tended to be transient. When times were good they would wander from camp to camp looking for cleaner ground, a better strip of timber and better food; when times were bad they would compete for scarce jobs with an army of other loggers.

All this changed once trucks started hauling wood and logging ceased to be dependent on the spring breakup. Over the course of the 1950s, the average worker at Abitibi put in more days of work every year, and by the end of the decade each logger was working 83 per cent more days than ten years earlier.[15] The seasonal nature of logging work was quickly eroded. By the 1980s, at least during times when there was a demand for pulp, paper and lumber, most woods workers were putting in a good nine months on the job.

As far as management was concerned, logging mechanization gave companies added flexibility in their attempts to bring down wood costs and boost labour productivity. Management's principal motivation was to ensure that there would always be an adequate supply of cheap wood in the mill yard. Gordon Godwin, a manager with Ontario Paper, reflected on company attitudes to wood and the forest when he addressed the Woodlands Section of the CPPA in 1968. Looking back on his experience with a group of superiors who were in turn under pressure from the owners of the firm — the proprietors of two big daily newspapers, the *Chicago Tribune* and the *New York Daily News* — Godwin told his Montreal audience of fellow woods managers:

> I suppose there isn't a production man in this room who hasn't been flattened periodically in the squeeze of the corporate wringer as pressure is applied to do something about wood costs. I can't tell you how to avoid this kind of pain in the future because no matter what you do, cost will always be too high. But the next time the inquisitors in the executive suite are about to put you through the press, you might say to your president, "Sir, do you realize that in 1945 wood cost was 31 per cent of the total product value for our industry and thanks to the good work of men like me, that figure came down to 26 per cent in 1968?"[16]

Gordon Godwin was one of a small group of people convinced that even better productivity and cheaper wood could be obtained by going beyond the chain saw and skidder towards completely mechanized logging *systems* that would use machines to cut the trees and transport them from the stump to the roadside. The hydraulic and diesel technology was already at hand. It simply had to be moulded into the right machine to do the job. But this was no easy task. Given the expense of research and development work, it was hard to convince the men at the top of such a conservative industry to sink money into entirely new concepts of machine design. There were no guarantees that new logging systems would cut costs in the way skidders had done. Mill-oriented managers, quick to invest money in profitable new pulping and papermaking techniques, had trouble seeing past their nearby woodyards to the forests beyond, and couldn't be convinced that substantial savings might be realized through further mechanization there.

ROSS SILVERSIDES IS WELL AWARE of the cautious approach of forest products companies in the forest. Silversides spent over twenty-five years with Abitibi, where he started out doing wilderness timber cruises and eventually became Director of Woodlands Development. After that he worked for the federal government's Forest Management Institute and the National Research Council. Now, although he has retired from full-time work in the industry, Silversides retains an active interest in forests and their exploitation, and writes and speaks about wood utilization, logging mechanization and the timber harvest.

Like his fellow advocates of mechanization, Silversides has had to fight against conservatism in the industry. For him, the argument for mechanization centres around low cost wood. He emphasizes that the only reason the industry mechanized was to reduce or hold costs. "On the whole," he says, "the entire effort has been to reduce the number of workers in the woods."[17] But he also knows that production managers, as key decision-makers, are skeptical of untried, unproven techniques. They prefer what they know to be tested and reliable methods of production. "Most organisms have built-in defenses to reject a foreign object," he says. But he thinks managerial resistance to change can be overcome: "If enough anti-rejection can be built into the system, they will accept and utilize such objects."[18]

Ross Silversides, Gordon Godwin and a small group of others working for both equipment manufacturers and forest products companies spent years trying to vaccinate the industry against rejecting the concept of a machine or a system of machines that would cut, delimb, top, section, pile and haul trees. And the obstacles were not always organizational and financial. Nature itself has an annoying habit of forcing new machines back to the drawing board again and again. Forests have highly variable physical structures combining mixtures of rock and mud, steep and flat terrain, dense and thin stands. Machine operators have problems with visibility and find that their big, top-heavy machines can be very unstable on difficult or uneven terrain. Specialized, expensive equipment cannot be permitted to remain idle due to breakdown for very long, so back-up repair facilities have to be readily available. Unpredictable variables like rain, fog and snow combine with adverse conditions to create an environment quite different from the controlled, predictable conditions of factory production. Clearly, the problem of replacing labour with capital in the form of new machinery was not an easy one. "It's a highly capital-intensive industry and your mistakes live with you for a hell of a long time," reflects Silversides.[19]

The efforts at developing multi-purpose tree-processing equipment did meet with some notable failures before a few reliable machines emerged, though some flops did ultimately contribute to better designs. As early as 1957 the Quebec North Shore company tried out the Vit Feller-Buncher, named after its inventor, Rudy Vit. The machine, with a hydraulically-driven chain saw, crawled up to a tree, grabbed it, cut it and bunched it up with other trees it had already cut. A load of whole trees could then be hauled off to a roadside landing. However, there were problems because processing equipment to limb and slash the trees at the landing had not yet been successfully developed. The process of manoeuvring the bulky unit up to each individual tree was also awkward and time-consuming. Only a handful of the machines were sold, though over forty were produced.

Perhaps the most extraordinary harvesting outfit was the Beloit Harvester. It looked like a power shovel with the usual caterpillar track. But instead of having an earth-moving bucket at the end of a hydraulic boom there was a mechanism designed to delimb a tree, sever its top and slice it off at ground level. The harvester would seize a tree with this device and, using the tree itself as a guide and support, send its cutting head up the trunk, slicing off the limbs and top just like one might do with one's fingers on the stem of a flower. An awe-inspiring sight, admittedly, to see the branches fly. But the 62,000-pound behemoth simply could not manoeuvre with sufficient agility in rough forest terrain. Beloit, a company more accustomed to designing pulp- and paper-making machines for use under factory conditions, withdrew from the logging equipment business, leaving forty harvesters and tens of millions of dollars behind.[20]

In spite of such failures, efforts at developing the ideal logging machine persisted as the costs of paying men and keeping them in camps continued to rise at a time when fewer people were inclined to work in remote logging camps. This trend, combined with the insatiable and always-growing appetite of the mills for more wood, prompted some forest companies to maintain their interest in getting the man with the chain saw off the forest floor. Eventually several concepts were transformed into viable machines that enjoyed some commercial success. Finally, instead of joining the buck saw as museum pieces as soon as they left the factory gate, these machines joined the

A full tree logging system delivers complete trees to the mill untouched by human hands. The Koehring Feller-forwarder can cut over one hundred trees in an hour.

wheeled skidder as common features in the woodlands garage. One of them, the Koehring Shortwood Harvester, was a complex machine that cut a thirty-foot swath through the forest, shearing trees and at the same time feeding them to its own "processing tower" to be limbed, topped and cut into sections. The pulpwood, ready to be shipped, was then carried back to the landing by the same machine, which could work on slopes of up to 43 per cent. In 1970 independent researchers labelled the shortwood harvester "one of the most promising recent developments towards highly-mechanized logging operations".[21]

Another success story, the Drott Feller-Buncher, was designed to shear trees and pile them in a selected place, from where they would be skidded to the landing. Drott's machine had two advantages over Rudy Vit's earlier feller-buncher. The Vit model was like a dog among so many hydrants, trundling up to each tree before it could shear it off. The Drott unit, with its hydraulic boom, could sit in one spot and seize several trees from there before it had to move on. It could thus work faster and more productively. As well, by the time this feller-buncher came along, processing equipment had been designed to transform entire trees into bolts of wood quickly and efficiently at the roadside landing.

The feller-buncher is part of what is known as a full tree logging system, meaning that the whole tree is cut down and hauled away to a central processing point. Many people who have been keen students of woods mechanization, including Ross Silversides, argue that this is the best way to go about things. The alternative, tree length systems in which delimbing and topping take place at the stump, is said to involve too many variables and potential problems. Better to do as little as possible in the woods, say people like Silversides. Once you get the tree to the processing station, more complex and costly machines that do not have to be designed for travel in tough conditions can do the job in a more controlled environment, and factory conditions can be more closely duplicated.[22] Under a full tree system, wood can be delivered to the mill untouched by human hands.

Following this notion, the Koehring company, which had found that its shortwood system* depended on too many variable functions — any of which could break down independently, thus stopping the entire process — proceeded to develop a machine that would cut and haul away full trees all by itself. Getting into the cab of Koehring's Feller-forwarder (KFF), a machine of no modest proportions, seems almost perilous, rather like climbing to the top of a set of lofty monkey bars. Initial assessment found that the KFF could cut 92 trees per productive machine-hour. Workers who operate the machine claim they can shear off anywhere between 150 and 180 small trees in an hour, especially when productivity is geared to a bonus and the trees are thick on the ground.[23] As they sit high above the forest floor manipulating various pedals, toggles and joysticks, the machine operators would no doubt appreciate the sentiments of W.J. McGee, that early philosopher of the Conservation Movement, who spoke of "consciously and purposefully entering into control over nature". Still, nature sometimes gets

* A shortwood system is the same as the old cut and pile system of logging used for so long by the axe and saw brigade of lumberjacks, who would lug fallen wood into piles after doing the topping and delimbing by hand. The Koehring Shortwood Harvester does the same thing, substituting hydraulic power for muscle power and delivering wood to the landing rather than piling it in the bush.

its way with even the largest of machines. At times the Koehring's twelve-foot tires spin free when the machine's belly, laden with ten tons of pulpwood, gets hung up on rock or bogged down in mud. "If you get this thing stuck, you've got yourself some fun," said one logging boss who had been forced to bring in two bulldozers and another feller-forwarder to get a KFF out of a jam.[24] Mistakes can be costly: When the cutting shears strike a rock, the $5000 butt shear cylinder can be irreparably damaged.

In spite of these problems the KFF has enjoyed some market success, simply because it can deliver enormous quantities of wood in a very short time. It cuts swath after swath through the forest, using its large hydraulic scissors to shear off up to half a dozen trees with each pass of its felling head. It then loads the complete trees onto its own back and transports its load — up to twelve cords of wood — to the roadside pile. After dumping the trees, it returns to the edge of the woods and once again starts to push back the margin of the forest. It does its work in about the same time that an expert lumberjack used to take to cut and pile a single cord of short wood in the bush. Not much more than thirty years ago such lumberjacks still cut all of Canada's pulpwood. Now those still around can only wonder in disbelief at the pace of technological change in their industry.

BEDFORD WHELTON AND LEO SISK are farmers and loggers who live in the northeastern corner of New Brunswick, a province whose origins are firmly linked with the timber industry. Around the small community of Black Rock, where their families settled when they arrived from Ireland in the last century, farming has never been easy. The land is not as productive as in other, more richly-endowed parts of the country — areas where in any case farmers in the 1980s are being squeezed into bankruptcy.

Whelton is over seventy years old and Sisk is a generation younger. With his heart condition, Whelton can't do heavy work and the doctor has told him to stop working altogether. But he's always worked outside and he still drives the tractor while Sisk pounds in cedar fenceposts with a large wooden mallet. Both take a few minutes from their spring fencemending to talk about their working lives in the fields and forests.

"Around here it always had to be that the farmer had to depend on the woods to a certain extent," Bedford Whelton observes.[25] "The farms aren't big and we haven't got the market for what we do produce. Winter and summer, whenever there's a spare couple of days, we make for the woods to make a dollar." Leo Sisk agrees: "You're darn right. If it wasn't for the wood we probably wouldn't be here today."

Both men have cut lumber and pulpwood on both their own land and Crown land, where they worked for companies holding government-issued cutting licences. In 1926, at the age of sixteen, Whelton started cutting long lumber for the Gloucester Lumber Company, during a time when the cross-cut saw and the farm horse were the principal tools. Later he joined a seasonal migration of New Brunswick loggers to Quebec's north shore where he cut pulpwood "in the buck saw time" for $1.35 per cord. Sisk began work in the 1940s and was co-owner of an early chain saw.

"When I started, at that time they wouldn't cut anything on the stump under eleven inches. Now there's not much in the woods *over* eleven inches," Whelton reflects with some astonishment. "The pulp companies are cutting it right down to three inches. Yes, they cut pretty well everything. What they don't cut down they tear down with their machinery. When I was first in the woods, after we were through cutting there was still good doings for another start. All the trees from ten or eleven inches down were left standing. Your horses didn't tear the bark off the trees or knock them down. We'd leave no stain on them."

Leo Sisk has his own skidder and uses it to haul the pulpwood he sells to the Consolidated-Bathurst pulp mill in nearby Bathurst. He is a little frustrated with the machine's performance in the bush, but acknowledges that it gets the job done. "When you go into the woods with a skidder, you hook onto a log and haul it out. OK, we try to do the best we can. You don't want to break down too much but you can't help breaking a lot of the trees down."

Both men know that the big operations of the pulp and paper companies now cut down everything as part of the clearcut logging system in vogue in most parts of New Brunswick. Such clearcuts have to be treated and carefully tended like a farmer's field if they are to produce another crop of conifers within a reasonable period of time. After all, the cutover areas were cleared with machines known as harvesters. Sisk and Whelton have heard about the full tree harvesting systems, the "big outfits" that can pick up a whole tree from one place and put it down in another. Sisk once saw such a machine on television. Both men think that this isn't the way to treat the forest, that too much land in New Brunswick is locked up by the pulp and paper companies under long-term agreements with the government.

"Nowadays," Bedford Whelton says, "The companies don't crop the land. They fairly mine it. . . . If the International Paper Company and the Consolidated-Bathurst Company say, 'We want this done and we want it done that way' — that's the way it's done, see." Whelton is adamant on this point. "The government may have it at the back of their mind, 'Well, we should be helping all these little fellas.' But they don't do it because the company says, 'Do it our way.' "

AS WITH BEDFORD WHELTON and Leo Sisk, the most common metaphor used by critics of how the forest has been and is being treated — as a nonrenewable rather than a renewable resource — is that of *mining:* the extraction of a raw material, a mineral for instance, from a quarry, with no thought for what will take its place. The phrase "timber mining" has particular resonance when you watch a machine like the Koehring Feller-forwarder at work in the woods. The machine certainly looks like it would be more at home in an open-pit mining operation where oversized vehicles are common. The research and development effort leading to the introduction of such machines was solely concerned with cost and productivity: what would end up supplying wood most quickly and economically. What was missing was consideration of the effects of the new technology on forest ecosystems and future forest productivity. The science of forestry was given scant consideration in the process of technological change.

Equipment designers, busy trying to conceive of practical logging systems that would kindle a spark of interest among cautious logging managers, couldn't take time to worry about the
long-term effects of their inventions.

The basic fact neglected is that forestry, like farming, is based
on the theory of ecological succession. Once a forest is cut,
nature takes over: Various new plants and animals populate the
former forest site; each community of natural life gives way to
another; the site in turn becomes less accommodating to the
earlier species. So the raspberries and woody shrubs that come
in first eventually give way to larger trees with bigger stems,
organisms better able to vie for the supplies of light, water and
nutrients that nature has to offer. Eventually one of two things
happens. The process of succession proceeds and ultimately
results in the formation of a climax or sub-climax forest* beyond
which no further succession occurs. Or some cataclysmic disturbance, such as a forest fire, a plague of insects or the intervention
of a feller-buncher, takes place and the process begins again at
square one with the raspberries and the woody shrubs.

Forestry and silviculture are concerned with manipulating
this natural progression of things, intervening at various points
to make sure that a "crop" of trees with commercial value develops as quickly and efficiently as possible. The logging methods
chosen in the first place to remove the original stand will have
an important bearing on future stand development. In fact, logging and silviculture are inseparable. Logging is the first step in
forest management and an integral part of silvicultural practice.
Every undergraduate forestry student learns this.

In the days when logging was carried out with horses and
there was general government and industry indifference to
future forests, foresters had to base their meagre silvicultural
efforts on the hopes that logging techniques were not dramatically disruptive to the forest ecosystem. They had to trust that a
new stand of commercially-valuable timber would grow up
without much assistance from themselves. These early foresters

---

* When forest communities evolve through the sequences of growth that make
up the process of ecological succession, that growth can culminate in the
climax forest — where two or three species dominate and make up both the
upper canopy and the young seedlings on the forest floor. A sub-climax forest
is a stand that never makes it to the climax stage, due to factors such as soil or
water conditions, or fire.

had little choice but to hope that since natural seed sources and a vigorous young undergrowth were often left after logging, the process of natural succession would take its course to re-establish good stands of merchantable timber. Sometimes this happened. Often it did not, because different forest species on different forest sites require different treatment and logging was carried out not with a view to silviculture but in relation to wood cost. Silviculture does not lend itself well to blanket prescription. Even old-fashioned logging often resulted in new stands of birch or balsam fir, not the spruce trees that forest and mill managers wanted. But still, the blanket prescriptions were applied because natural regeneration as a forestry philosophy permitted very little attention to be paid to active silvicultural measures. Using horses to skid logs from the woods in the winter was the cheapest and easiest way of going about the task. The fact that this particular system could also be justified in terms of the prevailing silvicultural philosophy of the time was merely coincidental.

When the horse was replaced by the wheeled skidder, and mechanized harvesting systems were introduced into the forest, there was no consideration of how the changes might affect the forests. Alexander Koroleff, the White Russian emigré who brought the time and motion study into the Canadian forest and provided the focus for much of the activities of the Woodlands Section of the CPPA, was a sparkplug behind the mechanization of logging in eastern Canada. By 1941 this energetic forester was convinced that machines should replace human labour in the woods, though at that time mechanization had not begun to gather momentum. Yet Koroleff was pleased with advances in mechanization on the west coast, where steam-powered cable yarding systems had been introduced in the early days to cope with steep slopes and big timber and by the 1930s had been augmented by bulldozers and trucks.

British Columbia had in fact been the exception to the long non-technological rule of human and animal muscle power in the rest of Canada. In British Columbia, from the earliest days of the industry there, huge trees and perilous slopes had pre-cluded effective use of draft animals and forced the introduction of small steam-powered engines known, ironically, as "donkey engines". These machines provided the power to what was called the "ground yarding systems", which employed a horizontal spool to wind cable in and out, dragging logs out of the woods along the ground towards the machine. This awkward method posed problems because logs would inevitably get caught on various snags, resulting in the airing of endless streams of profanities and oaths from the loggers on the job.

It wasn't long, however, before the ground yarding system gave way to "high lead" methods, whereby a tall spar tree was selected and rigged at the top with cables and pulleys. This gave the loggers a height advantage so that the big logs could be lifted up, clearing most of the obstacles on the forest floor. This enabled more wood to be extracted and resulted in significant gains in productivity. R.V. Stuart, who in 1910 was one of the first professional foresters to be employed by the new B.C. Forest Service, explained the difference between the two systems:

> The ground logging system was a selective logging system, but any similarity between that and the forestry definition of [selective logging] was purely coincidental. In those days it was dictated entirely by economic considerations. If you go out to any of those old areas that were ground-yarded, you'll find luxurious second growth. It was far better forestry than the 'high lead' that superceded it. . . . The high lead, while a far more destructive system than ground yarding, was God's gift to the logger.[26]

West coast loggers have continued to employ the high lead system and the same logging principles into the 1980s, although a mobile steel spar has been substituted for the spar tree.

But, about the kind of mechanization that took place across the country, Koroleff the forester had reservations, in spite of the progress that pleased Koroleff the logging engineer:

> It is indeed regrettable, however, that the benefits from logging mechanization were so often only temporary and resulted in heavy damage to permanent forest values. As we know only too well, much of the economy in logging has been achieved through methods of cutting and wood extraction which resulted in leaving the forest land in bad shape from the point of view of natural regeneration and protection. . . . My criticism is mainly on the score that in logging mechanization, silvicultural requirements too frequently were neglected even when they could have been considered.[27]

Twenty-five years after Koroleff expressed his concerns, skidders were just being introduced in the east and the more fully-mechanized systems of logging were starting to move from the drawing boards onto the forest floor. By the 1960s, some foresters saw emerging the same problems that Koroleff had identified. They were worried about the soil compaction, ground disturbance and erosion that might accompany the introduction of heavy equipment into the woods. The thin soils characteristic of many sites in eastern Canada would, it was feared, suffer loss of productive capability when their delicate structures were exposed to the ravages of heavy machinery. Problems of general soil disturbance might be compounded by actual loss of soil from erosion on some sites. There was particular concern expressed over the destruction of advance growth — the understory of young trees so crucial to the success of natural regeneration. Skidders and harvesters, unlike horses, have a tendency to destroy young trees by driving right over them. The full tree system, in which all of the limbs, needles and cone-bearing tops are carried away from the stump area, can also result in the removal of important seed sources from cutover areas. The depletion of the nutrient content of the soil can be another spinoff when rich foliage is removed from the forest, disrupting the biogeochemical cycle of mineral nutrition so important to forest growth.[28] Whether these concerns are well-founded is not yet known, because insufficient research and the variability of forest sites have not permitted any final conclusions to be reached.

In 1964 I.C.M. Place, a forester with the Canadian Forest Service, predicted that the notion of natural regeneration would have to be abandoned with the onslaught of new logging equipment. Place thought new methods of forest treatment might have to be adopted, but had his doubts about whether this would happen: "The initial Canadian reaction will probably be either to ignore the destruction of advance growth as being too expensive to do anything about and to hope for the best with natural regeneration after logging or to rely on artificial regeneration."[29] Implicit in Place's reasoning was a belief that forestry would have to undergo a change as a result of mechanization, that silviculturalists would have to start actively treating cutover areas — the large clearcuts necessary in order to make the investments in machinery pay off — instead of pinning their hopes on nature to provide the next forest of valuable timber. As new cutting systems adapted to the requirements of the new machines were introduced, more trees would have to be planted or the cutover areas would have to be seeded artificially after being scarified. The bigger and better forest road networks that threaded through the forests providing truck and logging equipment access to the woods also held out the opportunity for more intensive forestry. For the first time, the opening up of forests provided all-weather access for silviculture as well as logging. But Place was not hopeful about the priorities that the forest industry and foresters in general were likely to establish, even though mechanization had presented opportunities for new, activist approaches to reforestation: "I suspect that for some years logging foresters will be so mesmerized by technique in mechanization that silviculture will receive scant consideration and silviculturalists will find the experience harrowing."[30]

Nevertheless, the potential problems associated with the introduction of mechanized harvesting techniques became of sufficient concern for both foresters and industrial forest users that they started to conduct research studies into the relationship between logging methods and reproduction, even though such studies were not integrated with work on machine development. Research on items like feller-bunchers and feller-forwarders proceeded separately, apace.

An exhaustive study of the effects of various logging systems on the future forest was completed in 1978 by the Forest Engineering Research Institute of Canada (FERIC), an industry/government research centre which also tests new logging equipment for productivity and efficiency.[31] Three foresters investigated thirty-six logged-over sites in four eastern provinces to find out how the logging would affect future yields of wood. One of the researchers, Gordon Weetman, had set up the study of sample sites and had been monitoring reproduction on them for over ten years — the first extensive research effort ever undertaken in Canadian pulpwood logging to examine forest sites and their reaction to logging both before and after the removal of trees. Not surprisingly, the study found that it was extremely difficult to generalize about the effects of different cutting systems. It would have been surprising if the researchers had been able to come up with solid conclusions applying across the board because forestry is so very site-specific: Different conditions on particular sites give rise to different reactions by nature in the aftermath of logging. Different species, soils, levels

of stocking,* site conditions, types of machines and even operator attitudes complicate the picture.[32]

Nevertheless, Weetman and his colleagues were able to con-
clude that soil compaction and erosion resulting from the various logging systems used were not significant problems. However, as some foresters had suspected, they found serious
destruction of advance growth by logging machines, with 70 per
cent of advance-growth stems wiped out when skidders were
used. Skidders were apparently more harmful to advance
growth than other harvesting systems. "Invasion" of cutover
sites by hardwoods and unwanted scrub species which suppressed softwood growth was a problem, one that could have
been predicted by practising silviculturalists plagued by hardwood headaches in their attempts to promote the succession of
conifers on cutover sites. Gazing into the crystal ball with the
assistance of a computer-based simulation model, the FERIC
study speculated that, in fifty years, "Projected softwood yields
will probably be lower, the rotation ages to reach merchantabil-
ity longer and the number of softwood stems per cunit higher
than for previous stands."[33] In other words, the forest growing
up on sites previously cut for pulpwood would not be as attractive to the logging operator, because it would take a longer
period of time to produce a forest of inferior quality.

At the same time that he helped to inaugurate the series of
research studies leading up to these conclusions, Weetman was
disturbed by the way that technology had been applied in the
development of more productive mechanized logging systems.
He observed that company policies, rather than studying the
complexities of forest sites, developing ways of treating them so
as to ensure a succession of vigorous new stands and applying
logging systems compatible with these treatments, were just a
matter of "let's log and see what happens." Insufficient attention
was being paid to the results of introducing machinery into the
woods. "Speculation or sloppy empiricism are not good enough
to guide us in the use of machinery which can have such a
potentially deleterious effect on the future productivity of
cutover areas," Weetman concluded.[34]

---

* In this case stocking means how well forest areas were stocked with tree
growth before and after logging.

BEFORE THE ERA OF MECHANIZATION, accidents in the bush were often seen — particularly by the logging boss — as part of the job, just like the hearty meals and the seasonal work. In the years before chain saw and mechanical harvester, forest products companies tended to rely on independent contractors to supply their wood needs, and the swashbuckling logging boss, or "push", ran the cutting operations. This supervisor would in all likelihood be out there with the workers, overseeing the cutting and hauling, often taking an active hand in the tricky business of getting the wood out.

Accounts of the old days of logging are riddled with tales of loggers being crushed, maimed and killed. A stray log or a falling tree could deal a death blow with startling ease. A load of wood might careen out of control, burying a teamster. In the east the spring river drive required workers to wade about all day in fast-flowing, freezing-cold waters, shepherding logs downstream and unclogging log jams. It was not uncommon for dozens of men to be killed each season. In the west, where steam-driven winches pulled huge logs up and down hills with amazing speed, using steel cables as taut as bowstrings, things were no less risky. The "highballing" or fast-moving pace of the work was geared to maximum production and loggers had to be nimble and alert to avoid accidents. "You think people were pretty rough in them days," reflected one old-time logger from New Brunswick. "People wasn't so rough. They feared the woods. The lumber woods was a dangerous place at all times."[35]

There can be little doubt that the risky nature of the work was a factor when the industry woke up after World War II to find a shortage of loggers. The woods will always be a dangerous place to work, for the same reasons they have proved a difficult workplace to mechanize. Things are inherently unpredictable, with the uneven terrain, adverse weather and natural difficulties presented by the growth of trees in stands hardly designed for ease of access and freedom of movement. Many logging operations are undertaken in areas jammed with dense underbrush and tangles of dead and broken trees. These are not factory conditions easily altered for maximum worker safety. Yet loggers must face the uncertain forces of the natural environment every day with snow, rain, wind, steep slopes and trees leaning every-which-way, all just part of the job. It's little wonder that the loggers' lexicon is full of words like widow-maker, kick-back, sidewinder and bad timber.

With the advent of mechanical power, workers had to deal with new hazards that compounded the natural adversity they faced. They had to adapt themselves to new machines designed for maximum efficiency and productivity. The skidder dragging half a dozen treelength logs over uneven terrain at breakneck speed is an intimidating and often dangerous machine. The chain saw, combining light weight, portability and power, is one of the most dangerous tools anywhere, a tricky machine to operate even in the most controlled and stable work conditions. The image of the logger is no longer that of a fellow with a checked shirt, Popeye forearms and red suspenders with an axe slung carelessly over one shoulder. Woodcutters today wear steel-toed boots, brightly-coloured hardhats with earmuffs attached for protection against the noise of the chain saw, and facemasks to guard against flying chips and sawdust. They don special pants with knee and thigh pads to guard against the fast moving teeth of the saw. They have gloves of knitted nylon. Today's logger bears more resemblance to football player than industrial worker.

Protective equipment, along with more emphasis on job safety, has helped to reduce the risk of working in the bush. But logging remains one of the most unsafe jobs in Canada today.* In British Columbia, the most important forest province where authorities monitor logging safety closely, 2,188 people were killed logging between 1940 and 1980. In a typical year, over forty workers die in the forests of British Columbia and the total per year for this four-decade period has never slipped below twenty-eight. While forest workers make up about 10 per cent of

---

* Logging vies with mining for the unenviable top spot as the riskiest occupation. Some statistics show a higher incidence of fatal accidents in mining, others indicate a higher death rate in logging. In any case, the death rate in forestry is listed by Labour Canada as 129.4 per 100,000 workers in the period 1969-1978, well above the national average for all categories — 15 per 100,000 workers.[36]

Hydraulic shears are a common method of cutting trees today.

the provincial labour force, the group accounted for about 22 per cent of new compensation claims in one typical year, 1977.[37]

The forest environment presents so many hazards that experienced loggers take time to assess a stand before beginning to cut the trees. They take into account the slope, the number of dead trees and snags, the maturity and condition of the living trees, how they lean, the direction and velocity of the wind, whether or not the trees are frozen through. Even so, the unexpected can still happen: Logging must be unique among jobs in that the logger has to determine the fastest and easiest escape route before beginning. According to one logger, summing up what he feels is the essence of work in the woods, "You have to remember that a tree is bigger than a baseball bat and no one likes to get hit with a baseball bat."[38]

If a workplace is so inherently dangerous, it would seem logical to make the actual work as safe as possible, to design the production with safety in mind. In the case of logging, with its variable sites and conditions, the exercise of deliberation and care would seem to be important in keeping accident rates down. Contrary to the popular expression, accidents do not just "happen". They are caused by a complex interaction between a number of factors — the workers, the work environment, the organization of work, the machines being used and the method of production.

Of these factors, management is fond of focussing on the carelessness of workers as the major cause of accidents. Accidents happen, it is said, because workers do not obey the rules. In a 1980 speech the president of the Council of Forest Industries of British Columbia described the results of a survey he had conducted among operations managers in the industry.* "The opinion is strongly held by the managers that a principal cause of accidents is the unsafe act resulting either from worker carelessness or a refusal to follow safety regulations," observed the forest industry representative. "The opinion was universal that the worker had to be accountable to a greater degree for his own actions."[39]

Such a singular view, though widespread, has little to do with the real causes of accidents. In the forest, management behaves as in any other industrial setting, choosing the most

* COFI is the principal employers' association in the B.C. forest sector.

effective tools and organizing the work for maximum productivity. Safety is rarely a major consideration when these choices are made. Speed is of the essence. The method of payment is a good example of this tendency. In many parts of the country loggers are paid according to how much they produce. Whether the work is on a piece rate, a bonus system or simply carried out by independent operators supplying wood to larger companies, the results are the same. Workers whose pay is tied to their production naturally tend to work faster than those who collect a straight hourly wage. By linking pay to productivity in an inherently hazardous workplace, management makes a choice based on its own economic priorities. And, for economic reasons — more production equals more pay — workers respond accordingly.

These systems of payment by results are particularly pernicious in the woods where, according to long-time B.C. logger George Kofoed, in one hour a faller makes more decisions that his life depends on than the busiest executive in the world. Kofoed's years in the bush have taught him the hazards of logging. He has seen close friends and experienced loggers crushed to death by trees that failed to react as expected. Kofoed himself quickly learned about the innumerable factors the woods worker cannot control in the forest, and now emphasizes the importance of doing as much as possible about the factors that can be controlled. But, he says, "You don't have to have too much imagination to see that if the faller is on piecework he's not likely to take the time to figure out how to go about that job in the safest way. If he does, the next day in the crummy he'll be comparing scale slips with the guy beside him; 'Oh, I got so many cunits.' There's both a social pressure and an economic pressure to work fast and it lends itself to all kinds of problems."[40]*

Experience in Sweden, where the forest industry is also a pillar of the national economy, indicates that since payment by results was replaced by an hourly rate of pay, accidents among loggers have declined dramatically both in frequency and severity. A research study undertaken by a government health and safety board revealed a drop of just over 30 per cent in accident occurrence after the abolition of piecework, from 119.4 to 84.3 mishaps per million hours worked. The number of workdays

* A crummy is the vehicle used to transport loggers to the job. The scale is the measurement of the amount of wood cut.

lost per thousand working hours was also reduced, by 35 per cent, indicating that the accidents were less severe. "The cutters today take the time to listen to advice and instructions," observed the author of the Swedish study. "They're also willing to try new methods and equipment and don't have to look over their shoulder at possible loss of income as a result."[41] Once the posters-and-slogan approach to safety ("Don't stand under falling branches") favoured by management is abandoned and the nature of production is changed, workers are no longer forced to make choices between safety and earnings. The burden of the economic consequences of production is shifted to the employer.

But in Canada forest products companies have not been anxious to move in this direction. On the contrary, two of the most bitter and protracted labour disputes in the forest industry in recent years were fought over the method of pay for workers. In northwestern Ontario, the Boise-Cascade company successfully challenged the Lumber and Sawmill Workers Union; it simply shifted logging to contractors not in the direct employ of the firm and away from hourly-rated workers.

The management initiative did away with the hourly rate, resulted in violent picketline confrontations and revealed that corporate priorities had everything to do with lower wood costs, little to do with safety on the job. In 1980 the Confederation of National Trade Unions in Quebec launched a major effort to get rid of piecework in the bush, a method of payment the loggers realized was forcing them to cut corners on safety. A strike against three major paper firms — Canadian International Paper, Quebec North Shore and Donohue — lasted for over a year with the workers gaining financial and moral support from every corner of Quebec society. But though they made small gains the workers were ultimately unsuccessful in budging the companies from their insistence on payment by results.

Besides matters of safety, there are also health hazards to be found in the regular grind of forest work. In the mid-1970s, Canadian researchers began investigating an illness that had slowly been debilitating loggers since the first chain saws were introduced. Loggers call the problem white finger or waxy finger. The medical profession knows it as traumatic vasospastic disease, Raynaud's phenomenon or vibration-induced white finger. Whatever the label, it appears that the problem, due to the intense vibration transmitted from the chain saw into the hands of the user, affects loggers in epidemic proportions. The disease affects workers in cold and damp climates most acutely and research on its incidence and prevention was pioneered in the United Kingdom and Scandinavia. Canada, with its cold climate and huge forest industry, lagged behind somewhat but separate studies have recently indicated a prevalence rate of between 21 and 28 per cent among Canadian loggers.[42]

Loggers who suffer from vibration-induced white finger usually exhibit symptoms only after a few years on the job. Tingling, numbness and then painful blanching of the fingers are the successive steps in the development of the disease and many workers suffer severe, periodic pain and loss of use of the fingers as a result. It becomes impossible to fasten buttons, tie shoes, go fishing or carry out routine tasks, such as auto maintenance. In extreme cases the use of the entire hand is lost. But there is no known cure. Compensation claims have yet to become common and provincial compensation boards have not yet developed a consistent medical and legal approach to the problem. Still, there exists the potential for hundreds, if not thousands of claims by white finger victims.

Clearly, compensation is not the answer to the problem. It can only be solved by prevention. Under pressure from the authorities in the United Kingdom, in the early 1970s, chain saw manufacturers began to introduce anti-vibration saws, which help to cut down on vibration. But many workers still use saws without anti-vibration features or anti-vibration saws that are poorly maintained. Vibration standards have been established by the Canadian Standards Association but unions have criticized them as being far in excess of limits set in Europe, noting that the committee which established the limits was composed of Canadian chain saw manufacturers and representatives of large forestry corporations with no worker representation.[44] In Europe and Japan daily exposure limits have been established. The Japanese regulations stipulate that daily use of the chain saw should not exceed two hours. Canadian loggers have no such protection.

Dr. William Taylor of Scotland has been investigating chain saw vibration for over a decade and as a result has become an internationally recognized authority in the field. He says that intermittency of use is a key measure in the prevention of white finger. Expressing shock over the Canadian situation in which loggers routinely use chain saws for full shifts, Dr. Taylor adds, "[Prevalence] is very directly related to output. And it's made worse if you superimpose on that some sort of bonus system or scheme where you're paid additional money for productivity. We think this bonus tends to make the problem worse."[45]

IN THE PERIOD FROM 1945 to 1950, before significant advances were made in logging mechanization, 69 million cubic metres of softwood and hardwood were cut in Canada. The heavy demands of an expanding economy, together with the unrestrained zeal that forest products firms brought to the problem of getting more and more wood to their mills, resulted in the total cut of softwood *more than doubling* to 138 million cubic metres in the period 1975-1980.[46]

The technical breakthroughs in logging exposed new vistas of supply to a fibre-hungry industry. But technology is not simply the physical accomplishments of intrepid engineers in the fields of metal alloys, hydraulic lifting and cutting systems and diesel engines. People with explicitly partisan goals and interests made decisions regarding the introduction and use of new machines. In the case of the forest industry, such people want cheap wood. And they want it now — not at some point in the distant future a generation or more away. When the axe and the saw, the brute strength of men and animals can assure the supply, technological innovation need not proceed too swiftly. When labour costs rise at the same time that the demand curve arcs upward, technical breakthroughs occur, further taxing the limited resource. At the same time, rather than attempting to achieve a harmonious balance between the new technology and the silvicultural considerations vital to future productivity, the forest ecosystems are subordinated to the cost-based demands of the new technology.

"Every new, seemingly bold departure," concludes a recent study of the development of technology, "ends by following an already familiar path."[47] The trail established by the earliest timber operators in the valleys of the Miramachi and the Ottawa was again followed by the Woodlands Divisions of the pulp and paper firms like Abitibi and Consolidated-Bathurst. Only the tools, from broad axe to chain saw and hydraulic shear, had changed — along with the ultimate effect on worker and forest.

This black spruce stand was cut in 1964. The site is dominated today by unwanted hardwood growth which has succeeded the conifers.

6. Brush Wars

ENTION THE WORD "CLEARCUTTING" to many Canadian city dwellers and images of the rape of the land might spring to mind: visions of huge areas of denuded timberland, earth once covered with fine-looking evergreens now only a mangled, misshapen wasteland — certainly not aesthetically appealing. In response to this kind of public concern over clearcutting, industry and government forest managers usually react with a kind of patient, bemused tolerance. An uninformed public is usually told that clearcutting is the only way to maximize future forest values while at the same time economically removing the standing timber in support of a key, job-creating industry. Industry sees the problem *not* as one of a choice of an appropriate cutting technique but rather as a matter of the difficulty of communicating with a well-meaning but ignorant public.

In a talk urging the forest industry to use imagination and resourcefulness to show the public that their woodlands operations are compatible with a healthy and improved forest, a spokesman for one company, Consolidated-Bathurst, warned the Woodlands Section of the Canadian Pulp and Paper Association, "Unless the public travelling over newly-opened bush roads understands that the recent clear cut beside the road is the result of the harvesting part of the management cycle and is encouraged to stop and look at the young regeneration coming up through the slash, the industry is wide open to the familiar attack on the 'rape of the forest'."[1]

It was with its public profile in mind that the stolid, conservative CPPA, which represents the country's major forest corporations, began to take action. In an era when many Canadians had developed a sneaking suspicion that the country's forests — their forests — are being abused, overexploited, even "raped", the association began to display a considerably higher regard for public relations. In 1978, from its offices in Montreal's venerable Sun Life Building, the CPPA offered up a series of high-profile public advocacy advertisements to greet Canadians as they glanced through their morning papers.[2]

In the ads forest corporations informed readers, "We need profits the way trees need light." They said that though the trees may continue to grow, the industry might not. "Profit is growth money" the CPPA trumpeted in one ad, assuring any skeptical readers that profits are not just spent on mink coats and Maseratis. The ads said that, although profit rates in the forest business were low, those meagre profits were in fact being reinvested in items like big, new mechanical harvesters, to keep Canada competitive. The industry's importance was underlined: Exports of pulp and paper "enrich our economy . . . by about $1,000 a year for each Canadian family".

According to the corporations all was under control. No mention was made of an impending wood supply crisis, but we were told that the forest land belongs to us and that of the stumpage the industry dutifully pays — "more than $110 million a year" — a portion is "earmarked to pay for assuring the next crop of timber for future generations". There was the confident prediction that millions of seedlings would be planted to produce the healthy new crop. "Moose love us" was the message. And humans should too, because the industry's forest roads open the wilderness to enjoyment by campers, hunters, hikers and fishermen. The entire message was one of reassurance.

For those who find such fare a little hard to swallow, the CPPA made available a more detailed argument in a glossy booklet commissioned in 1966 in recognition of the crucial role the forest played in shaping Canada's industrial, economic, social and even artistic development. A Walk in the Forest is an attempt to explain in rather baroque verbiage the complex interrelationships that are characteristic of forest ecosystems: "In the forest there is mystery. There is magic. There is tranquillity and turmoil. There is delight. And there is drama." A lyrical explanation of forest flora and fauna explains the workings of nature's preordained plan. It takes the reader down a forest trail, revealing an interdependent web of life, with its insects, birds, animals, swamps, lichen, shrubs and trees. Soils are formed as organic matter decomposes and water and frost help to break down rocks into the mineral elements so necessary for the growth of plants and trees. Burrowing creatures help to aerate the soil and provide passage for vital moisture. Fallen trees decay, enriching the soil that nourished them in life. And, we are reminded, "man" is but a part of these interrelationships — "though he may consider himself above them".[3]

A Walk in the Forest concludes with the reminder that, given the demand for wood, conservation is a must. Conservation concerns not only the preservation of wildlife, but of all life: "Physicians are striving to lengthen the span of man's years. Statesmen are earnestly seeking to bring about world peace and to end the human slaughter. So it is with those whose workshop and laboratory is the forest." The experts — foresters and researchers — are doing everything possible to ensure that we use the forest wisely, according to the pulp company publication. Block and selective cutting, treeplanting, pest control and other measures are being employed by a partnership of industry, government and the university to use the forest crop more fully and efficiently, accelerating the growth of new forests. But, we are admonished, "There is no protection against the fool: the hunter who overshoots; the fisherman who overfishes; the camper who is careless with his fire; the hiker who smokes on the trail; the motorist who heedlessly tosses a burning match or an unsnubbed smoke from his car."[4]

The message behind this Smokey The Bear view of forestry is clear and simple: If we were all just a little more careful, if we trust the authorities, all would indeed be well in the woods.

AT THE SAME TIME the forest products industry attempts to convey reassuring images to the public, anyone who knows anything about the state of the forest resource also knows that the country's forest productivity is in serious jeopardy due to a combination of overcutting, underutilization, inaccurate inventories and insufficient regeneration efforts. The careless smoker is only a very small part of "man's" threat to the forest. Fire, like blight and insect infestation, is only an aspect of what people often perceive as a threat to the forest. As the CPPA publication acknowledges, human activity is just as much a part of the ecological cycle as the industry of the burrowing chipmunk or the foraging moose. Many of those who are aware of the critical state of the forest also know that something in the way of forest care other than fire and bug protection has to be done to salvage the future of the country's wood-dependent industries. They know that human activity has done more than anything else to bring about a situation in which words like "salvage" and "critical" can be used with no fear of exaggeration.

Since humans are a part of the forest's ecological makeup, it follows that their forest management efforts should be based on an appreciation of the particular ecology of each individual forest site to be managed. When a forest is cut, whether on a shelterwood, clearcut or selective logging basis, the principles of ecological succession come into play and a predictable series of changes gradually occurs. Lichen, mosses, raspberries, alder and a myriad of other plants can succeed each other and populate the cutover site. This is not, however, what the forest manager wants to happen. Although raspberries are a costly fruit for city-dwellers, there is, unfortunately, little money to be made in gathering them from recently logged scrublands. Nor is there a ready market for alder. It rests, therefore, with management or, often, the tree farmer to avoid the succession of unwanted species, and produce a marketable crop. In Canada this has, over the years, meant conifers like black spruce or Douglas fir — species that pulpmills and sawmills can use. This is why, according to some silviculturalists and civil servants in provincial resource ministries, NSR (not satisfactorily restocked) areas are called "silvicultural slums". These silvicultural slums of NSR land are the biggest burden of many a Canadian forest manager.

Hamish Kimmins, a forester who has explored the evolution of forest management practice in Canada from the ecological perspective, has attempted to develop ways of predicting how different forest sites will react to various methods of treatment. It is his contention that forest management evolves through three distinct phases. The first of these is familiar enough to

Canadians. It involves the unrestrained exploitation of the resource, with little regulation and no concern for the principles of forestry or future forest yields. Canada has only just recently emerged from this primitive period and has entered a second phase, which Kimmins refers to as an administrative type of forest management. This phase is based on recognition of the need to do something in the area of forest renewal; that need, however, has been translated into a non-biological approach to forest management. This attitude toward the problems of forest renewal must, in Kimmins' view, eventually give way to a third type of forestry: one based on an appreciation of the highly variable, biologically-complex nature of the forest.[5]

Kimmins, a forest ecologist at the University of British Columbia, warns that, should forestry measures be based on insufficient recognition or understanding of the biological mechanisms of the living forest, the result may be resource management "no different from the extraction of non-renewable mineral resources — an act of exploitation conducted without any thought for the future of the deposit".[6] Here again the notion of timber mining pops up. It is a reference that has been frequently — and accurately — affixed to forestry practices in Canada for the past century and a half.

Kimmins takes the example of clearcutting to explain the ecological complexity of forestry operations.[7] He points out that, though removing each and every tree from a given area may result in a visually offensive cutover, it does not necessarily bring about a radical change in the ecological function of the forest site. For forests are not merely trees. They are also the mosses, shrubs, insects, fungi and other forms of life. When trees are removed by people, the ecosystem is not destroyed, it is merely changed. The changes that result from clearcutting depend on many factors, not least of which is the type of forest site involved. When all the trees are removed from a big area, other plants are given the opportunity to flourish because more light, water and nutrients are available to them. In this way clearcut logging results in "successional retrogression": The process of natural succession is moved back several steps and the raspberries, alders or whatever take their turns dominating the area.

The speed of recovery in an area depends, again, on the kind of site involved as well as on the kind of actions forest managers take to promote conifers and suppress alders. If the area has been scarified, the nutrient-bearing mineral soil that is hospitable to seed germination becomes exposed. Scarification can also upset the influence of the mosses and humus that deter germination. In this way the conifers can get a head start in the race for water, sunlight and nutrients. Whether such forest management measures are necessary or fruitful depends on how well-developed the competing vegetation is. Whether clearcutting results in excessive erosion and resulting site degradation depends on the size of the area cut and the type of terrain involved. Large clearcuts on steep slopes are going to be more prone to producing erosion than small clearcuts or other forms of logging; they tend to set back forests to earlier successional stages. When huge tracts of forest land are laid bare of trees, the result is increased extremes of temperature, wind and humidity.

The successional character of logged-over sites also has important silvicultural implications. Kimmins notes that in dryland areas of southwestern British Columbia, the heavy disturbance accompanying clearcutting can lead to loss of soil nutrients, loss of nutrient and moisture storage capacity and a general drying up of the site. Such sites are likely to be slow to recover from clearcutting and it is very difficult and very expensive for forest managers to speed up the process of succession. On freshland sites with deeper, wetter and more nutrient-rich soils, Kimmins has observed that clearcutting is likely to lead to less extreme disturbances. Succession is generally faster. Should the recovery of this type of forest toward developing the commercially-desirable species be unduly slow, it can easily be accelerated at more reasonable cost using basic forms of site treatment, which might include drainage or scarification.[8]

So it is clear that in dealing with logging or any other forest management practice it is impossible and even dangerous to base actual practice on blanket prescriptions. Clearcutting is neither always bad nor always good. When any single technique is applied on a broad scale without reference to local conditions, it ignores the very essence of forests: the highly variable, highly complex mosaics of different sites. Forests all operate on the same principles. Trees need light, water and nutrients to grow just as automobiles need gasoline, oil and other lubricants to function properly. But to put gasoline into a diesel Mercedes or diesel fuel into a conventional Ford, or to attempt to fix both cars with exactly the same set of wrenches, would be folly. The same thing can be said of forests. According to Kimmins, "The successful management of any complex production system, be it a natural forest ecosystem or a man-made mechanical system, is of necessity based on a knowledge of the natural laws which control the operation of the system.... To operate the system otherwise is to court disaster."[9] Kimmins also observes, "Misapplication of the otherwise legitimate practices of clearcutting and slashburning can render a renewable forest condition non-renewable."[10]

Unfortunately, forest management in Canada all too frequently consists of the scattergun approach — the helter-skelter application of measures that are legitimate in some places but inappropriate elsewhere. The practice of clearcutting followed by planting is a high-profile example. Planting trees on large clearcuts is a good idea on many forest sites in Canada, including some on Vancouver Island, says Herb Hammond, a forester who used to work on silvicultural operations for Crown Zellerbach, a major multinational forest firm. When he returns to the area around Courtenay where he worked at one time, Hammond sees the makings of a healthy new forest thriving on the moist, deep soils there, the product of clearcutting and careful planting.

But Hammond, who now lives in the West Kootenay region of the B.C. interior where he teaches forestry and works as a forestry consultant, says that the same prescription is no good for many forest sites in Canada. The area he lives in now has an abundance of coarse-textured soils, which are quite moisture-deficient. As he looks out his dining-room window at the spectacular view, he sees more than the tourist's postcard vista. In one small area that stretches up from the valley bottom towards the top of the mountains, he sees larch, cedar, fir, white pine and Ponderosa pine. It's what he describes, with some zeal, as an ecological transition zone with a rich species diversity. "We shouldn't be planting many trees here," he says. "If we clearcut and then try to plant trees in this area it's like trying to plant tomatoes in your garden and never watering them. They die."[11]

This is where B.C. Chief Forester Bill Young's favourite graph* showing the dramatic rise in the number of trees planted by the B.C. Forest Service is rather misleading. In many cases, in the area Hammond is familiar with through his work as a for-

* See Chapter 4.

estry consultant, the planting never happened anyway and when it did the seedlings withered. Hammond finds it frustrating that logging operators and the Forest Service have not recognized that when logging systems are designed, implicit decisions are made about the later stages of forest management. When logging and silviculture are artificially separated, it leads to what Hammond calls "band-aid silviculture". While this may be good for his consulting business, it is certainly not the best thing for the forest in the long term.

"My life is solving problems," Hammond states. "Somebody says, 'Well Herb, we logged that — now what are we going to do with it? The trees won't grow there. Fix it up for us. Wave your magic wand and let's go!' The reason that the problem occurs is that they don't recognize that the decision to harvest and the decision to reforest are concurrent decisions."[12]

Instead of this cut now/think later regime, Hammond believes that a more appropriate and effective means of forest management would take into account the specifics of each ecosystem and manage things accordingly. In the part of British Columbia where he lives and works, Hammond recommends shelterwood cutting, selection cuts or very small clearcuts, techniques that could take advantage of the region's rich species diversity. Such carefully designed cutting would enable the forest to do a lot of its own renewal naturally, using available seed sources instead of nursery-grown seedlings. But to do this would require a break with current practices of sacrificing future yields in order to maximize present economic returns, and Hammond is convinced that there is insufficient money to practise even short-run forest management. "We don't manage the forests, we cut them down and plant trees. That looks good for the public," he concludes. "We've cut all the good stuff first and now we're looking at the rocks and the watersheds."[13]

When faced with this argument, the logging industry is quick to point out that it has not been standing still. Forestry practices have been changing and companies have realized that something has to be done if future wood shortages are to be avoided. In spite of crucial doubts about the continuity of government funding support, there is a generalized perception in industry and government forestry circles of the need to begin using intensive forest management techniques. The goal is to assure future supplies by increasing utilization and shortening the period of time it takes a new forest to become mature enough to cut: the rotation length. New, genetically-improved tree crops with shorter rotations would be nurtured under such intensive management. The current hopes of many highly-placed forest managers are pinned on these genetically-improved species, and on plantings, thinnings, fertilization, pest and disease control. They envisage a kind of agro-forestry or "green revolution" in the woods. Jack Toovey, the number-two forestry man at B.C. Forest Products behind Gerry Burch, told a CPPA meeting in 1979 that by the turn of the century these changes, coupled with new government policies, would hopefully lead to a "healthy forest industry, with bulging order files, and a forest land base that will reflect our leadership in the field of silviculture".[14]

In 1981 Les Reed of Environment Canada, speaking to the American Paper Institute in Homestead, Virginia, on the topic "Will There Be Enough Trees in Canada?", confirmed to the U.S. papermakers that intensive forest management was *the* basis for an affirmative answer to the question. Citing gains of 50 to 100 per cent or more in wood volume, the head of the federal forest service based his hopes on intensive forestry: "a combination of site preparation, use of genetically-superior planting stock, prompt planting after harvest or loss, suppression of competing vegetation immediately after planting, thinning and fertilization". Though he made no mention of the adoption of ecologically-based cutting methods, Reed did tell Canada's most important wood customers that intensive forestry would give rise to the allowable cut effect, which in essence means you can take more wood now in the assurance that later on there will be more available.[15]

Some foresters are not so confident that these measures, coupled with better utilization through complete tree harvesting, will be the answer to our wood supply problems. Hamish Kimmins, for one, does not share the heady optimism and is worried that this kind of "fibre farming" is likely to be part of the administrative, non-biological approach that could well create as many problems as it solves. The UBC ecologist is concerned about problems that have long been familiar to agriculturalists but that up to now have not appeared relevant to forestry. One of the most important concerns about agro-forestry centres around soil impoverishment. Once the whole tree — tops, branches and all

— is removed from a site, and once this happens with increasing frequency as rotations are shortened and forestry intensified, soil impoverishment can result. Agriculture, which in any case operates on soils far richer than those in the forest, is dependent upon regular applications of fertilizer to maintain soil productivity and fertility. Modern agriculture also depends on herbicides to kill weeds and insecticides to kill pests. As the new industrial farmers believe, they cannot produce sufficient crop yields if they don't also make generous applications of expensive chemical "inputs".

Utilization of the whole tree and its replacement with new crops of input-dependent supertrees cloned in nurseries will lead agro-forestry down the same path as industrial agriculture and present silviculturalists with problems familiar to farmers. Intensive forestry would also have to rely on chemical sprays to keep down the alders and poplars and kill those insects that like to gorge themselves on conifers. Once the complete tree is removed from the forest by machines like feller-forwarders, the nutrient capital of the forest soil may be depleted because the foliage, branches and tops that used to be left by yesterday's loggers on the forest floor contain most of the nutrients in the tree. What used to be slash contains valuable nutrients, such as nitrogen, potassium and calcium. The whole tree is currently being seen by forest planners as a source of fibre for the mills or as a biomass energy source. Full-tree chipping systems that grind the entire tree up at the roadside loom large in the full-utilization picture.

Since forest soils are basically far less nutrient-rich than agricultural soils in the first place, taking away the nutrients that used to be left in the bush may also necessitate agricultural solutions. And no one can know for certain what the results will be when massive fertilization efforts are applied to the forest. Kimmins and other concerned foresters think that declining soil fertility will mean increased fertilization. But, not only will the fertilization of tens of thousands of hectares of trees be very expensive, but also, this blanket solution may be biologically impractical. It may not even work. [16]

Once again the site-specific nature of the forest resource comes into play. One study of timberlands on the B.C. coast revealed that some plots treated with nitrogen-rich urea grew 30 per cent faster than untreated plots while other sites treated with the same fertilizer showed no response at all. Trying to predict how forests will respond to various treatments has proven very difficult for foresters. A productivity analyst for the B.C. Forest Service admitted, "We don't know anything about the effects of fertilizing in the interior [of the province]."[17]

In the eastern boreal forest Vic Timmer, a University of Toronto forestry professor, studied the effects of full tree chipping on forest soils. He found that on some of the deeper soils, the short-term effects of removing the nutrient-rich parts of the tree were not significant. But on shallow soils overlying bedrock, problems cropped up. Timmer sees problems with the ubiquitous application of any one forest management technique. "We have this blanket approach — black spruce everywhere. The black spruce syndrome. Monocultures. We don't have the expertise yet to distinguish one site from another. That's why this full tree logging is okay on certain sites — no problem at all. But you certainly can't do it on some of those shallow sites [that have] a thin, thin layer of soil. You just can't do it. It's irresponsible. It robs the land."[18]

On the west coast, Hamish Kimmins has developed a new way of predicting how forests will respond to more intensive management, by applying computer-based forecasting methods to forestry. In an attempt to remove some of the guesswork from forest management, he helped to design FORCYTE, a computer simulation model that can be used to predict the effects of intensive forest management on the productivity of the future forest. Kimmins wanted to be able to glimpse into the future and see how different ecological systems would react to all the various aspects of fibre farming, from clearcutting to the brush control with herbicides. The computer's ability to incorporate and interpret variable data when programmed to do so on a site-specific basis is something of a breakthrough in this important aspect of forestry. It is particularly valuable for forest ecologists concerned with the intricate interactions of all the components of the forest. The entry of the electronic age into the forest allows Kimmins to take all the variables into account: density, thinning, spacing, fertilization, rotation length, moisture, nitrogen fixation, levels of nutrients and organic matter, log size, weed suppression, slashburning, insect and fire damage.[19] The FORCYTE model can even incorporate variable economic cost/benefit ratios into its predictions.

The FORCYTE program was used by Kimmins to predict how an average Douglas fir site in coastal British Columbia would react to shortened rotations and more intensive management. It became apparent that 80-year rotations would give greater yields than either 120-year or 30-year cutting cycles. The most intensive 30-year rotations, coupled with complete tree harvesting, would result in a rapid drop in mean annual yields of wood. After three of these short rotations the yield would fall to a level of less than half that of the first 30-year cycle.[20]

What does all this mean? Simply that, once again, blanket prescriptions of new, improved management methods cannot be counted on to solve the problems of forest renewal. Kimmins and his fellow researchers concluded from their projections on this site, "Yield can be increased by switching from a 120-year rotation with no management [the practice up until now] to a shorter rotation with increased management and more intensive utilization, but . . . there is some point before complete tree harvest with intensive management on a 30-year rotation beyond which increasing our demands on the forest will reduce its yield."[21]

Foresters, however, have known for years that a finely-tuned approach that takes local factors into consideration produces much more wood than the indiscriminate use of the easiest and seemingly cheapest practices. Back in 1951 the CPPA itself published a study by its director of woodlands research, Alexander Koroleff, in which Koroleff predicted that blanket applications of cutting practices would lead to trouble.[22] He knew from his European experience that tree cutters were also tree breeders and he told his employers in the big wood corporations that decisions concerning suitable logging methods could not be made centrally, without reference to local conditions. Koroleff had an interesting label for the way logging was done by the big firms. He called it "nomadic logging" to convey a sense of the haphazard, migratory, cut-and-get-out practices he believed should be replaced by continuous use of managed forests. It was apparent to Koroleff's experienced eye that cutting methods which were silviculturally wrong would reduce future wood supplies and could even result in the degradation of the soil and its inability to support future growth at all. Although he knew clearcutting in particular could be a silviculturally sound practice in many eastern pulpwood forests, he reasoned: "No single cutting method can be recommended for general application, and the choice in each case should be made in light of pertinent biological, physical and economic factors. Even then it may not be an easy matter."[23] Alexander Koroleff and Hamish Kimmins were speaking the same language thirty years apart.

Unfortunately, it is a language that industrial forest operators have chosen not to understand. In spite of Koroleff's work and his cautions, things went on after 1951 just as they had for years. With the mechanization of logging — a development Koroleff keenly advocated — cutting practices became even more closely geared to the demands of immediate economy and short-term wood cost. The Russian *émigré* could have predicted this: His close association with the business had shown him the reason clearcutting was used all over eastern Canada was that it was cheap and easy. He noted "a decided preference of woods operators for clearcutting, chiefly for reasons of immediate economy and simplicity."[24]

A research study, which formed part of Koroleff's general overview of logging and forestry, indicated that this concern with immediate return was in the long run rather irrational. W.M. Robertson, who at the time worked for one of the two companies that dominated forest production in Newfoundland, compared clearcutting with selective logging within a ninety-year rotation period. He found that three selective cuts within the same rotation period would yield 45.6 cords of wood whereas a single clearcut would produce only 19.5 cords. Robertson's calculations were based on a hypothetical model of a good eastern pulpwood site. The costs of the two different systems were not that different. The average cost of a cord cut on a selective basis was $11.36 compared to the cost of a cord on a clearcut operation at $10.98. Robertson concluded that an extra investment of only about a dollar a cord in selection cutting would double the value of the wood harvested over the course of the rotation in comparison to conventional clearcutting methods.[25]

Robertson's analysis should not be taken as any final proof that one cutting system is intrinsically better than another, for his financial calculations as to the cost of the second and third cuts in the rotation did not seem to have been adjusted for either future inflation or technological change in cutting technique. Like many of his contemporaries, Robertson seems to have had a soft spot for selective cutting, at the time regarded by many as *the* solution to a lot of forest management problems. Perhaps this was a generalized reaction against past cutting practices that had not promoted good second growth. In any case, neither selection cutting nor clearcutting can be a general answer. But Robertson's estimates of dramatically increased long-term yields from selective cutting as opposed to clearcutting do merit some attention in that they confirm Koroleff's suspicion that pulp companies were sacrificing the future to satisfy the demands of the moment.

APPEARANCES CAN BE DECEIVING in forestry matters. To most of us, forest fires would seem to be one of the principal enemies of the forest industry. And it is usually only during an outbreak serious enough to make it into the national news that the nation's chronic forest problems come before the public eye. The image of tens of thousands of valuable acres going up in a sheet of flames inspires both awe and fear. Every fire season squadrons of government planes stand at the ready, loaded with fire-retardant chemicals. Small armies of firefighters are deployed in the hot, dirty and dangerous job of combatting wildfire on the ground. When the fire moves as fast as hot summer winds propel it, the forest inventory shrinks and pulp company owners eye their diminishing fibre supplies nervously.

There can be no doubt about the need to protect the forest against the depredations of fire. Yet at the same time fires are as much a part of the forest cycle as the black bear and the pine beetle. Much of the forest where industry cutting crews are operating today consists of stands that grew up in areas once destroyed by fire. Indeed, fire is a reproductive agent in many types of forest. It is one of nature's ways of dealing with forests that have become overmature: They are replaced following a fire. In a jackpine forest, a fire in standing timber will predictably give rise to another dense, even-aged forest of strong-fibred jack pine, one of the crucial pulpwood species in eastern Canada. To achieve similar silvicultural results after cutting the same forest would be a difficult and expensive undertaking for forest managers who are after the thick, even-aged stands ideal for extraction by mechanized logging.

Fire isn't the only natural forest enemy. A plague of hemlock loopers or spruce budworm can easily chomp its way through mile after mile of productively growing timber. This type of forest scourge has been around ever since the first settler lit a wooden match to clear the trees from a potential homestead. It was only when the forestry profession sprang up and the forest came to be studied and manipulated by expert scientists that foresters began to try to do something about the various insect infestations. In the 1930s, one early "forest engineer" graphically expressed his distaste: "Fat, greasy crawling worms everywhere... stinky, messy hairs hanging everywhere... motheaten woods with dead needles and excrement falling like rain... followed in a year or so by such an attack of borers — those ghouls of the dying forest, as has never been witnessed in Canada. To anyone in the budworm-ravaged forest at the time when the beetles were emerging, it was a nightmare experience."[26]

Such perspectives, if widely-shared, would certainly have presented no obstacle to the idea of blasting away the unwelcome critters. When demand for wood fibre escalated in the postwar period, with supply shrinking at the same time, techniques of pest control caught the imagination of the forest industry. One chemical in particular, DDT, became widely used in an attempt to eradicate the "greasy, crawling worms".

As their name fails to indicate, spruce budworm love to munch on the tender young growth of balsam fir trees. The spruces — white, red and black — are less popular with the budworm, which derive the second part of their name from the fact that the larvae of what eventually becomes a dull-coloured moth prefer the new buds of their host trees. When a stand of mature balsam fir develops, it provides an opportunity for the budworm to flourish and even reach epidemic proportions. This insect, like most every other forest creature, has its place in nature's scheme of things, helping to eliminate overmature stands so that the process of succession can start over again. Once the overhead canopy of a late-succession species like fir is decimated by a budworm attack, new forms of growth get a chance to establish themselves in the newly-available sunlight.

A government-sponsored report* in New Brunswick, where a budworm epidemic has been ravaging the province's forests, summed up the budworm's role in the forest cycle: "The picture here is of a biological system, including the budworm and its host forest functioning in a manner uniquely suited to the perpetuation of both insect and forest. Outbreaks and tree mortality are therefore perfectly natural and normal phenomena and have occurred periodically over a long period of time certainly predating European man. They are not new."[27]

Although there is professional agreement that the budworm is endemic to the forests of eastern Canada, the intensity and frequency of epidemics are a matter of some dispute. The official line in New Brunswick is that mature and overmature spruce and fir forests have been periodically devastated for thousands of years by the budworm. The provincial government's most recent intensive study of forestry, published in 1974, classes the budworm with such conflagrations as the famous Miramachi fire of 1825, pointing out that like the fire, the budworm has played a continuous role in shaping the forest. The report noted with "virtual certainty" that the budworm had been attacking the forest ever since there was balsam fir to eat. It described the insect as "a natural, 'built-in' factor in the normal forest succession in the region".[28]

The implication of these arguments is that the budworm has always been a big problem, continuously eating away valuable timberland. Both reports, one on forestry in general and the other on budworm control, agree that the province's long-established chemical spray program is the only way to hold the bugs in check. Although New Brunswick's forestry study admits that thirty years of spraying have probably simply prolonged and spread the current epidemic, it still says that "crop protection" (as in the agricultural sprays used on the province's potato crops) is the only answer, given the importance of the softwood forest to the province's pulp-based economy. Despite the admission that the contest between the spray and the worm is a no-win standoff, there is still the conclusion, "[Man] has a trans-

* The 200-page report of the task force for evaluation of budworm control alternatives reflects the intense interest in the budworm spray issue in the province. It is often referred to as the Baskerville Report after one of its authors, Gordon Baskerville, a University of New Brunswick forestry professor who became Assistant Deputy Minister of Natural Resources in New Brunswick and a principal defender of the spray program.

mogrified tiger by the tail, but there's no letting go. He must hang on in the hopes that nature or science will some day provide the reinforcements he must have."[29]

There is, however, another point of view, which maintains that the budworm problem has been getting worse over the years and says the reasons for this can be traced back to the cutting practices of the forest industry. Like the official position, this line of reasoning accepts the fact that the budworm has always come and gone in successive waves as part of the forest's ecological composition. But it diverges from the government line in its belief that the species composition of the New Brunswick forest has been changed dramatically over the past century. As a result of this change, the current forest provides ideal forage for the budworm. This in turn accounts for the intensity of the current epidemic.

The change in species composition goes back to the time shortly after the transformation of the eastern forest industry from a lumber- to a pulp-based enterprise. In the early years, the pulp and paper industry was based primarily on spruce, a species long-neglected by the timber sawmills. The lumbermakers preferred pine, when they could still get it. But the papermakers wanted black spruce, which would provide them with high volumes of good-quality fibre. After the turn of the century, logging became increasingly concerned with cutting as much spruce as possible, to the exclusion of other softwoods like balsam fir. For years fir was treated as junk wood in the same way that alder and pin cherry are now rejected by most industrial wood users.

While the forestry profession was getting established, foresters employed in the pulpwood logging industry started to notice that balsam forests were replacing spruce-dominated stands in the aftermath of logging. Balsam fir, a prolific species, is fast-growing, drought resistant and has more frequent seed years than spruce. Its seeds are also larger and less prone to being eaten by rodents. As early as 1909, a forester named Ellwood Wilson recognized, "As spruce has been a favourite wood for pulp, its removal has favoured the balsam, which is coming in rapidly everywhere and crowding out the spruce."[30]

Although it will probably never be proven conclusively that the forest now contains more balsam fir than it did two hundred years ago, many researchers and observers are convinced that the pattern of insect infestation was profoundly altered after logging changed the anatomy of the forest. New Brunswick's own Forest Development Commission of 1957 acknowledged that forests containing a good balance of species are less prone to devastation by insects than those whose natural composition has been badly upset by industrial logging.[31] Even before the 1950s, forest researchers had believed that the earlier budworm attacks were restricted both in time and geographical extent, and that they only became a widespread problem and a source of worry for industry after industry itself promoted the growth of balsam fir in the wake of its cutting practices.

J.D. Tothill, not only one of Canada's first forest entomologists but also one of the country's first forest scientists to study the historical evolution of budworm epidemics, thought that two nineteenth century outbreaks in New Brunswick were small, relatively localized and caused little damage in comparison to the infestations he personally observed in the 1920s.[32] Two scientists working for the federal government in the 1920s also believed that the selective cutting of spruce for the pulpwood industry had led to a heavy preponderance of fir in the forest and consequently more severe and extensive defoliations by the budworm.[33] So it seems that in the twentieth century the budworms have enjoyed a far more abundant cornucopia of their favourite food than they ever had the pleasure of dining upon previously.

Common sense and a solid understanding of the necessity of forest management based on the biological realities of the forest point to obvious budworm control measures. Since the predator likes fir, one possibility could have been an adjustment in logging methods combined with other silvicultural efforts aimed at limiting balsam growth. At the same time forest managers could have promoted the growth of mixed, uneven-aged stands of budworm-resistant yet commercially valuable species such as pine and black spruce. It is not as if they were unaware of the causes of the spreading budworm menace. The chief of forest biology for the federal government, J.J. deGryse, had pointed out in the late 1940s when the industry was beginning to suffer wood losses through insect manifestations, that production of a more diverse forest, through appropriate forest management, would reduce those losses. A senior U.S. government silviculturalist, Marinus Westveld, argued that shorter rotation periods

A spruce budworm. In New Brunswick spraying programs aimed at beating back the budworm continue despite efforts by citizens concerned about the environmental effects.

would help. Westveld was pushing for less clearcut logging and the associated long rotations, a practice he felt encouraged development of large stands of fast-growing balsam. It was better, he argued, to use silviculturally-based cutting techniques that would reduce the forest's susceptibility to budworm attack and at the same time increase the amount of wood available.[34] The goal of such logging-based management would be the development of budworm-resistant stands, not the promotion of budworm fodder that was being allowed to flourish on neglected cutovers.

But to the contrary, unrestrained industrial logging, totally unconcerned with its silvicultural implications, was turning the eastern Canadian boreal forest and particularly the once-diverse, rich Acadian forest of New Brunswick into a vast breeding-ground for the budworm: a feedlot for future larval plagues. Alexander Koroleff, whose study of Canadian logging practices, published by the industry itself, put forward the views of J.J. deGryse and Marinus Westveld, was perfectly clear on this point. He knew that planned forest management would heighten the living forest's natural resistance to infection by its natural predators in the same way that human health is best maintained through a combination of sound preventive practices, such as good care of the body, knowledge of the causes of disease and judicious vaccination. Koroleff appreciated the fact that vaccination of the woods would also involve preventive measures. Suitable partial cutting when required and other procedures designed to inoculate the forest against everything from fire to insects and fungi was the answer to the spreading menace. Koroleff was convinced the result would be a "forest always kept in a vigorous condition . . . better able to resist its enemies. This is not so under nomadic logging, when vigorous trees are taken, decrepit ones left and, because practically all merchantable wood is cut at once, the area is covered with heavy slash and becomes a fire trap and a favourable breeding place for parasites."[35]

But such advance planning is not something that, historically, industrial forest users and their government associates have been noted for. A myopic, after-me-the-deluge attitude has always prevailed, and continues to hold sway. The case of the highly-charged budworm spray controversy in New

Brunswick is perhaps the most persuasive example of this phenomenon.

NEW BRUNSWICK'S RURAL RESIDENTS have over the years grown accustomed to several rites of spring. On the coastal seaways, the lobster season opens, offering a few weeks of employment and a few invaluable weeks of unemployment insurance credits to part-time fishermen. In the woods, spring signals the start of a fresh cycle of new growth and some New Brunswickers take advantage of the opportunity to harvest the newly-uncurling tops of the Ostrich Fern. People come from as far away as Montreal for a few days of fiddlehead picking. And of course the larva of the spruce budworm wakes up and starts to chew away at the fir. It is soon chased around by insecticide-laden spray planes. The race is essentially between the companies and the budworm and the prize is the balsam and spruce timberland logged decades earlier, land whose silvicultural treatment was neglected by both companies and government after the logging was through. Former Abitibi forester and Lakehead University professor Ken Hearnden describes the companies as "running around pursuing the nuptial flight of the budworm, trying to salvage what they can".[36]

What the companies fail to salvage remains in the form of feathery, grey skeletons of budworm-killed fir, something Rachel Carson might have had in mind when she wrote the book *Silent Spring* in 1962. The American biologist's book stirred millions of people into a recognition that insecticides like DDT were being mindlessly sprayed over millions of acres of swamps, crops and forests around the world, upsetting and perhaps permanently warping natural systems. The image of the silent spring foretold a time when there would be no more birds left to sing. U.S. President John Kennedy told the press that Carson's book had played a crucial role in raising concerns about environmental degradation at the same time as he announced the scientific investigations that would lead to the eventual ban of the chemical in both the United States and Canada. The last forest spraying with DDT in New Brunswick took place in 1968.

Rachel Carson herself did not live long enough to be told about this small victory. She died of cancer in 1964. But not too long before her death she gave an interviewer her thoughts on the human place in the environment: "I truly believe that we in this generation must come to terms with nature. And I think we're challenged as mankind has never been challenged before to prove our maturity and our mastery — not of nature but of ourselves."[37]

Earlier, in 1922, J.D. Tothill also made a prediction. The entomologist had studied the patterns of budworm epidemics and noted with some interest their increasing intensity.[38] Accordingly, he foresaw a large, generalized outbreak of the pest in New Brunswick within about thirty years — time enough for the balsam fir to flourish in sufficient quantity to provide the budworm with a rich bill of fare. And in the early 1950s Tothill was proven correct. A budworm infestation was spotted in the Upsalquitch region of the northern part of the province. But by this time the pulp and paper industry had reacted to the changing composition of the forest. Having already cut much of the good black spruce, the industry was forced by its need for fibre and a strong demand for pulp and newsprint to turn to balsam fir as an alternative feedstock for its mills. The government of New Brunswick found itself faced with the problem of sustaining a supply of this budworm-threatened timber to the industry.

The fact that the government of New Brunswick had always had an intimate — some would say shady — relationship with the forest products industry made this problem all the more of concern. The dubious quality of government-industry dealings had long been a matter of public knowledge. When the pulp and paper industry was just getting started in the early days of the twentieth century, the Premier of the province, James Kidd Flemming, was forced to resign after a Royal Commission inquiry revealed that one of his trusted bagmen had been collecting money from the timber interests for an electoral "reptile fund". One financier, Angus McLean, who started what eventually became part of the Consolidated-Bathurst empire, testified that he gave Flemming's associate a "contribution" on the understanding that this would ensure the renewal of his timber limits.[39] Such close associations, coupled with the substantial,

"official" revenues from the forest industry, made it quite predictable, if rather lamentable, that New Brunswick would
declare chemical war on a bunch of bugs that threatened the
paper industry's profits. Despite the fact that there had been
ample opportunity to conduct the battle of the budworm on a
biological basis using silvicultural techniques, the province
opted for the quick chemical fix: the curative rather than the
preventive measure.

Starting in 1952 and continuing for the next sixteen years, the
province sprayed its forests with the insecticide DDT, at a total
cost of $48.7 million. During this period the spray program
developed its own institutional momentum, a noticeable tendency among such centralized initiatives and particularly self-
sustaining when backed by all the principal corporations in a
small, poor province's most important industry. Even after DDT
was banned in the late 1960s, the powers behind the New
Brunswick forest spray program were not to be deterred. The
program continued and grew, using an organophosphate insecticide called fenitrothion that the jointly-controlled
government-industry spray company, Forest Protection Limited, had introduced the year before the DDT ban took effect.

Combined with the solid political and financial backing of the
government and the scientific/ideological legitimation provided
by a willing forestry profession, the chemical fix proved a hard
combination to beat. Yet the provincially-sponsored Baskerville
report of 1976 admitted, "The continued use of chemical lar-
vicides appears good in the short run but is not considered a
wise long run approach, whereas the forest management solution looks better in the long run but offers no help at all in the
short run."[40] The year the report came out, the spray program
reached new heights: A record 10.3 million acres were sprayed at
a record cost of $17 million.[41] In May of 1982 the program went
ahead again, as planned, in spite of growing opposition. The only
direct loss of human life in that year involved the crash of one of
the province's venerable Grumann Avengers, whose pilot died in
the gasoline and fenitrothion soaked wreckage.

But though since the DDT ban fenitrothion has been the principal chemical used against the budworm, its introduction did
nothing to allay intensifying public concern over the use of
insecticides and the general abuse of the environment. The pulp

and paper industry was a particularly obvious target for those who were concerned about pollution, as anyone who has ever visited a pulp town and smelt the air or looked at the river will acknowledge. In New Brunswick pressure against the spray program started to increase steadily in light of growing evidence that some of the chemicals in the spray recipe used to kill the budworm can also kill children.

The battle against the budworm was transformed into a political struggle, waged with contending scientific studies aimed at proving or disproving the threat to human health of fenitrothion and the other components of the insecticide spray. The contending forces in New Brunswick were the "environmentalists" led by the Concerned Parents Group and the government/industry/professional nexus. At first it appeared to be a mismatch. But in fact, a poorly-financed group of volunteers successfully fought against an entrenched, well-organized combination of interests including the most powerful business outfit in New Brunswick, the Irving empire. K.C. Irving's family business includes the leading forest company in the province, and Irving power in the forest sector is matched by its control over much of the provincial media. While Irving information outlets are not noted for their strident opposition to the spray program, Concerned Parents still scored frequent minor victories. The province was even persuaded that it should warn parents in advance where and when spraying was to be conducted and it agreed that the planes would stay away from human settlements. In the DDT days entire communities could be sprayed without warning. By the late 1970s, the government had been forced to shuffle about conducting studies, issuing denials, commissioning task forces and changing chemicals in its attempts to resist pressure to stop spraying the budworm-infested forest.

Concerned Parents were concerned because emulsifiers used in the spray had been definitively linked to Reye's Syndrome, a rare but deadly disease affecting children that starts with flu-like symptoms and ends with death caused by swelling of the brain. One nine-year-old Newcastle-area child, who died in 1979, had such strong convulsions that his father, a muscular pulpmill worker, had to get help just to hold him down. Fenitrothion itself is a mutagenic compound that has been linked to chromosome damage and birth defects. In the public mind chemical sprays became increasingly associated with cancer: a nagging fear most Canadians live with and recognize as a personal threat, especially in light of the Terry Fox phenomenon. Soon after Fox ran through Nova Scotia and New Brunswick on his Marathon of Hope in 1980, it was revealed that New Brunswick had new cancer rates one-third higher than Nova Scotia. The incidence of Reye's Syndrome was nine times higher in New Brunswick than in Nova Scotia. [42]*

Faced with such evidence, the government stonewalled. Its attitude was perhaps best typified by the response of Health Minister Brenda Robertson to queries about the disease rates in the two neighbouring provinces. At first Robertson speculated that New Brunswick doctors were simply doing a better job of disease detection than their colleagues in Nova Scotia. When she was informed that there was one doctor for every 560 patients in Nova Scotia and one for every 922 in New Brunswick, the minister of a government blindly committed to its spray program responded, "It's very easy to say that [New Brunswick doctors are] spread more thinly, but I can't agree that their diagnosis is going to be less accurate. I would suggest that our doctors work a lot longer hours than if we had more doctors."[43]

The fight against the spraying attracted the attention of the national media who are keener than the Irving-controlled outlets in New Brunswick to jump on the latest revelations of sickness and spray links. Even *Pulp and Paper Canada,* a trade journal, headlined: "New Brunswick's forest industry, public and government act out community drama."[44] In early 1982 more comparisons between New Brunswick and Nova Scotia were drawn, this time in the pages of a Halifax daily and written by former Nova Scotia Forest Minister Vincent Maclean. The Cape Breton legislator had helped resist paper company pressure to start spraying the Cape Breton highland forest in order to stop a budworm outbreak. Opting instead for what he called effective forest management, Maclean revealed Canadian Forestry Service statistics on budworm egg-mass counts. The federal government forest researchers had found that egg-mass counts rose

---

* Research at Dalhousie University in Halifax revealed incidence of Reye's Syndrome of 0.75 per 100,000 people in New Brunswick, 0.09 in Nova Scotia and 0.37 in the entire United States. New Brunswick has used several different emulsifiers and solvents in its spray programs as it searched for a compound that could be used effectively and safely. Forest Protection Ltd. shuffled the chemical deck, moving from Toximul to Atlox, Aerotex to Dowanol, but none proved satisfactory. The long-term effects of these preparations on human health remain uncertain.

to a peak in Cape Breton in 1976 as part of the budworm's natural cycle but had fallen off dramatically by 1981 as the cycle continued. No spraying was done in Nova Scotia in this period. At the same time Maclean noted that New Brunswick, which in 1981 increased the acreage sprayed by 18 per cent over the previous year, saw egg-mass counts in sprayed zones *rising* an average of 29 per cent between 1980 and 1981.

The New Brunswick policy of poisoning the budworm and the rest of the ecosystem seemed to be having the effect of extending and prolonging an infestation that could have been allowed to run its course and decline. The former Conservative minister from Nova Scotia concluded, "Spraying has kept some of the trees green in New Brunswick, but it has altered the cycle of the budworm, thus ensuring its survival."[45] Maclean praised Nova Scotia environmentalists who he said had more of the public interest at heart than pulp industry executives. One such executive, Robert Weary of the Bowater Mersey company, had written in the same Halifax paper that the environmental movement was using "scare tactics" to manipulate the public. In an unfortunately ironic choice of words, Weary had recommended that Nova Scotia step into line with New Brunswick and "spray the cancer where it sets in".[46]

A key reason for the enthusiasm of mill owners for chemical spraying can be found in the fact that the spray programs help to keep down their costs. And mill owners are generally more interested in cheap fibre than in human health or ecologically-based forest management. From this perspective it makes corporate sense to have the government pick up the tab for what one radio documentary dubbed "the poison mist". The twist is that budworm damage does not necessarily lead to big reductions in wood supply to mills, as long as the logging interests are willing to do active salvage logging, which means getting at the dead trees before they are blown or burned down, or decayed. But the companies are not keen to do salvage logging. An example of this is the forest industry in Newfoundland, where chemical spraying is strongly pushed. An Economic Council of Canada study of the economics of Newfoundland forestry sums up the reasons why: "The forest industry benefits from protection [from the budworm] because logging costs are lower as a result of less salvage logging and less disruption of logging to undertake salvage operations. Manufacturing costs are also lower with

Spraying with Simazine and Amitrol. Herbicides are widely used in Canadian forestry to suppress the growth of commercially undesirable trees.

less salvaged material.* The timber supply is increased, and utilization need not be so tight."[47]

In Newfoundland Premier Brian Peckford decided in 1981 to begin a comprehensive chemical spray program as a result of the recommendations of a Royal Commission — the fifth since 1955 to look into the problems of the forest industry. Newfoundland forest policy has been so pitifully inadequate that since the turn of the century the government has not even collected any stumpage revenues for the pulpwood cut by the paper companies. The industry, now dominated by Abitibi-Price and Bowater Newfoundland, paid two-thirds of the cost of the spray program but the rest was borne by the people of the province through their taxes. The people also have to sustain all of the environmental costs of the spraying.

* Good pulpwood cut from living trees is cheaper and easier to convert to pulp than budworm-killed timber.

Since these costs are distributed so unevenly, the companies predictably push massive spray campaigns like the one in New Brunswick even though it has been known for years that pesticides do absolutely nothing for the long-term health of the resource. This has been proven to foresters by New Brunswick's DDT/Fenitrothion debacle and its success in making the budworm infestation last longer. Forestry professionals working for industry were told as long ago as 1948 that spraying was no substitute for sound forest management. In that year, at a government-sponsored meeting of company foresters held in the Ottawa Valley, the head of the Dominion Forest Service gave his opinion of the effectiveness of the miracle DDT insecticide, which industry was touting as part of the answer to its impending wood supply problems. D.R. Cameron told the assembled foresters that budworm spraying "is a palliative which may serve to protect a small area of high volume, but as a means of stopping an epidemic where population pressure has built up to enormous proportions, my opinion is that it is foredoomed to failure, whatever the extent of effort might be."[48] Cameron's position was backed by G.G. Cosens of the University of Toronto, who said that since the budworm was indigenous to many Canadian forests, it would make sense to look for a natural form of control. The only dissenting position at the meeting was that of W.A. Delahey of the Ontario Forest Industry Association, who advocated spraying the budworm-infested balsam stands.

The industry position soon prevailed with the inauguration of forest spraying in several provinces. The reason was that the companies had all the political clout and those foresters who did see the folly of the spray initiative had none. In any case most of the foresters were industry and government employees who could be relied upon by their superiors to go along with the insecticide operation. For the next thirty years the forestry profession provided the scientific/technical rationalizations needed to support continued spraying.

So it was not the foresters who challenged the government of New Brunswick and forced it to at least move towards rethinking its policy. Only when the environmental movement and groups such as Concerned Parents began to apply pressure did the province go through the motions of studying the problem once again and looking for alternative ways of killing the

budworm. For one thing, the groups pointed out that fenitrothion was one of the chemicals tested and approved for safety by a
U.S. firm known to have faked test results. By 1982 the public
opposition had been reinforced by mounting scientific evidence
about the health effects of the spray and an intense media barrage.
According to some observers of the New Brunswick political scene,
the issue had become hot enough to cause the government of
Richard Hatfield to delay a planned election.

Against this background it must have been distressing for
the government when, a month before the spray planes were
again scheduled to take off, the New Brunswick Federation of
Woodlot Owners (NBFWO) adopted an anti-spray resolution at its
annual meeting. The organization, representing thousands of
small landowners who supply 25 per cent of the fibre needs of
the province's pulp companies, had previously been regarded as
a safe source of political support for the continued use of insecticides in the forest. The manager of the Federation, a young
forester named Dave Curtis, was more than a little surprised at
the reaction of Gordon Baskerville to the NBFWO's stance. Baskerville, assistant deputy minister in charge of forestry, had for
several years lent his professional forestry credentials to the
support of the pro-spray forces. When he heard about the resolution drafted by Curtis and adopted by the Federation, Baskerville fired off a letter to the present of the organization telling
him that the budworm would not go away because of resolu-
tions passed by "well-meaning though ill-informed groups".
Baskerville told the woodlot owners that they had a stake in the
future of forestry and concluded, "I was therefore disappointed
to see their pronouncements on this important matter sink to
the level of alchemy used by the anti-spray groups."[49]

Environmental activists are used to being subjected to
accusations of being irrational, or worse. Catherine Richards, a
key member of Concerned Parents, notes: "We're always being
accused of being emotional. I think it's because we call ourselves
'parents' and a lot of us are women that the label is so easy to
apply."[50] But Dave Curtis is not accustomed to such labels. A
University of New Brunswick forestry graduate who quit a job
with the provincial ministry because he was disillusioned with
the kinds of forest management it practised, Curtis was at pains
to project a reasonable, careful image in order to lend credibility
to the Federation's position. Because of that, he put some dis-

tance between himself and the anti-spray groups. He wanted to avoid aligning the NBFWO position with that of what he called the "pressure groups" and so swing the maximum political weight he knew the woodlot owners could wield on the issue. Curtis was understandably miffed when Baskerville paternalistically referred to the Federation policy positions as "ill-conceived statements from people who should know better" and "downright silly".[51]

Curtis could only respond by reiterating the position of the small proprietors' sector. In his view, the woodlot owners were stuck in the middle of a simmering political fight, which was heating up to the boiling point. While he did regard the anti-spray position as "extreme", Curtis didn't think much of the industry/government/professional line that held forestry as akin to agriculture, thus in need of crop protection, thus in need of spraying. The real solution could only be based on a reduction of the balsam fir content of the forest and its replacement by a more diversified species mix, he believed. Curtis was clear on what he felt was the real answer to a problem that had become chronic — both ecologically and politically — in New Brunswick: "Our position derives from the concept that a budworm epidemic starts due to the nature of the forest. It's been postulated and in fact proven that budworm outbreaks start when there is an overabundance of mature fir. That's what initiates an outbreak. So if an outbreak is related to the nature of the forest, then any long-term control must also be related to the nature of the forest. Otherwise you just battle a symptom instead of the cause of the problem."[52]

As a Federation representative, one of the people Dave Curtis speaks for is Aurele Mallet, a woodlot owner from St. Sauveur in the northeastern part of the province. Mallet is a short, wiry fellow, an Acadian who has been using his small, 150-acre parcel of timberland to supplement his income as a carpenter for over three decades. He cuts pulpwood and makes maple syrup products to help buffer the chronic economic uncertainty that reigns in his poor corner of a have-not province. Mallet shares with many other New Brunswickers the suspicion that the budworm spraying destroys as much of what is good in the forest as it kills what is bad. He worries that the natural predators of the budworm are also affected by the spray and thinks that there are less birds and squirrels around these days than there used to be. He says that back in 1955, three years after the DDT spraying started, he first noticed that the birds seemed lethargic and sick. Unlike Concerned Parents, Mallet has a direct personal and financial stake in the wood industry. But like the anti-spray group, he is opposed to the spraying. The Concerned Parents have claimed that not only are the beasts that hunt the budworm adversely affected by the insecticides, but that the budworms that do survive are hardier. Since there is less competition for available food, the surviving worms become healthy moths capable of flying further and laying more eggs for future infestations.[53]

Gordon Baskerville has acknowledged, "Spraying has virtually no impact on the [budworm] population — it just saves trees."[54] Aurele Mallet believes that though a lot of people are against the spray program, the government is for it and that's what counts. Reflecting on his experiences at sap-gathering, he notes that whereas he often used to find squirrels drowned in his sap buckets, now he finds none. Mallet offered his own appraisal of the overall situation: "Put a man and a budworm in a bottle. Spray them and the budworm is going to live and the man is going to die."[55]

A lot of Aurele Mallet's neighbours are small farmers who, like their fellows elsewhere in Canada, have had to give up agriculture or practise it on a part-time basis. Canadian agriculture has become agribusiness, with ever more powerful centralized companies controlling the production of food and the many inputs that modern, intensive cultivation is dependent upon. At the same time many farmers have become worried about the effects of heavy applications of pesticides and chemical fertilizers on their health and the health of their farms. Forestry faces some of the same problems, as control gravitates into the hands of integrated forest products firms and big government departments. The type of non-biological forestry that Hamish Kimmins worries about becomes the order of the day. Spraying agricultural or silvicultural crops may produce short-term gains in productivity. But in the long run, as human intervention attempts to dominate complex natural systems rather than proceed in harmony with them, such practices may also backfire.

Herb Hammond, a B.C. forester, measures the age and growth of a tree with an increment borer.

Tree Huggers and Ghost Towns

Colonies of ancient murrelets. Peregrine falcon eyries. Rhinoceros auklets. Mature, virgin ecosystems of the Queen Charlotte Islands. Subzone of the Western Hemlock Biogeoclimatic Subzone. Aboriginal forest utilization. Salmonoid enhancement. Ecological reserves and direct job losses. Wilderness preservation.

THE WORDS ARE NOT exactly everyday language, but they are familiar enough to anyone who followed the fights over logging on the Queen Charlotte archipelago off the north coast of British Columbia. At stake was the valuable timber of the Charlottes, an extraordinarily beautiful group of islands that attracts loggers and nature lovers alike. The cedar, spruce and hemlock forests that have long flourished in the moist, temperate climate represented valuable sawlogs to a forest industry fast running out of big timber. At the same time one island, Moresby, had a portion of its bush selected by federal parks officials as one of three spots in Canada worthy to be called World Heritage Natural Site. A report commissioned by the B.C. forest ministry labelled the Charlottes as the key environmental "hotspot" in the province, potentially "the biggest single public relations crisis the Ministry has ever faced".[1]

Logging on the Charlottes, like in the rest of Canada, has had a long history. The islands were first opened up to large-scale logging by the demands of war: The rich stands of Sitka spruce provided light, strong material for airplane construction in World War I, and Canadian and British pilots flew biplanes constructed of wood from the rainforests of the Charlottes. But

191

things have changed since the days when H.R. MacMillan, founder of the MacMillan-Bloedel colossus, helped to administer a Queen Charlotte spruce boom when he was assistant director of the Department of Aeronautical Supplies of the Imperial Munitions Board. More recent battles were no longer being waged with Sopwith Camels and Snipes. Instead, the struggle became a matter of public meetings, press releases and feverish lobbying.

Into this environmental dispute came two opposing organizations whose names reveal their respective orientations: Western Forest Products* and the Islands Protection Society. The conflict was over logging of the company's Tree Farm Licence No. 24 — to the public, another in a familiar round of contests between the wilderness preservers and the forest industry. In many respects the affair was representative of many similar fights that have developed in Canada over the past ten or fifteen years, pitting "environmentalists" against "loggers" — perhaps a false distinction, given that if you scratch a logger you sometimes find an environmentalist, and vice versa. Nevertheless, on the Charlottes the lines seemed clearly drawn.

The forces aligned with the Islands Protection Society wanted to preserve parts of the archipelago in a wilderness state and thus protect important wildlife sanctuaries and preserve the scenic beauty for all to see. The preservation of the entire Windy Bay drainage area on one of the Charlottes, Lyell Island, became a particularly high profile issue. The Islands Protection Society also wanted assurance that the entire southern portion of Moresby Island would be protected from the negative effects of logging. Its supporters argued that they weren't asking for a lot. They stated that 95 per cent of the productive forest land in the province was open to development, with only about 5 per cent locked up in parks and ecological reserves. The IPS position held that if the provincial forests were properly managed there would be no need to log sensitive sites on the Charlottes.[2]

A native organization on the Charlottes, the Skidegate Band Council, also pointed to the fact that the traditional Haida lifestyle had been adversely affected by resource extraction. The Haida once lived in and from the products of the forest and

---

*Western Forest Products is a creature of three larger forest products corporations: B.C. Forest Products, Doman Industries and Whonnock Industries.

indeed saw themselves as one with the forest. The giant cedars of the Charlottes were particularly important for Haida culture. The Skidegate band believed that Western Forest Products could not operate without being extremely harmful to the environment and was particularly concerned with the effects of clearcut logging on steep slopes.[3]

For its part, Western Forest Products was quick to point to job losses it said would result from the establishment of an ecological reserve in the area in question: a portion of land around Windy Bay in the southern Charlottes. The company came up with a figure of 123 "man-years" of employment that could be lost annually should the IPS proposal be accepted by the provincial government and logging in the area prohibited. Western Forest Products also speculated that total losses to the provincial Gross Domestic Product might exceed an astonishing $330 million over a whole forest rotation — about the equivalent of a human lifespan — should the wilderness preservers get their way. "We suggest that the Queen Charlotte Islands has more than its share of ecological reserves and resulting lost productive forest land," the company stated.[4] It preferred a "multiple use" approach to accommodate both timber and recreational/environmental considerations.

In the period 1979-1982 this struggle over forest use attracted regional and national media attention as both sides sought to sway the provincial government one way or the other by rallying other organizations to their side and displaying the relative strengths of their positions. The IPS came up with a province-wide petition signed by fourteen thousand people and enlisted the backing of Local 4 of the Pulp, Paper and Woodworkers of Canada, a union representing millworkers in nearby Prince Rupert. The environmental group also secured the support of Local 28 of the United Fishermen and Allied Workers Union. Western Forest Products countered with the backing of the International Woodworkers of America (IWA), the biggest forest union in British Columbia. The IWA was particularly vociferous in its defence of Tree Farm Licence No. 24, trotting out the old shibboleth of fifty-cents-out-of-every-dollar earned in the province being generated by forestry. IWA loggers working for Western Forest Products felt threatened by the wilderness proposal, so their regional council waded into the fray on the side of the employer.

The IWA position started from the premise of timber as a renewable resource: a logical enough assumption. The union reiterated the belief that trees are a crop just like corn or wheat. It underlined its oft-repeated support for environmental protection through proper logging methods and good forest management. If logging regulations weren't strict enough to protect the environment, the IWA said, the rules should be changed and strengthened. But it was scornful of those who would try to set up untouchable wilderness areas, portraying them as a narrow interest group of cruising yachtsmen and kayakers. As an IWA publication put it, "There is already plenty of wilderness for these types of people to play in." The loggers' union analyzed the wilderness preservers' strategy as one "hoping to make enough noise and advance phoney ecological arguments using phrases like terrestial ecosystems, dentritous cycles, micro diversity etc. to force a moratorium on logging the Windy Bay Watershed."[5]

RELATIONS BETWEEN THE IWA and those seeking more stringent controls on logging had been severely strained in 1979 by an incident that cast some doubt on the union's commitment to forest management and careful logging.

Over the years logging on the Charlottes had proceeded much as elsewhere in Canada. It was a familiar pattern: The easier and more profitable logging was carried out on the flat, stable terrain on the east coast of Moresby Island and on the central part of Graham Island. That was where big firms, such as MacMillan-Bloedel, chose to situate their Tree Farm Licences, leaving the more difficult steep slopes for the Public Sustained Yield Units.* These slopes tend to rise sharply out of mountain streams and creeks, making them not only difficult to log but also near impossible to log while avoiding soil erosion and massive landslides. When logging does take place in such places, the roots of the stumps quickly rot away in the wet climate. On the

* See chapter 3 for details on the introduction of these forest tenures in British Columbia.

west coast of the Charlottes it is not uncommon for six inches of rain to fall in the same place over the course of a couple of days. Such weather conditions, combined with the precipitous, unstable slopes and the removal of the trees that helped to anchor the soil to the bedrock, mean that what were once complete forest floors can easily go tumbling downhill into the streams.

Many of these streams provided vital breeding grounds for salmon. Those unfamiliar with the ways of fish might think that fish fry are shore-lunches or backyard picnics. But fry are also the young, recently-hatched fish living in the tiny spaces between the stream-bed pebbles where they were first hatched. When a forest floor gets flushed into a stream, the silt has the effect of paving the stream-bed, making it impossible for the young fry to continue their cycle of development into mature salmon. And, because the livelihood of many communities on the B.C. coast is intimately linked with either the forest industry or the fishing industry, or both, it makes very little sense for valuable forest land to get dumped into valuable salmon streams. Renewable resources become non-renewable when the ability of the forest to reproduce disappears along with the soil and when the salmon's ability to proliferate is also destroyed. Yet this happened with some regularity on the Charlottes.

In March of 1979, Q.C. Timber, a unit of C. Itoh,* one of the *zaibatsu* or trading companies that control much of Japan's booming economy, started to log their Cutting Plan 144 at Rennell Sound on the west coast of the Charlottes. The B.C. Forest Service had authorized the cutting plan, over the objections of the federal fisheries department. The Ottawa officials who have responsibility for the maritime fishery were worried that the logging would cause heavy stream siltation and endanger an already severely-depleted salmon fishery. The fishery officers were particularly alarmed because they knew the creeks draining Q.C. Timber's licence area spawned a quarter of all the pink salmon on the west coast of the Charlottes. Riley Creek was of particular importance, because it had been classified by the International Salmon Commission as a significant producer.[6]

Within eight months of the beginning of logging at Rennell Sound, following heavy November rains, thirteen slides occurred.

* C. Itoh is the third largest of these trading companies. Its capitalization is nearly double that of the Toyota automobile company and over three times higher than the Sony corporation.

Two of these slides found their way into Riley Creek. One fisheries officer, Kip Salter, visited the site immediately after the slides and reported mud up to five feet deep at the bottom of the slope, as well as substantial siltation. "I think it is pretty obvious [the slides] were caused by logging," Salter later told a reporter. "Slope failures do occur in unlogged timber but not with that kind of frequency." Salter was accompanied by a technician for the provincial environment ministry. When environment ministry Regional Director Don Smuin surveyed the site, he commented that, though he was unfamiliar with coastal logging, words failed him because of the "mess". Smuin was puzzled at the B.C. Forest Service's action in permitting the logging to proceed. "When these major slides occur they usually go to bedrock and as a result there is no soil left for regeneration of forest cover. This, I would think, should be of much concern to the forestry people themselves."[7]

Yet the logging by Q.C. Timber had been approved by provincial forestry officials the previous March, precipitating a dramatic confrontation involving a federal/provincial jurisdictional tussle and the International Woodworkers of America. The controversy had been simmering for months before the logging go-ahead, with federal fisheries officers warning of the harmful effects of steep-slope logging at Rennell Sound. Under the Fisheries Act they had the power to stop activities that would result in harm to the salmon fishery. Soils experts from the provincial Forest Service had acknowledged there would be landslides and even admitted these slides would make it difficult for the sites in question to produce another crop of timber.[8] But they thought there was no danger of sedimentation of Riley Creek.

Still, by January 1979 it seemed that the various regulatory agencies involved had reached a consensus that it wasn't worth Q.C. Timber taking the chance on cutting the trees it wanted from its Cutting Plan 144. So it naturally came as a surprise to federal fisheries people when they learned in March of the Forest Service's decision to allow the logging to proceed.

At this point a confrontation erupted. Under the authority of the Fisheries Act, federal officers moved in to arrest loggers falling timber on Cutting Plan 144. Soon sixteen loggers had been charged, along with Q.C. Timber itself. Still the province refused to halt the logging and seemed bent on challenging the federal law in the courts. The IWA reacted vehemently. Its leader, Jack Munro, threatened a province-wide forestry strike if the charges were not dropped. Given the importance of the industry ("fifty cents-out-of-every-dollar") this tactic worked. Charges against individuals workers were soon dropped. The affair prompted one B.C. business magazine to observe, "Funny things have been happening on the labour beat. Or, it's hard to tell who's in bed with whom."[9]

The fact that the IWA had sided with its frequent adversaries — Premier Bill Bennett and the forest corporations — was notable since the union could have framed its response around the argument of bad cutting practices that would result in a valuable forest site being lost to future timber production. The IWA was and is formally committed to sustained yield and proper forest management. Instead of adopting a position critical of government and industry, the union simply backed an employer who was knowingly sending loggers in to work where they would be arrested. The IWA's position stood in sharp contrast to that of another big provincial union, the United Fishermen and Allied Workers Union, which had opposed the logging on the grounds that it was harmful to the fishery.

THE VARIOUS CONTROVERSIES over logging on the Charlottes pitted environmentalists against the Forest Service, forest products companies and IWA. Twenty years ago such disputes would probably have never erupted. Logging then was carried out far from the public eye in remote regions of the country. It has only been through the increase in public consciousness of what can be classified loosely as environmental issues that the practices of logging operators have come under any popular scrutiny. After decades of operating out of sight in places like the Charlottes and the wilds of the eastern boreal forests, the forest industry suddenly found itself confronted with demands articulated by people questioning everything from cutting practices and spray programs to the use of the forest simply for its timber values.

Why this new and, for the industry, unfamiliar political challenge to its longstanding hegemony in the woods?

Years earlier, phrases like "land use planning" and "resource planning" would have brought quizzical, astonished expressions to the faces of logging bosses, men who tended to consider trees as abundant as hay and almost as cheap. Very few people, except for the odd maverick forester or naturalist, ever had the time or the opportunity to gain a critical perspective on forest practices. For a long time, instant communications networks and the electronic media weren't available to bring home to people the potential ill effects of standard logging industry practices.

For example, over a century of driving logs down rivers in eastern Canada certainly took its toll on the river environment. The spring drives coincided with the breeding period of much aquatic life. Bark and other debris clogged river beds and the resulting decay used up valuable oxygen needed by fish. The large numbers of logs floating downriver could destroy the vegetation on river banks, promoting erosion and siltation. Changes in the aquatic environment resulting from transportation of wood fibre to the mills also adversely affected water fowl. Nonetheless, hardly a peep was heard about these sacrifices made to bolster the important economic position of an industry that continued to use the rivers from the Miramachi to the Nipigon as private sluices. As late as the 1950s, when the beginnings of mechanization were bringing an end to river driving, pulp and paper companies in New Brunswick were still legally exempt from paying damages to property owners who might suffer loss from destruction of their boats, camps or docks by floating pulpwood. [10]

Provincial governments have a history of going out of their way to facilitate the assault on the environment by forest products corporations. In years past when there were few environmental watchdogs this was particularly easy to accomplish. The famous case of the Kalamazoo Vegetable Parchment Company (KVP*) springs to mind. In 1949 a group of landowners along the Spanish River, downstream from KVP's Espanola, Ontario operation, got fed up with KVP's effluents, which made the water so putrid it was unfit to bathe in, let alone drink. Using Ontario's Lakes and Rivers Improvement Act, the landowners obtained an

---

* This firm is now owned by E.B. Eddy.

injunction from the courts restraining KVP from fouling the river. The company appealed the decision right up to the Supreme Court of Canada, but lost. While the case was before the high court, Ontario's Tory government amended the Act to force the courts to consider the economic factors involved before issuing injunctions against the companies. But the Supreme Court ruled the new amendment did not affect the KVP case because it was passed after the court's ruling. So the government, led at the time by Leslie Frost, passed a special new law dissolving the injunction and giving the Kalamazoo firm permission to pollute. Leslie Frost joined the Board of Directors of KVP soon after his retirement from active politics. [11]

Such a cagey finesse might be rather more difficult to pull off in the 1980s, due to the political embarrassment it could generate. Many Canadians had become more environmentally sensitive than in earlier days. They'd acquired leisure time, often using it to get out of the cities and into the country's wilderness areas. Ironically, the growth in urbanization, which drew labour from the woods in the forties and fifties and was a principal cause of logging mechanization, the building of more forest roads and the decrease in river drives, had also exposed the forest industry to unprecedented public perusal. City dwellers wanted to get away from the smog, noise and bustle on a regular basis and those who could afford a break in the wilds would take it. New forest roads — the Canadian Pulp and Paper Association puts the figure at 12,000 miles, three times the length of the Trans-Canada highway — made more wilderness accessible to hikers, hunters, canoeists and anglers. In the period 1963-1973, the number of visits to Canada's national parks doubled. [12] The visitors could see what was happening in the bush and many of them had developed a preservationist ethic. As a result, more and more people began to demand additional parks and wilderness areas. More and more people became critical of corporate forestry practices.

In addition, with a new widespread awareness of urban sprawl, with over-industrialization and a shrinking agricultural land base, more and more people began to demand land-use planning. They saw that farmland and forest land were rapidly disappearing from production. And the ideas of people like Rachel Carson helped to spawn an awareness of the threat posed by chemical agents like DDT. Governments even started to create separate ministries to deal with environmental concerns. The pollution of air, water and land was suddenly an important public issue. Organized political initiatives aimed at reversing these trends developed rapidly.

The recent history of the herbicides 2,4-D and 2,4,5-T stands as an example of the change. In Ontario the provincial government had most frequently used a combination of the two chemicals for its forestry spray programs, at least until the late 1970s.[13] During that time the compound 2,4,5-T developed its own particular notoriety, based largely on the fact that it contains one of the most deadly toxins known, a form of dioxin (TCDD 2378) used by the U.S. military in the infamous Agent Orange applied to Vietnamese jungles and people, and even inadvertently to American GIs. When popular pressures resulted in the use of 2,4,5-T as a herbicide being severely restricted in Ontario in 1979, the province managed to sell its remaining 800 gallons to J.D. Irving Ltd. of New Brunswick.[14] The Irving interests evidently judged the chemical safe for their private forest lands or the public forests they manage for the government of New Brunswick.

Some citizens, alarmed at the looming threat posed by herbicides, have taken direct action to stop the application of the chemicals. In the summer of 1982 a public outcry erupted in Nova Scotia over the aerial spraying of both 2,4-D and 2,4,5-T. The provincial government had issued permits to several paper companies allowing them to conduct spray operations aimed at killing off hardwood growth on spruce plantations. Cape Breton Island residents reacted strongly with a series of public protest meetings.

When it looked like the spraying was going to proceed, members of the Micmac reserve at Whycocomagh decided to do something about the threat to their community. Chief Ryan Googoo and others from the band paid an uninvited visit to a Nova Scotia Forest Industries' spruce plantation, where they ripped up a thousand or so young spruce trees, and warned that they'd continue the action if the spray permits were not revoked.

This and other protests were enough to push the province into issuing a temporary ban on aerial spraying — although ground spraying was still permitted. The cabinet decision, such as it was, displeased lands and forest minister George Henley, who called the groups protesting the spraying "ridiculous" and said they were obviously not interested in maintaining jobs in Cape Breton.[14] Henley also argued that 2,4-D and 2,4,5-T were "safe as water" — a statement not calculated to greatly reassure the native people of the Micmac reserve, who were concerned about contamination of the band's drinking water from runoff. The president of the Union of Nova Scotia Indians replied, "If Henley wants to drink the damn stuff, let him drink it and we'll see what happens in a couple of years."

The growth of the environmental movement soon had its effects on forestry and industrial cutting practices. Companies began to employ "environmental foresters" to communicate the corporate perspective and answer querulous citizens agitated about the spraying of chemical poisons and clearcutting. Some residents of forest-based towns, people who were the most directly affected by the operations of the forest companies, made the loudest noises of protest — especially about the community instability that was characteristic of transient cutting operations or what Alexander Koroleff called nomadic logging. A few even took a look at the historical record of the forest industry in promoting the growth of ghost towns, found it disturbing and started to clamour for better forest management as a means of community preservation.

The onslaught of public attention and political pressure caught the forest industry and various governments flat-footed. Forest administrators were used to operating in the peaceful solitude of a receding forest frontier, where they could go about their business of supplying wood fibre to the mills and stumpage revenue to government without bothersome meddling from outside.

This was not the first time the forest industry had been challenged about the manner in which it was conducting its affairs. Half a century before the spread of the environmental movement in the 1960s, a conservation movement had had an important effect on forestry in both Canada and the United States. It was concern over lack of efficient resource management that led to the establishment of the forestry profession in North America. With the coming of the conservation movement around the turn of the century, industry and government both began to acknowledge that, yes, sustained yield forestry was the only way to go if the resource was to be managed to produce wood fibre in perpetuity. At the time this constituted at least a theoretical recognition that forests were renewable, a notion remarkably absent in nineteenth-century forest treatment. The conservation movement called for rational forest management, for putting resource development on a sound business-like footing.

This was not exactly what many of the modern-day challengers of the forest industry had in mind. The environmentalists talked about preservation of the integrity of the ecosystem, adapting industrial initiatives to fit in harmoniously with the cycles of nature. Many were motivated by a growing awareness of the obscene spinoffs generated by North American industrial capitalism — the poisoning of aquatic systems with substances such as phosphates, dioxin and mercury, the air with sulphur, lead and asbestos, the forests with chemical toxins like DDT and fenitrothion. Acid rain, smog, the paving over of productive land — these have been the issues around which the environmental movement has mobilized.

So the new movement stands in rather sharp contrast to the conservation movement, whose leading lights were businessmen, politicians and intellectuals under the impression that technical solutions and a little business ingenuity were all that was needed to set things straight. In 1909, Gifford Pinchot, an early forester who along with his friend President Theodore Roosevelt was a key figure in the American conservation movement, told the Canadian Forestry Association that the ethic he was espousing had nothing to do with love of nature or any such stuff. "Beware of the sentimentalists who would make you believe differently," Pinchot reminded his Canadian audience. "Forestry with us is a business proposition. We do not love the trees any less because we do not talk about our love for them. . . . Use is the end of forest preservation, and the highest use."[15]

Forest use has also been of concern to the environmental movement. But the movement has seen other virtues in the forest aside from the value of timber. Wilderness preservation, recreational use, the preservation of original genetic stock, the forest as a source of pure water and clean air in an age when both are in short supply — these concepts reveal a somewhat broader conception of the uses of the forest. And the environmental movement has had a somewhat broader political base than its conservationist predecessor. Though both crusades have tended to be urban-based, the environmental movement has enjoyed wider active public support to back its demands.[16] Modern communications have helped, but in addition the urgency of the issues and a more informed public have led to a widespread consciousness of the necessity for change before untrammelled economic growth and industrialization lead to irrevocable environmental damage. The institutional leaders of the conservation movement had little consciousness of, nor interest in, environmental integrity, preferring rather the soundness of a healthy balance sheet.

It is no surprise, then, that a normally complacent and conservative Canadian forest industry was taken aback by the upsurge of public concern over what it regarded as its exclusive affairs. But, after all, it was logging on public land and fouling the rivers and the air everyone breathes with its mill effluents. So the industry should not have been too shocked when public pressure prompted governments to move towards making it clean up after itself. Some of the most highly publicized environmental cases in Canada have involved the forest products industry. The pollution of the English-Wabigoon river system with mercury from Reed Paper's Dryden mill in northwestern Ontario resulted in the destruction of an entire native fishery, fears of poisoning of native people with Minamata disease and a huge public outcry. The furor was great enough to stop the Ontario government from handing over a huge tract of public land to Reed. Similarly, dozens of local, less known land-use skirmishes and disputes over cutting practices have dotted the Canadian political landscape.

Some early twentieth century advocates of conservation were labelled "denudatics" by those logging operators who felt they were going too far in their concern over denuded land and lack of "rational" forest treatment. Similar epithets have been flung at wilderness preservers, not only by forest companies but also by trade unions justifiably concerned over job losses they feared could result if cutting operations were curtailed.

One union, the United Brotherhood of Carpenters and Joiners of America,* felt threatened enough by environmentalist criticism of forest practices to publish a defense of clearcutting as a

---

* Although a U.S.-based building trades union, this organization includes in its membership most of the organized loggers in Ontario through its affiliate, the Lumber and Sawmill Workers Union.

forest management tool: "Super-conservationists may make the working man the endangered species, instead of the trees they believe they are protecting," declared the Carpenters' magazine. The loggers were worried that since clearcuts look so bad, it was difficult to defend this cutting practice against the criticism of environmentalists — "every one of them with camera, leading several politicians and newspapermen along by their beards, and happily pointing to 'the rape of our forests' ". This type of anti-clearcut hysteria, argued the union, was the same sort of sentiment responsible for the hanging of witches at Salem, Massachusetts. The union argument, though, was as flawed as any that attempts to prescribe blanket treatments across the board in forestry. Clearcutting for this union was just a silvicultural practice to harvest timber and replace it with a new stand. As simple as that: no reference to careful application of harvesting techniques geared to varying forest sites. The union had fallen into the trap of defending corporate forestry practices against environmentalist critics, "People who," according to S. McNeil writing in *The Carpenter*, "five years ago thought ecology had something to do with glands have now become instant experts and at cocktail parties and when writing letters to the editor mouth phrases like 'ecosystems' and 'biodegradable' and 'the nutrient pool' and 'excessive siltation'."[17]

Forest products firms have also reacted defensively to criticisms from the environmentalist side. They have often regarded the new public concern as a simple communications problem, one that could be solved by educational and public relations campaigns under slogans like "Moose Love Us" and "Profit: Jobs". Such initiatives would presumably explain their side of the story in light of changing attitudes toward business and the environment. In 1970 a Consolidated-Bathurst executive told his colleagues at the Canadian Pulp and Paper Association that they would have to learn to appreciate changing social values, the new emphasis on recreation and the threat posed by environmentalists who were causing phrases like wilderness seeker, multiple use and user conflict to "creep into use" at the time. The Consolidated-Bathurst man warned that because the industry had been doing such a poor job of explaining things like the forest cycle to the public, a small minority of single-use recreationists was in the process of winning over the great mass of campers and casual holidayers to their anti-industry side: "The recreation users of forest areas are a rapidly growing, organized force which can draw heavily on public sympathy by using references to common interest in 'protecting our heritage' etc.," he said. "The forest industry must improve its public image and explain the economic and forest management benefits which it provides."[18]

Faced with wilderness advocates and environmental militancy, forest firms have focused their own campaigns on the local communities likely to be most directly affected. They have advised workers and their fellow citizens in remote, resource-dependent communities about the vulnerability of local economies. They have also attempted to appeal to northerners on the grounds of an alleged threat to their leisure activities.

IN NORTHWESTERN ONTARIO, where one forest controversy after another has been perking ever since the Reed Paper/mercury poisoning atrocity boiled over in the mid-1970s, Great Lakes Forest Products launched its first-ever advocacy advertising effort in 1981. In essence, the campaign warned local anglers to beware the wilderness preservers who would reserve for themselves vast tracts of boreal forest land.

Like many Canadians, people in northwestern Ontario enjoy fishing, and their northern homes provide them with access to well-stocked lakes. If you visit a northern milltown at the end of the day shift on a sunny May afternoon, you'll see a steady trickle of cars towing motorboats as workers head off for their favourite lake. Great Lakes knew this when it issued its appeal to anglers. Its advertisement featured a woebegone would-be fisherman, "Poor Henry", a kind of northern everyman earning a living in the forest industry, a victim of the wilderness buffs. Of course, the company may have been more worried about its dwindling timber reserves and the fact that it has to haul pulpwood over three hundred miles to its mills than it was about the chances of "Poor Henry" hauling in a big catch.

At the same time that it was attempting to fight off groups such as Environment North, Parks for Tomorrow and the Algonquin Wildlands League with this type of tactic, Great Lakes Forest Products was also complaining that it could not find enough experienced loggers to employ because people like to live in southern cities where there are more abundant recreational opportunities. But many people abandon Canada's resource hinterlands only reluctantly, because of the insecurity of employment there and not because they want to. When the ore runs out, or "market forces" result in layoffs, or when the mill cannot get enough wood, jobs evaporate. Former residents of Ocean Falls, B.C., and Uranium City, Saskatchewan, know this. Both places are now modern ghost towns, complete with hockey arenas. Great Lakes Forest Products' operation in Dryden, Ontario, may suffer a similar fate. The company bought up a Reed Paper mill there in 1979 and invested $335 million in rejuvenating it.* But even as it spent this money, the firm was privately aware that wood supplies for the mill were likely to become tight before it was able to write off the investment. So Great Lakes played for time, keeping its eye on the short-term wood supply problem while launching its "Poor Henry" ad compaign and publicly assuring area residents it had enough spruce and pine available to keep Dryden open "forever and a day".[19]

Not all appeals by the industry are so subtle. Ken Greaves of the Ontario Forest Industries Association took a leaf from the opposition book and told a northern Ontario municipal federation that if Canada were going to occupy its proper leadership niche among the nations of the "free world", the threat to both agricultural and forest land would have to be eliminated. He argued against what he called "single purpose withdrawals for uses such as wilderness" and reminded his audience that 76 per cent of the region's economy was represented by the forest products industry. Greaves, who lives in Toronto, was puzzled by a Ministry of Natural Resources planning process that he thought was ignoring the needs of both residents and the indus-

---

* This was the mill responsible for contaminating the English-Wabigoon River system with mercury. To help pave the way for Great Lakes Forest Products' acquisition of the facility, the Ontario government agreed to underwrite any claims for pollution damages that GLFP might inherit with its purchase of the archaic mill. This surely pleased GLFP immensely, because it also inherited the inside track on a piece of forest land almost the size of Nova Scotia — the original "Reed tract", which had been the subject of bitter controversy when Ontario initially announced its intention to license the land to Reed.

try.[20] It was Greaves who stated, "If we cannot make money, then the forest is not worth anything."[21]

Appeals to a sense of community and personal security are well-grounded. In northern Ontario towns such as Smooth Rock Falls and Iroquois Falls over half the workers are employed in pulp and paper company operations, in these particular instances by Abitibi-Price.[22] In the early 1980s, Abitibi began mill modernization programs in towns like these, programs designed to increase productivity and cut costs and pollution. In doing this it was assisted by provincial and federal government grants of $22.5 million, with the Ontario money coming from the province's Employment Development Fund. Given the name of the fund, the government at Toronto was anxious to point out that modernization would stabilize over five thousand jobs. In fact, Ontario officials revealed in 1981 that the government-assisted modernization at Abitibi would mean the loss of 183 jobs.[23] Ultra-modern pulpmills require only a few workers on the shop floor, because much of the machine tending has been automated and can be carried out in front of centralized instrument panels. Modern timber harvesting operations are designed to remove the worker from the forest floor and place him (and now for the first time, her) in harvesting machines. In both workplaces there are fewer people employed. So concern over job stability expressed by absentee-owned forest corporations rings rather hollow for some residents of northern communities.

Thunder Bay is another such city. In contrast to many northern centres, "the Lakehead" has a relatively diversified economy and acts as a service centre for much of the northwestern region. But one worker in ten is employed by the pulp and paper industry, which has been a crucial part of the economic fabric of the area ever since Howard Ferguson's government in the 1910s and 1920s ignored its own laws in its haste to concede Crown timber to the paper companies. The export of resources continues to dominate the economy and the skyline, with grain elevators loading prairie wheat and pulpmills processing timber. The surrounding woods of northwestern Ontario have long provided jobs for countless loggers, and in particular for a large number of Finnish immigrants who came to the area in the years before and after World War I to cut pulpwood. The Finns were especially crucial to the organization of the loggers into the Lumber and Saw union.

By the 1980s the giant Great Lakes Forest Products complex in Thunder Bay was gobbling up a continuous, year-round flow of pulpwood. Each year the Great Lakes mill was processing over 200 square miles of the boreal forest.[24] Area residents who have tried to ensure that some wilderness is preserved for other uses, such as tourism, in a more diversified economy soon became alarmed by the speed at which the forest resource was being depleted. Those who agitated for more parks in turn alarmed industry people who know the resource is finite. The fight is between what the "environmentalists" see as a dwindling wilderness offering more than timber values and what industry sees as its diminishing fibre base. As in the Queen Charlottes, the battle is in part over the allegiances of the local population and a broader provincial population. The terrain of the fight is the press and public meetings. The prize is public opinion. The government, the owner of the resource, is in the middle, trying to convince people that its planning process can satisfy both sides.

Part of the provincial mediating effort in Ontario has been performed by the Royal Commission on the Northern Environment, set up in the wake of the mercury pollution scandal to study northern environmental problems. The Royal Commission is headquartered in Thunder Bay, but the real decisions around forest use and timber sales are made by the Ministry of Natural Resources in Toronto. MNR has a curiously ambiguous role. It has worked out Forest Management Agreements assigning huge areas of timberland to pulp companies to manage on the basis of sustained yield. At the same time it is the ministry responsible for designating provincial parks and wilderness areas. A group of lawyers who conducted a study of provincial laws and policy for the Royal Commission on the Northern Environment found that MNR was favouring multinational resource firms and that government policy was having the effect of driving small forest operators out of business while depriving the north of jobs that could be created in secondary industry. The study of resource policy in the north concluded, "MNR must be relieved of its dual role as custodian and resource developer. The internal conflict inherent in such a dual role almost ensures that one or the other takes low priority."[25]

Bill Addison of Kakebeka Falls on the Trans-Canada highway west of Thunder Bay is one northerner who thinks MNR places timber values above all others in its resource planning activities. He helps spearhead Parks for Tomorrow, a northwestern Ontario parks advocacy group. Addison used to work for MNR as a fisheries research biologist and in his view the ministry is not a neutral arbitrator. He says the government's role as a mediator between contending forest uses has resulted in decisions that favour the forest products companies. The most important park in northwestern Ontario is Quetico, a canoeists' paradise that hugs the Minnesota border. In response to industry claims that the creation of parks will eliminate jobs, Addison likes to tell the public: "The timber industry eliminates, through the creation of NSR land, an area of productive forest land equal to Quetico Park every three-and-a-half to five years. Since the end of World War II, industry and government have eliminated more land from production than has ever been dreamed of for parks."[26]

While some northern residents see MNR as the "narcs of the bush", the forest industry has not been content to sit by and let the planning process unfold without pushing its jobs versus wilderness position. Robert Loughlan, a colleague of Ken Greaves at the Ontario Forest Industries Association, enumerated industry's enemies to one northern Chamber of Commerce in 1982. He started with the "dreamers in canoes", a group who, if they had their way, would flush jobs down the drain. Too much "anti-industry tripe" was also being preached by university professors, he added. And Loughlan even lambasted government land-use planners who he thought were far too casually marking up their maps with potential parks. "By what reasoning do the planners arrive at these decisions?" the industry man asked his small business audience. "Are they themselves wilderness buffs? Do they have friends who are wilderness buffs? Have they been imbued with wilderness philosophy at their mother's knee, or in some cases, her kennel?"[27]

Although such virulent rhetoric is not to be found among the more polished industry lobbyists, who probably cringe at such references to government planners, the forest industry position can usually be distilled into one that offers a choice between jobs or the environment. One or the other.

Ken Hearnden may well be one of the university professors Loughlan had in mind when he railed against anti-industry sentiment. Hearnden has a reputation around the Lakehead as an outspoken critic of government and industry forestry practices. He has lived in the region for over thirty years, working on forest management for Abitibi and then teaching forestry at Lakehead University.

Hearnden has two predictions to make about timber supply in northwestern Ontario. Firstly, he thinks that within ten or fifteen years area pulpmills will be facing a severe wood fibre shortage as stands of black spruce and jack pine become less accessible and more expensive to get at. This, he believes, will lead to the closure of at least one area mill. Secondly, Hearnden fears that this loss of wood supply will be increasingly accompanied by industry threats to close mills and put people out of work unless more wood is made available. Northern Ontario will be left with fewer forest-based jobs, more logging trucks clogging the highways on their longer and longer runs and a legacy of patchy, poorly-stocked cutover land — the result of half-baked silvicultural efforts. According to this forester, companies like Great Lakes Forest Products, Abitibi-Price and Domtar will be forced ever-northward in their search for fibre, a search leading to harvesting operations on land with a very thin mantle of soil, where the roots of spruce trees spread out over the bedrock in search of little veins of life-sustaining earth. Once such sites are cut, they are likely to become permanent forest deserts, "Not Sufficiently Restocked" lands unable to sustain further growth for hundreds of years.[28] Some of these low-potential sites lie in areas Bill Addison and Parks for Tomorrow would like MNR to reserve for non-timber uses.

Ken Hearnden would approach the supply problem differently, aiming for a more diversified type of forestry in a more diversified economy, instead of dependence on big, automated, single-product pulpmills. "When they've finished all this and when the economic supplies of wood are all gone, what then? They'll close the door and walk away. All those towns along the north shore of Lake Huron, like Sprague and Spanish, once had great roaring sawmills going day and night, based on white and red pine. Where are those towns, now that that's all gone? Sitting there in that scrub." Hearnden, like many a longtime observer of the forest scene, is a little wistful and resigned when talk turns to this state of affairs. He has heard the industry line too often. "I've no sympathy for people who argue that wilderness areas are a waste, that we can't afford them and that we'll run out of timber if we set them aside. All that does is suggest to me they're confessing indirectly that because of lack of management we are going to confront timber supply problems."[29]

Yet timber supply headaches are not the only ones facing Canadian resource hinterlands like northwestern Ontario. Along with the truncated, short-term development associated with reliance on resource extraction come disturbing social problems. In 1980 the seven Children's Aid Societies in northern Ontario received a report they had commissioned on child welfare in the north. The area's social workers received statistical confirmation of what they already suspected from their heavy caseloads. Suicide rates among children in northwestern Ontario were 8.19 per 100,000 people compared to a provincial average of 1.3. Alcoholism in the north exceeded the provincial average by nearly 50 per cent. Infant mortality was 50 per cent higher in the northwest than in the province as a whole. Curiously, even though the north as a whole had a higher birth rate than the rest of the province, it had a lower population growth rate. The reason? More emigration by citizens with little confidence in the economic future of the region. The report laid the blame for these social problems on the volatility of what it called a "pre-industrial" resource economy. Even people with jobs found that life in isolated communities or temporary accommodations was contributing to family breakdown, so job turnover rates were high.[30]

Forest industry personnel managers, secure in their southern suburban homes, find it a problem recruiting permanent workers willing to commute from home and family to isolated logging camps on a daily or a weekly basis. Few people like living in the cramped mobile homes so characteristic of Canadian resource communities from Hearst to Prince George. The uncertainty of employment and lack of southern social amenities lead to the high incidence of social problems the northern social workers must face every day. Small wonder, then, that northerners often choose to move out, leaving logging managers pondering how best to mechanize the abandoned jobs. In addition, undiversified, dependent resource economies are subject to market forces, technological changes, the possibility of resource depletion, a whole host of factors over which people in the areas affected have little or no influence. "Control of many of these factors lies outside the region and often outside the province and the country," noted the report on child welfare needs. "The inhabitants of the region who are most immediately affected by the decisions taken have the least influence in the determination of these decisions."[31]

Against this background it did not seem unusual for the Lakehead Social Planning Council to publish a report on the state of the forest industry from a social planning perspective. The report, written by a carpenter and a pulpmill worker, seemed to the forest industry to be just another attack similar to those mounted by the "environmentalists". The Social Planning Council was harshly critical of government and industry over-estimates of forest inventory as well as the highly-touted Forest Management Agreements between the industry and the provincial government. The Council was critical of the FMAs for giving too much power to an industry controlled outside the region by large companies that were always getting larger. At the same time it was pointed out that public participation in the formulation of forest policy had been negligible. The Council argued that the forest companies and the provincial forest planners should be directly accountable to the people of the region. In what must have irked both corporate and Ministry people, the Council put forward its first recommendation: "That in order to ensure the financial and job security of northwestern Ontario, it be recognized that substantial control of area resources is a right and a necessity of the people of the region."[32]

By 1982 MNR had responded to its critics with a series of "open houses" to explain itself and to receive public advice on the land-use planning exercises it was using to decide finally just how much parkland there was to be in the north. But at the same time it kept on signing FMAs, in the best tradition of Howard Ferguson. Great Lakes Forest Products of Thunder Bay, the only pulp firm with a head office in the region,* answered with its "Poor Henry" advertisements. It also made representation to the local United Way social agency about the funding of the Lakehead Social Planning Council. This initiative resulted in the establishment of a sort of negative allocation system, which made sure company dollars would not find their way into the coffers of the social planning agency.[33] It appeared that the forest industry's views on social planning were similar to its views on

---

* Actual control resides somewhere between the Montreal and Calgary offices of Canadian Pacific.

land-use planning. Ten years prior to these events Thunder Bay had hosted a Canadian Pulp and Paper Association seminar on the subject of the forest environment. The principal conclusion contained a worrisome prediction about the future of resource conflicts: "Social change and environmental concern are the primary causes of resource use conflict in Canada. The conflicts will grow and result in diminishing wood supplies and increased costs."[34]

OF COURSE, NOT ALL INDUSTRY representatives display attitudes that are crude and confrontational. The more thoughtful and sophisticated men at the top would never dream of hurling abuse at environmental activists. They prefer instead a cooperative approach including discussion and compromise.

In British Columbia environmental awareness is very widespread — not only on the lower mainland but also, more important for the forest industry, in communities dependent on logging. This is perhaps in part due to a political culture in which both the main provincial political parties retain the vestiges of populism. It may also have a lot to do with the fact that many B.C. population centres are long valley-islands in a sea of mountains. This geographical reality breeds both a regional consciousness and an awareness of all the benefits that nature has to offer to people outside of the cities. In these local areas there is an acute public awareness of the old saw about the "fifty-cents-out-of-every-dollar" forest industry, because many communities are entirely dependent on that industry.

But, for whatever reasons, the men at the top know they're faced with a challenge they can neither ignore nor simply malign. Gerry Burch of B.C. Forest Products is conscious of this and thinks industry has moderated its initial hard-nosed responses to the demands of the environmentalists. Burch believes that accommodation and dialogue represent the way out of land-use fights and demands for more local control of forestry. "Most of these people aren't lower class yahoos or anything. These are articulate people. In most cases these people want to be heard. They want somebody to talk to them."[35]

Up in the area around Smithers, in the northwest interior of the province, this type of person abounds. Smithers is a town like many others along Highway 16 — the "Yellowhead Route" — which cuts across the wilds of "Super, Natural" northern British Columbia. The towns, including Terrace, Prince George, Houston and Vanderhoof, all have one thing in common. In spite of provincial government attempts to publicize the natural beauty of the mountains and to promote tourism, there is an overwhelming dependence on the forest industry. In Smithers a ski resort and an ersatz Swiss townscape have helped to mitigate this dependence. But still the wide valley and the lower mountain slopes produce the spruce, hemlock, pine and balsam vital to the health of the sawmilling industry.

One forest business journalist wrote in 1981 that Smithers had a reputation as a town with more environmental activists enjoying more popular support than anywhere else in British Columbia. While such a claim might be disputed by activists in other regions, there would be no quarrel with the assertion that executives in the northern forest industry "shudder at the thought that the ideas popular in the town — like the concept that the townspeople should have the final say on what happened to the forest — might spread".[36]

Richard Overstall is one of the Smithers-area people who believe in community control of the forest as the only real means of perpetuating a resource so long treated like an ore-body. He has been a sawmill worker and a land-use researcher for an area Indian band as well as an active member of the Telkwa Foundation, a group whose magazine bears the slogan also used frequently by Les Reed at Environment Canada: "Land is not something we inherit from our parents but something we borrow from our children." Overstall has been an active member of the Smithers Forest Advisory Committee (SFAC), a body set up by the B.C. Forest Service in 1976 to resolve or at least defuse conflicts over forestry.

Overstall got involved with SFAC at the start because he thought that local high-grading would soon leave the area short of good timber, that the old historical pattern of "cut the best and leave the rest" would lead to familiar industry warnings of impending mill closures. When this happens, according to

Overstall, the relationship of forestry and logging practices to land use and environmental issues becomes clear: "When the mill shuts down . . . then there is the cry, in the extreme case, to go and log the nearest park or critical wildlife habitat. Here are two hundred people out of work who don't know why so you pick the thing nearest to you."[37]

Concerns about environmental issues and jobs led to an intense local interest in the SFAC in the years immediately following its creation. The committee, including both concerned citizens and local sawmill owners, met frequently to talk with provincial government foresters about the critical issues necessary for an understanding of local forestry problems. Richard Overstall and the others soon grasped the fact that the pivotal issue affecting forestry was the Allowable Annual Cut. The way in which the AAC — the key element in sustained yield forestry — was determined also affected land use, reforestation and all the other elements of forestry. Once the committee understood the importance of the AAC, it was ready to express its concerns and ideas for forestry improvements to the B.C. Forest Service.

The Smithers committee did this several times between 1977 and 1979.[38] This was a critical period in the development of B.C. forest policy; it followed on the heels of the release of the exhaustive report of the Pearse Commission on forestry.* It was a period of intense public discussion surrounding the development of the new policy that eventually was to be enshrined in the 1978 Forest Act. The gist of SFAC's concern centred around the way in which the government was calculating the AAC. The committee knew the Forest Service established the allowable cut on the basis of timber volume but that industry, being a profit-and-loss endeavour, based its logging practices on value rather than volume. This meant that industry naturally went after the best timber first. In the Smithers area spruce and pine was being logged in preference to the less valuable hemlock and balsalm. Loggers also preferred to cut the stands with the highest wood volumes per acre. Such above-average stands were obviously not representative of the forest as a whole, so cutting them first resulted in a gradual decline in quality and net value of the forest sites that remain untouched by chain saw and skidder. In mining, the practice of extracting the richest ore first is known as

* See chapter 4.

"high-grading". Though this term is also used in forestry, the practice is also referred to as "creaming", in reference to the days before homogenization when the rich cream could be skimmed off the top of a quart of milk.

But whatever the practice is called, the Smithers committee was anxious that the Forest Service start to regulate wood quality as well as quantity. The committee wanted the Forest Service to ensure the net value of the wood cut would be representative of the average quality of timber in the entire area covered by the AAC guideline. Once this was done, the Smithers people hoped, the stability of their community would be fostered, because long-term yields would be sustained in value, not just in volume. They felt there was no sense in staking their future on low-value stands of trees like hemlock, species not as commercially attractive as others.

This was the sort of constructive advice the province was supposedly seeking when, in response to public concern over forestry matters, it set up its system of local public advisory committees. Indeed, the District Forester for the B.C. Forest Service wrote to the Smithers committee in May of 1978, telling them, "Our general reaction to this recommendation is that it has merit."[39] The provincial foresters knew that in 1976 the average wood volume per acre of stands logged in the Smithers Public Sustained Yield Unit was 51.9 cunits while the average volume per acre of all the mature coniferous stands in the administrative unit as a whole was 35.5 cunits.[40] They also must have known that it is more profitable in the short term to log a dense stand, or a stand on a lower slope closer to existing roads. But the provincial administrators soon told SFAC they could not obtain the funds needed to carry out a detailed study of the proposal to change the basis of AAC calculations and thanked the Committee for its "considerable effort".[41]

While this was happening in Smithers, the provincial government in Victoria was busy making crucial decisions about forestry. Ignoring the hard work of the committee, the ruling Social Credit Party steered a new Forest Act through the provincial legislature and replaced the old PSYUs with a category called Timber Supply Areas. By the time Smithers people realized that the changes did not answer their concerns about high-grading, it was too late. In a 1979 brief reflecting the frustration they felt after sixty meetings, SFAC members complained to the Minister of Forests of their inability to get anywhere with local officials, who simply told them to address their concerns to Victoria. SFAC told the Socred forest minister, who, ironically enough, came from a mining industry background, that it "feels it has provided sincere and informed input to the forest use planning process in the Smithers area. However, the response of the Forest Service at the provincial level has been insufficient for the committee members to feel their recommendations are having any impact on forestry decisions."[42]

As a veteran of the whole affair, Richard Overstall feels a little frustrated, but no more than many other former participants in the process. He has continued to work on resource issues in the northwest, while some of the other SFAC participants have dropped out of the picture. Overstall has looked over the timber supply analysis reports put out by the province under the new Forest Act and notes that there isn't a dollar sign in them in spite of the fact that logging is very much an economic activity. In other words, SFAC's concerns about planning based on timber values have not been answered.

Bill Young, Chief Forester for B.C., and Gerry Burch of B.C. Forest Products are not so pessimistic about the public advisory process. They both acknowledge that things do not always work out to the satisfaction of all parties concerned and that some people do not get what they want from the process. Young believes that, though he is not satisfied with the way all public involvement initiatives have turned out, the process is still essential.[43] Gerry Burch is a little more candid: "These Public Advisory Committees, even though they're only advisory . . . I believe that in those that haven't worked particularly, it's been the environmentalists who have perceived them to be a government-sponsored game to involve them in a multiple-use [exercise], and they don't want to be involved in it. They want to be fighting in the public sphere."[44]

Richard Overstall agrees. The experience of SFAC has taught him that the public involvement game has been designed to help the government pour oil on waters previously stirred up by environmental activists. "It relieves a number of pressures on the Forest Service. Before, the critics had a certain amount of power through the press and shouting at public meetings. The Forest Service sees the Public Advisory process as part of the bureaucratic sausage machine — information is fed in, ground up and emerges... but it doesn't go anywhere."[45]

SFAC eventually went into limbo, the result of state-initiated consensus politics taking power away from local activists. But Overstall still believes in more localized control — not just public participation — as a prerequisite to any rational, long-term resource use. In order to achieve this goal, he is also convinced there will have to be a lowering of net income currently derived from the forest in the form of taxes and corporate profits. Until this happens, the number of jobs per cunit of wood harvested will continue to decline in the face of increasingly capital-intensive logging and milling operations. In the past the effects of such declines have been mitigated by expansion in the volumes of wood harvested — expansion that cannot continue given impending wood shortages.

MICHAEL TREW WORKED for the B.C. Forest Service during the time C.D. Orchard held the top forestry job in Victoria. Having worked with the logging industry in the 1930s and noticing that company forestry was another word for timber extraction, Trew moved over to the government side in hopes that things would be different there. In the course of twenty years with the Forest Service, he realized that the government was simply allowing companies to log as simply and as cheaply as possible — a system usually involving clearcutting and perhaps planting. He wasn't satisfied with this either but, though he is a vocal critic of industrial forestry, Trew still says things that might disturb the average wilderness preserver. Starting from the premise that logging is the main tool of the silviculturalist, the only way to manipulate the forest, he even goes so far as to advocate logging in parks, providing such logging is carried out in an ecologically-based manner.[46]

Trew is one of a small group of foresters who gives the impression of being really excited about the subject. A passionate foe of clearcutting methods, Trew is of French extraction — this last fact perhaps reflected in his European approach to forestry. He was involved in the high-level discussions surrounding the development of forestry and forest policy in the important watershed period of the forties and fifties. Given this background, he is an effective critic of industrial and government forestry practices. Though he no longer holds a forestry job, Trew has not really retired from forestry. He is constantly sniping at the B.C. Forest Service. But he is equally critical of environmentalists who do not frame their demands as part and parcel of good forestry practices. Trew refers to these people as "tree huggers" and argues that it is their strict preservationist perspective that produces such defensive reactions among foresters. "This is the reason foresters talk continuously of the 'shrinking land base' and see park reserves, wildlife habitat areas and green belts along salmon-spawning creeks as counterproductive land withdrawals from *their* timber preserves," Trew notes as he scolds tree huggers for lack of political savvy. "It is this negative attitude that conservationists must learn to challenge and they must do so by learning to argue forestry and the economic fact that intensive forest management means more, not less, timber jobs and community stability."[47]

Even though the environmental movement has been the first to challenge in an organized way the practices and prerogatives of forest corporations, its demands and the terrain it occupies politically have often limited its effectiveness in the communities dependent on forest operations for their survival. Since logging is usually carried out in the remote regions of a regionalized country, it takes place in a context in which local people feel alienated from the political and economic forces that shape their communities and affect their lives. Centres such as Rouyn-Noranda in Quebec, Terrace in British Columbia and Bathurst in New Brunswick are literally the hewers of wood within a country that, as a whole, is itself frequently characterized as such. So their resentment about being "ripped off", a feeling many Canadians have about their country's relations with the United States, also holds true for people in hinterland areas within Canada. It is a part of the country's political fabric. People in Kapuskasing, Ontario are often peeved at the mention of southern Ontario's "Golden Horseshoe" from where big business and big government direct the affairs of the north. In British Columbia it's the Lower Mainland that's the villain in the regional piece, while in New Brunswick the Acadian north frequently sees the southern counties as being a favoured power centre.

In forestry these fissures are readily apparent. The country's forests — far from the financial and political capitals of the country — are as firmly under the thumb of absentee landlords as Latin American latifundia or the forests of medieval Europe, reserved for the exclusive use of the landed gentry. In modern Canada the controlling interests are the provincial resource ministries and the corporate forest users. It is no surprise that things powerful and things central are cause for complaint in the forest regions of the country. The forest is a variable, site-specific resource different in subtle but important ways from one ridge to the next, from the valley bottom to the mountain slope. This is why thoughtful foresters are highly critical of blanket prescriptions for forest treatment. They know the type of management to be undertaken is best determined by people closest to the forest, those on the front line of forestry who tramp through the woods on a regular basis — not those in the faraway office tower. This is why the forest is ideally suited for and even *requires* a more decentralized type of control than it has experienced up to now. It just makes more common sense to run things on a local basis in forestry.

Part of the popular resentment of outside control common to Canada's resource hinterlands stems from insecurity about jobs and community stability. In single-industry towns, there is always that nagging worry about the mill closing down or the mine stopping production: decisions made by people who in Newfoundland would be seen as having come "from away". But politically the issue of insecurity and dissatisfaction is a double-edged sword. Those who could be loosely grouped under the banner of "environmentalists" can and have used arguments for local control of the forest resource in their quest for more rational, long-term forest management aimed at environmental quality, community stability and job security. But where parks advocates and wilderness preservers do not take careful note of these political realities, when loud cries for conservation drown out local worries about job security, or where the environmental demands are issued exclusively from major urban centres where there is admittedly strong political backing for them, then Michael Trew's fears about the environmentalists being out-flanked politically become relevant.

Gerry Burch knows this quite well. "There is a pressure point now — needing industry, needing jobs, more than so-called recreational reserves, particularly wilderness. That's so strong that the government is becoming more hard-nosed all the time," observes the senior executive. "The unions are starting to get into this. And, incidentally, if I were an environmentalist I would worry more about the unions than I would about industry."[48]

Burch seems to sense that the jobs card is a potential trump in the industry hand. Michael Trew, in his personal quest for better forest management and less ubiquitously-applied clear-cutting, has also given these matters some thought. He quit the Forest Service in British Columbia and went to work on aid projects in the Third World, having given up trying to change forestry from the inside. Trew, now retired, lives on a quiet street in Victoria, across town from the headquarters of the Forest Service. Instead of working on trees, he now takes obvious pleasure in cultivating a city allotment garden. He knows that in the forest regions of the province it is vital for the environmentalists to win over the small business interests and the forest workers to their side by attempting to show that solid, environmentally-sensitive forestry can create more, not less, jobs in the short and long terms while preserving the productivity and integrity of the forest. This makes good sense for forestry, for securing the future viability of the industry and thus the provincial economy. Perhaps most importantly, it also makes good sense politically. Trew thinks it should not be a matter of jobs *versus* the forest environment. It is one of both jobs *and* the forest environment.

"The logger knows the options," Trew says.[49] According to him, when a logger sees environmentalists putting so much pressure on the way forest land is used, and how much land they want to close to industry, "He opts more to support the companies than he does to support the environmentalists. But his interests are really with the environmentalists."

Trew adds: "My argument with the environmentalists is — you can do nothing until you get the logger on your side. There are arguments to get the logger there. He has a family and he lives in a community. When you get an Ocean Falls or a Honeymoon Bay,* you've already got a good part of the population that knows the score."

* Ocean Falls and Honeymoon Bay are two B.C. communities that have been decimated by mill closures. Ocean Falls presents a dramatic picture: isolated,

Michael Trew thinks the only thing he can do as a forestry critic is to continue to warn against entrusting forest management to the big companies and to advocate community-based forestry. His reasoning is based on the assumption that people in forest regions have a vested, long-term interest in the continuity of timber production, whereas corporate interests are centralized, with loyalty to no single community beyond that of the shareholders. "I often wonder why I keep going," Trew reflects. "I guess I do so because I believe we're coming to the crunch time. The crunch will come before I go. Somebody will remember that these things were predictable."

Nearly two generations younger than Michael Trew, Herb Hammond shares Trew's experience and much of his thinking. From where he lives with Susie Hammond and their two children in B.C.'s Slocan Valley, the issues surrounding the forest environment take on added clarity and importance — more so than out in Victoria. Though there aren't quite five thousand people in the entire valley, the residents of the area have still managed to raise a clamour over forestry, loud enough to be heard in the provincial capital. The residents of the Slocan Valley have pushed the province into its first-ever attempt at integrated, long-term resource planning. Government resource inventory reports were ordered and public "input" solicited as the local Regional District political authority got together with the province in what was a novel process.

"In Victoria, when they agreed to this plan they categorized people who live here incorrectly," figures Susie Hammond. "Either as being ignorant Russians who don't speak English or hippies who've blown their minds on something and can't think anymore, even if they could once. Well, it just didn't happen that way."[51]

Susie Hammond's defiant tone is nothing new to this part of the Kootenays. Russian Doukhobor settlers were among the first

---

halfway up the coast between Port Hardy and Kitimat, inaccessible by road, its aging pulpmill and townsite now deserted in the wilderness. The newsprint mill, first opened in the early 1900s, was for decades the basis of the town's prosperity. But it floundered in a wood supply squeeze in the 1970s, prompting the NDP government to buy it from Crown-Zellerbach. In 1980 the mill was forced to close down, in the words of the *Financial Post*: "starved to death for lack of wood".[50] Honeymoon Bay is not so isolated. It is located near Cowichan Lake in the middle of some of Vancouver Island's best timberland. Nevertheless, its sawmill also closed down in the midst of a wood supply crunch.

whites to set down roots in the area after an initial influx of people interested in silver mining in the late nineteenth century. Mining activity has declined steadily since its peak during World War I but the Doukhobors stayed on, and worked hard to establish the first firmly-rooted agricultural settlement in the valley. Their dilligence paid off in the successful farms they cultivated. But internecine turmoil among the group resulted in a high incidence of arson as the Sons of Freedom sub-sect made their points about religious doctrine in a forceful fashion. By the early 1950s the sect was bombing bridges and railroads, an activity that, to say the least, began to shake up the public authorities. The forces of order intervened and hundreds of Doukhobors, along with their children, were jailed. Mass internment was nothing new to the Kootenay area, however. It was also the forced home for seventy-five hundred Canadians during World War II, when people were herded into camps because they were unlucky enough to be of Japanese extraction.

By 1982 these controversies had blended into the background as public attention locally shifted towards land-use conflicts. The best known issue concerned a proposal by the Valhalla Wilderness Society to preserve from logging the Valhallas mountain range, which rises majestically from the west shore of Slocan Lake. The Valhallas — a range deriving its name from Norse mythology as a magnificent palace, home for dead warriors, ruled by the god Odin — have only recently emerged from the glacial era and in fact glaciers are still present on the mountains. Soils are young and, although there are stands of timber, those stands are expensive to get at, because roadbuilding on the terrain is an expensive proposition. Herb Hammond thinks that the scenic slopes offer only marginal timber values. The Valhalla Wilderness Society, based in New Denver just across Slocan Lake, has estimated road costs at $100,000 per mile. Hammond put the figure at $200,000 on average, although he says some locales would present engineers with challenges that would push road costs as high as $400,000 per mile. The forestry teacher and consultant noted that road costs could not be justified given the limited amount of timber: "What you need is an elevator to get up to where the trees are."[52]

At the southern end of Slocan Lake sits the town of Slocan, a community of modest size where Slocan Forest Products runs a sawmilling operation. One of the hot controversies surrounding

the Slocan Valley plan has been whether the park proposal for
the Valhallas would put a wood supply squeeze on the Slocan
sawmill, an important employer in the valley. As early as 1976
the B.C. Forest Service warned that the removal of the Valhallas
from timber production would cost over $700,000 a year and
could result in direct loss of twenty-nine jobs and the indirect
loss of forty-two more.[53] By late 1980 Ike Barber of Slocan Forest
Products was issuing gloomy forecasts of shrinking forest land
base, reduction of the Allowable Annual Cut, less logging and
less jobs. In early 1981 Barber's company sent a letter to all its
employees and contract loggers predicting possible job cuts if
the Valhalla Wilderness Proposal went through. Barber's letter
went on to urge workers to write their provincial parliamen-
tarians and express their concern.[54] This tactic was enough to
draw protests from the local International Woodworkers of
America and activists organizing public participation in the
formulation of the joint provincial/regional land use planning
process.

Such a perspective did not sit well with provincial
The Slocan Valley has been something of a hotbed of agitation for community control of resources since at least 1974,
when a group of local residents completed a detailed study of
forestry in the Valley. The Slocan Valley Community Forest
Management Project found that trees in the area took an average
of eighty-eight years to reach the point at which they could be
marketed for timber. The citizens' study contrasted this to the
life of the previous provincial (Socred) government, which was
in power for twenty years. It also focused on the fact that the
previous two logging companies in the local Public Sustained
Yield Unit were each there for a span of just six years. The final
report of the study summed up the implications of these factors:
"The local community represents the only visible group with a
binding interest in the long-term sustenance of this valley's
resources, for it is they who will have to live with the results of
our management policies, good or bad."[55]

Such a perspective did not sit well with provincial
authorities, who ignored the report's principal recommendations that a resource management committee of local agencies
and residents be formed to manage all the valley resources and
take charge of budgets. The Slocan Valley residents were concerned about budgetary matters because their research had
revealed significant capital leakage from the region. In 1973 the

Corky Evans, a logger from Winlaw, B.C., advocates more local control to ensure better forest management. "There are people all over B.C. who perceive they're being ripped off to service the Lower Mainland."

Victoria government spent $235,000 on resource management in the Slocan PSYU but collected $545,000 in stumpage revenue and over $1 million in total revenues from all logging and milling activities there.[56]

But though the report was not greeted enthusiastically by the province, the government could not ignore the continuing political heat being generated around resource issues. So it agreed to set up the land-use planning program and, pending the completion of the planning process, slapped a moratorium on logging in the Valhallas.

When Susie Hammond said she thought the government was using this local planning process in an attempt to put one over on a group of Russians and hippies, she was referring in the latter case to an influx of young urbanites who arrived to settle in the Slocan Valley in the 1970s. Generally speaking, this group was looking for an alternative to the frenetic pace of urban life and the pollution of industrial society. Some of these people brought with them the ability to articulate their dissatisfaction with the way the environment was being abused. They found in the Slocan Valley an existing community of people who were practising small-scale agriculture — growing crops and keeping a little livestock — to supplement their incomes. They found this type of local self-sufficiency an attractive alternative to city life, in much the same way that the Doukhobors had sought freedom from religious persecution in Russia.

One such Slocan Valley resident is Corky Evans, a contract logger and local community activist who worked on the preparation of the community forest management plan in 1974. His experiences cutting timber, fighting forest fires and doing research on the management of the valley's timber resources have propelled him into a key position in the development of a political coalition built around the notion of local power in the development of local resources and participation in the planning process. Evans sees the conflict over resources very much in regional terms, as a contest between the centralized power of the B.C. Forest Service and the aspirations of the Slocan Valley people he represents on the Regional District political authority. "We're not unique at all," Evans observes as he looks out over the valley from his home just above the town of Winlaw. "There are people all over B.C. who perceive they're being ripped off to service the Lower Mainland."[57]

In an attempt to bring a fresh approach to logging, Evans and his partner attempted to make a living by using horses to skid the logs they had cut. Their hope was that this would enable them to log certain stands in need of selective thinning, a task skidders or bulldozers (caterpillar tractors, or "cats" to the initiated) could not perform, being too bulky and cumbersome. According to Evans, the experiment failed when the Forest Service would not agree to the more flexible stumpage arrangement that would have made the venture a paying proposition. After a couple of years working with their Percherons, Evans and his partner were forced to abandon the experiment and buy their own cat. The affair served to confirm Evans' suspicions about the Forest Service as an inflexible, over-centralized institution concerned primarily with collecting revenues for the provincial government.

Evans' hopes for the viability of a return to the horse as a logging tool were based on his analysis of the microclimate and how it affects some Kootenay forest sites. Like fellow valley resident Herb Hammond, Evans believed that logging had to be designed to suit the forest. He felt he should be able to use horses to log some of the gentle slopes at low elevations — sites which, with heavy water retention early in the year, germinate large numbers of trees. These trees grow rapidly for thirty or forty years, until they overstock the site, monopolize all the sunlight and take too much water from the soil. When this happens, growth slows down and the trees start to become stunted. Nature's response is to thin the forest by itself, using tools such as tree mortality brought on by conditions like Douglas fir root rot and white pine blister rust. Once this happens the timber becomes useless for conventional commercial applications. What Evans wanted to do with his horses was to move in and selectively thin such stands before the wood became unuseable. This would have yielded a marketable volume of timber while at the same time opening up the forest enough to enable the remaining trees to flourish for another sixty years, eventually producing another healthy crop.

"It was our belief that there was a niche for horses around here," Evans recalls, noting that there are 100,000 acres of this type of forest site within travelling distance of his mountainside home. "The system isn't applicable to the steep slopes or the deep mountain valleys. There's a lot of places it doesn't belong and a lot it does."[58]

The scheme made sense in forestry terms and could produce economic wood, so Evans was eventually able to secure the backing of local government foresters. But a proposal to get into it in a big way on an area licensed to a nearby firm floundered because Forest Service accountants refused to allow it. According to Evans, they could not see their way through to permitting the proposed operation to pay a lower stumpage than conventional logging with cats or skidders. The money men were anxious about establishing a precedent which would have allowed different logging systems to pay different tax rates.

As it turned out, the structure of the system was too rigid to allow for the flexibility the forest resource needs if it is to be treated in a rational and sustained manner. Evans' plan would have produced benefits in the short term (logs thinned from the forest) and in the longer term (a healthy stand six decades down the line). But when the idea was scuttled Evans and his partner, under a heavy debt burden, were forced to sell their horses, buy a cat and haul logs from the forest just like the other small logging contractors in the Kootenays.

Afterwards, when he wasn't out looking for logging jobs, Evans continued his involvement in the local planning process, hoping that local resource control would pave the way for the versatility that sound forest management requires. In 1981 he ran against an activist from the Valhallas Wilderness Society in a local election. While the two candidates, on the surface, shared the same environmental concerns, the wilderness advocate ran a campaign centred primarily on the Valhallas park proposal. Evans, pushing for integrated local resource control, thought it would be a mistake to decide the wilderness park issue in isolation from other Slocan Valley resource questions. Evans won the election, but the struggle over who would have the final say in resource management continued.

CORKY EVANS, SUSIE AND HERB HAMMOND and many of their Slocan Valley neighbours involved in the dispute with the province have been basically fighting for the stability of their community and along with it the perpetuation of the plant and animal communities so important to their economic survival. They don't want to repeat the history of the defunct silver mines of the Slocan Valley and the ghost towns which have become something of an area tourist attraction. In the political wrangling over environmental and resource issues, many people think there are only strict choices between primitive wilderness preserves and degraded, cutover forest sites. But Evans has a different notion. "Don't listen to people who say 'He's an ecofreak' or 'He rapes and pillages the forest'," he warns. "Environment, ecology and economics all come from the same root word meaning 'household' — and it's all about community."[59]

But this perspective is not shared by the powers that be in Canadian forestry. Their reaction to the environmental crisis and the environmental movement has been to see the problems as difficulties in communication, to be solved by imparting their objective expertise to a gullible public easily led astray by the scare tactics of "environmentalists". Edward Fellows, a mainstream forester who was once president of the Canadian Institute of Forestry addressed these problems of communications in his 1975 Weyerhauser Lecture* to the forestry faculty at the University of Toronto.

In a talk called "The Moulding of Public Opinion on Forest Management: What Public? Whose Opinion?" Fellows urged his audience of foresters to be more aggressive in using their "objective" expertise to inform the public about the state of its forests. He seemed a trifle defensive about the image of foresters that "a few glib, unperceptive, self-appointed experts" had created by promoting images of environmental degradation. "Somehow we have to convince the public that we know far more about the forest, its components and its functions than the handful of writers and broadcasters who expound and moralize on these subjects with fulsome self-righteousness," he urged. "We shall not succeed by resorting to oversimplification or scare tactics; that is the route the media have chosen and which has fostered so many misleading and sometimes invidious misconceptions."[60]

Rachel Carson, who played an important role in the public creation of environmental awareness, saw the same tendency toward public misconceptions that Fellows worried about. But she saw the trend from a different perspective. In 1962 she wrote in *Silent Spring* that the general public, confronted with clear evidence of environmental damage due to pesticides, is often

---

* Washington-based Weyerhauser is one of the world's largest forest products corporations. The firm tries to cultivate a good public image in the same way it cultivates trees and enjoys a reputation as being very concerned with environmental issues. *Audubon* Magazine titled an article on the firm: "The Best of the S.O.B.s". The company is on the cutting edge of intensive agro-forestry in the United States. It is also quite aggressive in selling its products. In 1979 *Forbes*, a U.S. business magazine, reported that Weyerhauser had been hit with $54 million in fines and damages by the U.S. government for illegal price fixing.

"fed little tranquillizing pills of half-truth". But Carson did not blame the media. "This is an era of specialists, each of whom sees his own problem and is unaware of or intolerant of the larger frame into which it fits," she concluded. "It is also an era dominated by industry, in which the right to make a dollar at whatever cost is seldom challenged."[61]

8, All Fall Down

EORGE MAREK paces the corridor in the downtown office highrise twenty-one floors above Toronto's Chinatown. The only sign of vegetation is a dry-looking indoor fern flourishing in the fluorescent glow. The veteran Ontario forester would prefer to be out tramping about in the bush surrounded by something other than potted office plants. His unease is betrayed by a fidgety manner and a number of forcefully-voiced complaints about the effects of the big city on his stomach condition.

Marek hates the city but he has come to town on a late summer day in 1982 to give testimony supporting Don MacAlpine before a provincial grievance settlement board. MacAlpine worked under Marek in the government forestry offices of the Nipigon district until the younger forester was fired by the Ministry of Natural Resources (MNR) for allegedly breaching his oath of office. As soon as MacAlpine was let go, in March 1982, Marek immediately and publicly rose to his support. Marek has never been too popular with his bosses.

The MacAlpine case made a lot of waves around the Lakehead, creating ripples felt as far off as Toronto. It was a complex story. At issue were timber rights on the Black Bay peninsula, a finger of land jutting down into Lake Superior near Nipigon in northwestern Ontario. Local operators of small-scale logging outfits had been led to believe that the area was being reserved for their own use, a fact confirmed by the chief of the ministry's Timber Sales Branch.[1] And, according to government correspondence that Don MacAlpine later leaked to his provincial member of parliament, Jack Stokes, MNR had in April 1981 turned down an application by Domtar for cutting rights on and around the Black Bay peninsula because the government already had "other commitments" there.

George Marek and Don MacAlpine were more than a little surprised, then, when a memo came down to them six weeks later, on June 5, 1981, from the Deputy Minister in Toronto. The memo instructed ministry staff to give "top priority" to a request by Ken Buchanan's timber interests for wood in the Nipigon area. Buchanan, a blossoming local entrepreneur, was known to have been putting the heat on the foresters at the Nipigon MNR office to come up with timber for him in the Black Bay area. The memo from head office in Toronto promoting Buchanan's application made no mention of the small operators who also needed timber there.[2]

The affair presented an interesting conjuncture of forestry and politics. George Marek and Don MacAlpine felt they did not want to be rushed into allowing the Buchanan interests to start cutting around Black Bay. Their reasoning was simple. The government's Forest Resources Inventory (FRI) for the area was, they felt, drastically overestimating the amount of available wood. If a cutting licence were issued to Buchanan on the basis of such an inventory, the principles of sustained yield forestry would be defeated. The FRI is used to calculate the Allowable Annual Cut, itself the basis for managing the forest for perpetual yield. Developing an AAC on the basis of an overinflated forest inventory would be like trying to live off the interest of an ever-dwindling bank account — a losing proposition in the long run.

In spite of the unease the front-line foresters felt about the amount of timber actually available, the administrative foresters in Toronto kept the pressure on MacAlpine to go ahead and use the inventory anyway. Apparently, middle management officers were feeling the pressure from their superiors to help out Buchanan with his wood supply problems. MacAlpine testified later at the Toronto hearings that one of his bosses, in urging him to get on with the task at hand and develop a licence that would accommodate Buchanan, told him that Buchanan "had connections".[3]

After details of the story were leaked to the press in late 1981, small-scale contract loggers around Nipigon were, not surprisingly, upset about the possibility of losing what limited timber the Ontario government was making available to them. Ever since the government started signing Forest Management Agreements with the big, integrated pulp and paper companies, independent operators had been feeling a timber supply squeeze. David Bak, a logger from Pass Lake who helped start the North Shore Citizens' Committee for Responsible Forest Management after the MacAlpine affair became public, says he was told for years by MNR that he could not expand his operation due to lack of timber. "Then all of a sudden they started considering giving this whole Black Bay peninsula to Buchanan," Bak says indignantly. One of his fellow contractors, Lief Gran, calls Buchanan "the last of the timber barons". Gran, a mechanic by trade, considers that to be a small logging operator you have to be a jack of all trades — faller, skidder operator, mechanic, driver, forest technician. "But the most important thing is to have a sharp pencil," Gran concludes. "Buchanan has a very sharp pencil."

"And a long arm to work it with," adds David Bak wryly.[4]

Talk of timber barons, political influence and declining timber reserves seems to be a throwback to the heyday of the buccaneering timber operators, when the "old Tory timber ring" ran the show around the Lakehead. To get your hands on a timber berth back then, you had to have an "in" with the local Conservative Party bagman.[5] It is now the Progressive Conservative Party but campaign contribution records for the 1981 provincial election reveal that Buchanan interests paid $1,000 to the campaign of Leo Bernier, a Tory politician in the region and former Minister of Natural Resources who later became Minister of Northern Affairs.[6] *Plus ça change . . .*

But the entire incident was more than a revelation of yet another timber scandal — one of many dotting the historical landscape in Canada. The characters and issues involved reveal much about the actual state of forestry today and the way the government treats the public forest. The forestry profession, the administration of public timber, wilderness conservation and control over the resource are all factors connected with what became an important regional affair but never quite made it onto the national stage.

North of Lake Superior, George Marek practised forestry for the Ontario government for over 30 years before being squeezed out of his job. "Our system is built on maximizing exploitation today. The system is going to exploit it right down to the last."

KEN BUCHANAN WANTED TIMBER from the Black Bay area, known
to contain stands of red and white pine, in order to supply a
sawmill he ran at Sapawe in the Atikokan area west of Thunder
Bay. In 1981 Buchanan had bought the sawmill from Domtar, the
same company he apparently edged out in both the contest for
Nipigon area timber and the jockeying for a sympathetic ear at
the top levels of the Ministry of Natural Resources. Domtar,
number two in the Canadian forest industry behind
MacMillan-Bloedel, had sold out to Buchanan because the
Sapawe mill was facing timber shortages and was in need of an
expensive refit of its equipment. The big Montreal-based firm felt
the half-dozen years of wood supply remaining could not justify
the capital expenditure necessary to get the aging mill into competitive shape.[7]

The mill at Sapawe had been facing wood supply problems
since the early 1970s, when Bill Davis' Tory government, faced
with pressure from wilderness buffs who wanted to maintain
the unspoilt character of Quetico Park, prohibited logging in
that canoeists' paradise. The announcement of the logging ban
was a high-profile event, coming as it did in the midst of a
strong public campaign by the parks advocates. By the end of
the decade the Atikokan area had been hit hard by the closure of
Canadian Pacific's Steep Rock iron mine in 1979, when six hundred jobs evaporated. The next year another local employer,
Caland Ore, shut down, putting another four hundred out of
work. The additional threat of timber shortages at the biggest
sawmill in the area, then, was surely a major concern to a government faced with a province-wide economic tailspin.

But any move to allow Buchanan to start logging in Quetico
would certainly have been politically embarrassing, especially
given the pristine reputation of the park and Davis' previous
logging ban. In addition, the organized wilderness lobby was
pledged to defend the concession wrung from the Tories a
decade earlier. So it seemed natural for Buchanan and the government to cast their eyes eastward toward the unallocated
timber in the Black Bay area. If Buchanan could come up with a

timber licence, he could take it to the bank as collateral for the loan he needed to spruce up the Sapawe mill.[8] Again, it appears things hadn't changed much since the 1920s when Premier Howard Ferguson signed over huge tracts of Ontario timberland to paper companies in order to satisfy their Chicago bankers. The forest was still an adjunct of the mill, necessary for a loan guarantee.

Back in the days of the timber barons, forestry considerations were not too important. There still seemed to be trees for all. But by 1981, with growing unease over impending timber shortages, the public was likely to become rather edgy when the facts surrounding backroom timber dealings came to light. When Don MacAlpine was fired, the citizens' committee that included David Bak and Lief Gran was able to gather fifteen hundred signatures on a petition in support of an individual who the small logging operators felt was standing up for his principles and at the same time defending their interests.

Don MacAlpine had been engaged in forestry work for MNR for less than a year when he became so frustrated with the pressures from his superiors — pressures he knew were politically motivated — that he felt compelled to take the matter to his own political representative. Time and again he had told his bosses (as later time and again he would repeat to the grievance board hearing his appeal) that he could not in good professional conscience work out a licensing plan for the Black Bay area on the basis of the existing forest inventory.

Both MacAlpine and George Marek had firsthand reasons for believing that the FRI was seriously askew. Marek had walked the peninsula frequently and knew there was not very much timber on the ground. The inventory itself is derived from aerial photographs, sometimes updated by computer. When MacAlpine sent out teams to cruise the timber in Hele Township at the top of the peninsula, they came back to the Nipigon office complaining that trees recorded in the FRI did not exist, that species were often mislabelled in the inventory and that timber density estimates were far out of line. When MacAlpine walked through the area a month later he saw the discrepancies for himself, further heightening his concerns about the inventory.[9]

Yet senior forestors at MNR, who MacAlpine said never questioned his timber estimates, continued to press him to move the licensing process along quickly. And the Buchanan interests kept coming up with timber supply figures far above those MacAlpine had developed. The young Lakehead University graduate could only continue to insist that he could not trust the FRI, that things would have to wait until a detailed ground survey was completed. Marek and MacAlpine even came up with 27,000 cunits they said Buchanan could take as a "liquidation cut". But in November 1981 MacAlpine got a call from Toronto. On the line was the Regional Forester from the MNR office in Thunder Bay, who wanted MacAlpine to back up his concerns about the accuracy of the FRI and told him to be in Thunder Bay three days later to do so. At that meeting, MacAlpine was told about Buchanan's "connections" and instructed him to come up with a ten-year licensing program based on the existing forest inventory. A frustrated MacAlpine could only respond that the directive was "professionally unacceptable" to him. He drove back to Nipigon and wrote a memo to the regional officer reiterating his concern and refusing to accept responsibility for any licence issued. When George Marek passed MacAlpine's memo on to their boss, George Koistonen, the statement was rejected as being "too emotional".[10]

At this point MacAlpine felt stonewalled. He later told the board hearing his appeal that, faced with political pressure, he felt he had no choice but to take the matter to his own political representative, NDP member for Nipigon Jack Stokes. MacAlpine provided Stokes with copies of MNR documents backing up his case and the matter was soon aired, both on the floor of the provincial legislature and in the local press. MacAlpine also filed charges of professional misconduct against the Regional Forester, the Deputy Minister of Natural Resources and two other foresters from the Thunder Bay office. The charges were sent to the licensing body for foresters, the Ontario Professional Foresters' Association. Three months later MacAlpine was fired (or, in delicate administrative parlance, "terminated") for breaching his oath of office. Fortunately for MacAlpine, though, the Ontario Public Service Employees Union backed his appeal against this action on the basis of freedom of information and the public's right to know what government was doing.

DON MACALPINE RECOUNTS THE STORY from the beginning to
end in painstakingly explicit detail, his fingers working nervously. The hands aren't those of an administrative forester.
They're rough and cracked from working on a treeplanting contract he successfully bid for in an MNR tender offer, after his
dismissal. He lives with Patti MacAlpine and their two pre-
school children in a double trailer in Nipigon, just across the bay
from Domtar's Red Rock mill. Patti MacAlpine saved up enough
money doing home daycare to afford the airfare to attend the
grievance hearings in Toronto. She has a derisive appraisal of
the entire situation: "Any idiot can see what's going on here —
politics." Another MNR forester, Glen Swant, came down from
northern Ontario with the MacAlpines to testify on Don's
behalf. Swant made the journey from Red Lake with the knowledge that his support for his colleague would not exactly
enhance his career possibilities. "I'm already euchred just
because I'm sitting here," he observed during the hearing. "But
Don is doing a magnificent thing. I hope it works out."[11]

What Swant was getting at is the inclination of many government foresters to go with the flow, not to rock the boat when
faced with the kind of tough choices MacAlpine made. For those
with degrees in forestry from one of Canada's six professional
schools, there are few career roads open. A young graduate can
work either for industry or for government. Most other opportunities, such as teaching or consulting, present themselves only
with experience or further education. Given such limited possibilities it is perhaps understandable that few young foresters
— especially with family obligations — are vocal critics of industry and government forest practices — at least in public.

Career paths for the "successful" are conventionally seen as
leading upwards to administrative positions, with raises in pay
the further you get from the forest. Most ambitious young foresters advance quickly from the level of the practising silviculturalist and soon lose the ability to find the time or opportunity
to walk about in the woods. The unit forester position Don

MacAlpine occupied in 1981 was subject to a 30 per cent turnover rate in 1974, according to Ken Armson, Chief Forester for MNR when MacAlpine was fired. Armson noted that achieving solid management at MNR would be "an uphill struggle in light of such major movement."[12] In its dissection of provincial forestry in 1947, the Kennedy Commission observed of local staff in the north: "They are lucky if they see a division chief for a few hours once a year and several years may elapse between visits from a Deputy Minister." Armson found that this tendency had become more serious since that time with the expansion in the number of head office specialists.[13]

When he disclosed documents supporting his concern about the adequacy of the forest inventory, Don MacAlpine knew the action could well result in his being hung out to dry. No provincial forestry service would likely hire an individual fired from another government, with a reputation as a troublemaker. And the private sector would be reluctant to take on such a forester, partly because company foresters have to spend so much of their time dealing with their opposite numbers on the government side, working out the day-to-day details of licensing, cutting and management. Blackball might be too strong a word here. Perhaps "informal proscription" would be more appropriate.

It all boiled down to a wrangle over inventory accuracy and the resulting validity of allowable cut estimates, which were being pushed through to satisfy the Buchanan interests over the protests of local logging operators. To forestry insiders, such a dispute came as no surprise. It has been widely recognized for years that Canadian governments have only the most vague notions of how well their forest warehouses are stocked. In his landmark 1978 study of forest management in Canada*, forest consultant Les Reed recommended a complete overhaul of the inventory system, noting serious deficiencies that were impeding forest management. Reed called for a "wholesale reassessment" of allowable cuts in light of these defects, pointing out that for decades Canadian forest policy has been "of an informal character".[14]

The MacAlpine affair presents a case study in how this informal policy works: backroom political dealings, administrative decisions unconnected with forestry principles or the actual

* See chapter 4, p. 100

situation in the woods, lack of accurate data. Don MacAlpine attempted to follow the formal rules of forestry he had been taught at Lakehead University, rules he still believed in. In doing so he apparently ran up against an unwritten rule governing forestry in Canada: Shut up and obey orders even if you think they contribute to the butchering of the bush. But MacAlpine believed he had responsibilities over and above his duty to do as he was told.

"They were preparing a management plan to lead people down the garden path, convincing them that everything is okay," he said in his quiet, straightforward fashion. "That's wrong. It's the public forest. The public pays my wages. I'm responsible to them."[15] This particular civil servant's belief in his responsibility to something beyond the wishes of his bureaucratic and political masters got him fired.

At his appeal hearing MacAlpine faced a hostile line of questioning from government lawyer Christopher Riggs. Riggs attempted to sketch a picture of MacAlpine as a young, inexperienced and naive employee who just wouldn't do what he was told. He argued that MacAlpine should simply have gotten on with the job and come up with a licensing plan for the Black Bay area that would ensure jobs for the workers at Buchanan's Sapawe Mill.

When Riggs' questioning took a paternalistic tone, inferring that Bill Foster, Deputy Minister of Natural Resources, and the other government foresters were far more experienced than MacAlpine, it seemed to upset the young man's sense of what constituted a real, practising forester. The usually soft-spoken MacAlpine jumped on Riggs' inference, refusing to acknowledge that the Toronto administrator was an experienced forester. When Riggs persisted in this direction, referring to MacAlpine's "foot-dragging" in the face of explicit instructions from his experienced bosses, MacAlpine became uncharacteristically acerbic. He reiterated his concern about the reliability of the inventory and pointed out that his bosses had "questionable experience". But in one sense he did agree: "If you call experience climbing a ladder, then yes, they are more than I am.[16]

MACALPINE'S IDEA OF WHAT CONSTITUTED an experienced forester most likely emerged from his dealings with his immediate superior, George Marek. Marek is something of a curiosity in Canadian forestry. For one thing, he has seen fit to remain working in the same local forest region for over thirty years, ever since he came to Canada from his native Czechoslovakia in 1950. In the old country, Marek's father was a forester and his grandfather both a forester and a gamekeeper. The European tradition of forestry is evident in Marek's approach to forest management, in a way similar to that of Michael Trew, the former B.C. forester.

Marek, a spry sixty-plus years of age, likes to spend his holidays walking around in the forests he manages, hunting birds and generally taking in the scenery. Marek brings what he likes to call a "holistic" approach to forestry, a view that sees the forest as a set of interrelated natural cycles including not only trees but also wildlife, shrubs, insects and a host of other flora and fauna.

Marek comes to this approach via the historical evolution of European forestry. In contrast to Canadian forestry, introduced as a field of technical specialization into an emerging capitalist society around the turn of the twentieth century, European forestry has its roots in feudal and even pre-feudal times. In Germany, where forestry is often said (especially by German foresters) to have first developed, the forest of the pre-feudal era was still common property, which could be used by people who needed both wood and game to survive. In this way ownership of the forest was regarded in much the same way as it was by Canada's native peoples.

But with the growth of a more centralized feudal power, the nobility established their large baronial estates comprising not only arable land and pasture but forest as well. The new forest "owners" wanted to restrict access to the forest to preserve an abundant supply of game. Indeed, "riding to hounds" and the right to the chase are often associated with the landed gentry and their exclusive right to hunt on their woodland preserves.

Those at the top of the feudal heap needed agents to enforce these rights against the incursions of the common folk. Gradually the role of gamekeeper emerged, as the enforcer of feudal restrictions, a policeman of the bush who tried to keep out poachers. These agents also administered the chase and gradually, as the right to control the hunt was extended to the right to collect wood, came to be administrators of the growing forest. By the eighteenth century in Germany there were two types of forest supervisors: the forest guards (holzgerechte Jaeger) who were developing a practical knowledge of wood and forests; and the cameralists, men from the upper echelons of society who had little practical knowledge but in any case were responsible for recording information filtering up from below. This initial growth in the written body of knowledge came at a time when the importance of the hunt was starting to give way to a recognition of the forest as a vital source of wood fibre for shelter and heat. [17]

George Marek's grandfather was perhaps an heir to this tradition, for as feudal power waned and the accumulated knowledge of forests slowly grew into a separate science based on the cultivation of trees, there also developed a group of silvicultural specialists who still had an appreciation of all the other aspects of forest life. Marek, who was "doing forestry" steadily since his childhood, brought that knowledge to Canada. Now he sees himself as a renegade swimming against the mainstream of Canadian forestry, particularly the conventional approach of industrial forestry that has everything to do with specialized expertise and little to do with a general appreciation of the natural forces at play in the forest — an appreciation that only comes after years of practical experience. It's the experience Marek has developed by staying in the same place for so long that sets him apart from many of his colleagues.

Clearly, Marek has not followed the well-trodden path to the top. A scrappy individual with a pronounced accent that doesn't prevent him from getting his point across in a rapid-fire manner, he boasts about being the Ontario government's longest-serving field forester still on the job. Marek knows he will never be promoted: He has sentenced himself to stay where he started. But that's the way he wants it. "The guys who started with me are now superdirectors making fifty thousand a year," he says. "They think I'm a stupid jerk. 'Look at that crazy Czech living twenty-five years in Beardmore, bringing up two kids' — that's what they say when they talk about Marek. But my two kids are both studying forestry. . . . I don't mind."[18] Though a minority perspective, Marek's is a valuable one, an outlook that would do more than innumerable consultants' reports and new funding programs if it were shared by more foresters and put into practice on a broad scale.

In the Kootenays of British Columbia, Herb Hammond, a generation younger than George Marek, tells the same story. Hammond reflects that he's worked in the forest for fifteen years and every year he is amazed at all the new, simple, practical things he learns by spending as much time as he can in the bush. "I'm glad — my pocketbook might not be glad but the rest of me is glad — that I retain that bias, that I'm happier out there doing my job," Hammond observes. "As long as my legs and my lungs can still do it, then that's where I want to do the job. Because otherwise it won't get done right." Hammond says this view of forestry is not shared by too many of his associates. "I'm looked at like, 'Who the hell wants to go out there for four months in the summer and walk straight up and down hills? You gotta be crazy, Herb! You're forty years old. Why do you do this?'"[19]

The reason he does it, Hammond says, is that a forester is "a bastardized sort of creature" who knows something of soils, plant physiology, road engineering and ecosystem management. Canada seems short of such creatures. When they emerge, they do so after making a conscious effort *not* to follow the customary paths to what are generally accepted as the pinnacles of success in the profession. One of the principal reasons for this may well be that in order to develop the practical expertise it's necessary to stay in hinterland Canada. This frequently means remote or northern communities, or at least communities far from the major cities.

Helen and George Marek *want* to stay in their small home in Beardmore, a dwelling the visitor from the south can easily pick out because of the potted spruce seedlings sitting on the hood of the pickup truck parked in the front yard. But it can be very hard for families to remain rooted in these towns for a long time, especially since there are very limited opportunities for women at a time when many families need two incomes. "Up north it's primarily a man's world," says Helen Marek. "And it's tough on women."[20] She came to northern Ontario from Toronto as a Red Cross nurse before Beardmore got water and sewage, when the town had an economic base consisting of mining and logging. There was a working gold mine nearby, and Domtar and Abitibi were running up to ten logging camps between them and employing hundreds of pulp cutters. By the 1980s, Beardmore had shrunk and like many northern towns had become a fuel stop on the highway for southern Canadian motorists travelling to somewhere else. Logging trucks passed through regularly, also on their way to mills elsewhere. But the signs of past prosperity were evident. An abandoned and forlorn-looking movie theatre recalled Peter Bogdanovich's *Last Picture Show*, a movie about a decaying community in the Texas desert.

But at least in the early 1980s the Lake Nipigon fishery was still operating and there were a few steady government jobs and more than a few make-work government job programs. Beardmore still supported five hundred people, had a library, a bar and an active social life. But the fact remains, its people would have had a more secure future had the productive forest sites in the area been treated as renewable resources by the government and by Abitibi and Domtar.

As a longtime resident of Beardmore, George Marek hasn't found it difficult to link the stability of the community to the logging and forest management practices he's so familiar with. He points to fire-derived stands of jack pine growing well in some places, to second-growth stands of poplar, aspen and birch mixed with jack pine in untreated or poorly-treated cutovers. Marek uses 2,4-D as a herbicide to help keep down the poplar growth. In direct competition with the conifers, poplar shoots up quickly, retarding the development of the desired fibre that pulpmills are designed to use. The herbicide acts to disrupt plant growth, causing sporadic cell elongation, and killing the broad-leaved species off temporarily. Marek is uneasy about using the chemical because he doesn't know its effects on other aspects of the ecosystem. He doesn't know if it will harm the nitrogen-fixing bacteria that help to enrich the soil. He does know that untended clearcut areas will produce trees, but not necessarily the species, sizes and shapes desired. Untended land often becomes "Not Sufficiently Restocked" land. As a result, under "conifer release programs", Canadian foresters, along with George Marek, use herbicides to weed their forest farms.

George Marek has a pragmatic attitude towards the application of the defoliants. "I don't like to do it but what the hell?" he says. He would rather promote the growth of conifers by tailoring cutting methods to discourage the growth of deciduous trees in the first place. But, he says, "I am presented with this mess of poor management for the past thirty years. I'm trying to get something growing, doing my best to establish a crop."[21]

So Marek tries to do what he can, making the best of a bad situation. His outspokenness, his eagerness to stay in one place for so long, his accumulated practical knowledge — these characteristics have earned him the respect of many of the foresters he works with. Vic Timmer, a forestry professor and researcher at the University of Toronto, says when he works with Marek he can draw on Marek's knowledge of what a stand has been or is likely to become rather than being handicapped by only looking at the forest at a single point in its development. He compares Marek to a farmer who can see exactly what is happening over the course of a crop rotation. "George spent twenty-five years in one area and never got higher," says Timmer. "He couldn't get higher. He's been red-circled for all those years."[22]

Marek is indeed up against a stone wall, just like the one his young protégé Don MacAlpine faced over the Black Bay peninsula issue. His long-range view, coupled with his experience in the forest and the bureaucracy, have allowed him to survive in the system. Yet he finds it frustrating. The tensions have given him recurring stomach problems. When he admonishes industry to give silviculture a chance, when he warns about the problems with simply clearcutting and replanting — "any fool can do that" — Marek is confronted with the harsh political realities of forestry in Canada. He tells of the time years ago when he was told by the president of one forest products company, the Marathon Corporation, "Mr. Marek, you talk about ecology. Do you know what I call ecology? Ecology means jobs in our mill. I hope we're going to keep a good relationship with MNR."[23]

George Marek has a colourful assortment of epithets to pin on foresters who don't rock the boat and who conform to the demands of the men who run the mills, executives he calls the "draculas" and "sharks" of the industry. Depending on his mood, Marek refers to his conventional colleagues variously as *busboys* and *lackeys*. Any label connoting subservience will do. The term busboy as applied to foresters, however, isn't unique to Marek. It was also used by University of British Columbia forester Jack Walters in his wrap-up speech to a national forest regeneration conference in 1977. The outspoken professor reflected at the time that the "busboy" professional foresters were not saying much about the deteriorating forest situation because they were looking for tips at a government-hosted forest banquet.[24]

In the midst of this metaphorical onslaught the most appropriate handle to describe the role of the forester has also been coined by George Marek. Bumping along a forest road, pointing out carefully-managed stands of conifers — "That's nice spruce. Isn't it beautiful?" — Marek refers to foresters as "warehousemen".[25] The image is telling: the forest as an industrial warehouse, a source of supply for other branches of industry, tended by a body of individuals whose job it is to supply wood on demand. The inventory in the warehouse is finite, but that is of little concern to the directors of the enterprise, private sector and government managers who tell the warehousemen how much fibre they need and when they need it.

When a forester is reluctant to fetch some more fibre from the warehouse, it can go poorly for that individual — witness Don MacAlpine. When MacAlpine was fired and orders came down to all staff not to comment on the case, Marek felt he had to publicly support his colleague because he believed MacAlpine was doing the job the way it was supposed to be done. Marek's own job was saved, apparently because of his long experience and reputation. But still he remained unrepentant, testifying with enthusiasm on MacAlpine's behalf as the junior forester tried to get his job back. In fact, Marek's public support of MacAlpine rankled his superiors and as a result of the affair he was shunted aside within the ministry, banished to an obscure posting with little responsibility. Relieved of his former position of authority, the most experienced practising silviculturalist within the provincial forest service could no longer make the same contribution to the forest management effort nor make waves and embarrass the government.

In the end, both MacAlpine and Marek were vindicated when MacAlpine won his grievance against the government.*

*MNR, less than pleased with this decision, subsequently appealed to the courts in yet another attempt to get rid of MacAlpine.

The grievance settlement board ruled that MacAlpine should be offered his job back and noted that he had been motivated by a sincere desire to uphold the sustained yield policies of the ministry.[26]

Despite this small victory, Marek is himself both unsure and uneasy about the future of the forest resource. His enthusiasm for his job vies with his experiences in the woods and his critical feelings about the government-industry nexus. Marek worries about what he calls the naïve optimism abroad in Canada, a sense that things in the forest — and in other fields — will somehow work out. His experience tells him you can't leave things up to government and business. And he gets frustrated when people tell him not to be so pessimistic.

"I say — those trees are dying on me," he gestures excitedly. "I like to be optimistic when I can. But when I see the run-down forest, the problems on a daily basis — how can I be an optimist? Everything I touch every day tells me I have problems."[27]

TWO OF THE MOST WELL-WORN CLICHÉS about Canadian forestry are that it is very important and that it is at a crossroads. Certainly, forests are vital to the nation's economy, the health of its environment and the enjoyment of its people. But it is far from clear that the crossroads has been reached. For in the industry procrastination has always prevailed. Even yet, in the words of Dr. Marcel Lortie of Laval University, "Forest management hardly goes beyond the harvesting of wood."[28] But the questions remain: What is the future of forestry in Canada? Is there a bright future for the woods or are the prospects as bleak as George Marek's experiences illustrate?

There are those who look at the changing nature of the traditional markets for Canadian forest products and see a shrinking demand. Various images are invoked. The electronic, paperless office. The death of the daily newspaper in the face of instant access to information through the home video screen. The use of video terminals to do home-shopping, and the associated use of electronic catalogues that would bring a reduction in paper-based advertising. The metal stud displacing the traditional softwood two-by-four. Such technological innovations, combined with the historical record of forest depletion and the continued complacency around forest renewal, point towards a forest-based industry in decline. Such a downturn would only happen over the long run, because the changes in the forest and the broad transformations affecting wood use would take years to manifest themselves. Should those changes eventually take hold, though, the future of many mills would indeed be bleak. And along with the mills, communities dependent on them would stand to lose. Other problems, particularly acid rain, could have profound effects on forest productivity. In the case of acid rain, factors such as site variability, species diversity and long time-frames for growth have made it difficult to pinpoint the exact effects. But it is feared that acid rain could contribute to accelerated leaching of valuable nutrients from the soil. [29] Since certain Canadian soils can be fragile and low in nutrients to begin with, they are highly likely to be prone to the ill effects of increased acidity.

Yet Canada's forest-based industries have never been static, judging both by the products turned out and the different species used to transform wood into saleable and useable goods. The products have run the gamut from naval masts to reconstituted building products like particleboard. The species used have included everything from oak and white pine to hemlock and even the much-maligned poplar. In recent times, people who have given thought to the future of the industry place a good deal of hope on fast-growing hardwood trees, which can be used for biomass energy production. New pulping processes have been developed to use "junk wood". Poplar, which grows with vigour on marginal farmlands in the east, lands now lying fallow in the wake of failed farming efforts, can even be used for the production of synthetic fuels.

In the past, uses for wood often changed as a result of technical and economic developments in other fields. Demand for square timber disappeared when the age of sail on the world's oceans was replaced by the age of steam power. Over the years wood heat gave way to warmth generated by coal, electricity, gas and oil. Lath for plaster walls is now a thing of the past, supplanted by drywall or gypsum. The wooden barrel has become merely a decorative item and even the brown paper bag, formerly used to wrap everything from groceries to garbage, has fallen from favour in post-industrial society, superseded by the plastic bag. Packaging now usually contains a mixture of plastic and cardboard.

In many of these cases, especially since World War II when the age of plastics arrived, the products that replaced wood were derived from non-renewable resources. Like the cheap energy that fuelled postwar industrial expansion, plastics are generally produced from fossil fuels. And in an early spate of petro-chemical optimism, there was oil to be found everywhere, from the Persian Gulf to Venezuela, from Nigeria to Alberta. Or so it seemed.

Now that it has become more apparent that the world's resources are finite and that non-renewable resources are on a rapid road to depletion, as well as getting more and more expensive, a renewable resource like wood is gaining increased attention. If carefully managed, a renewable resource can be made to last. One of the most obvious examples of the re-emergence of wood is in the field of space heating. A trip to any Canadian community close to a forested area will illustrate this. Over the past ten years, large woodpiles have once again sprung up in many backyards, replacing or supplementing oil tanks and electric heat in cities from Fredericton to Sudbury and Nelson. With people turning back to wood to save money and gain security in the face of much-publicized energy shortages* and volatile prices, the wood stove and furnace business has boomed. The solar energy stored in wood represents a reliable alternative to ever-increasing monthly hydro or fossil fuel bills. Besides, being able to cut your own winter fuel supply brings a welcome feeling of autonomy from powerful oil companies and monopolistic public utilities.

Of course, urban Canada and industrial Canada will never be able to rely on wood as a source of fuel. There, wood can sometimes be used to supplement other energy sources. But forest-based energy can do much to help bring the country closer to energy self-sufficiency. The forest industry has finally awoken from decades of self-satisfied slumber to the fact that it has been literally throwing or burning away tons of waste that could have been used for fuel. Gradually, the beehive burners that for years incinerated mill wastes are being replaced by co-generation sys-

*Whether or not the energy shortages were "real" is a different story.

tems by which mills use their own sawdust, bark and chips to provide some of the energy needed to power the mill. In Hearst, Ontario, one plywood mill uses a fluidized-bed gasification system to produce gas from wood waste and in turn uses the gas to help make the plywood. In the process, conventional fuels are replaced. The engineers who developed the system have high hopes for its application in other forestry-related operations as well as in burning everything from peanut shells to cotton-gin trash, and producing gas.[30] Down the road in Hearst, a plant owned by Shell Oil produces dried wood pellets from sawmill wastes. The pellets look like animal feed and in fact are produced in the same type of pellet mills used to manufacture pet and livestock food. The pellets are sold to pulpmills to replace petroleum, and the refined biomass fuel can even be marketed for residential space heating.[31] All across the country the forest industry is catching on to the energy potential of its principal raw material.[32]

Another potential use for wood is, ironically, in the production of the plastics that have in the past captured markets from wood. Fibres, adhesives, plastics — these widely-used products are derived almost entirely from fossil fuels. But both wood and fossil fuels have the same chemical base. The conversion of the carbohydrate polymers in wood to ethanol through fermentation is a step in the production of ethylene, one of the organic chemicals in widespread use as a building-block for plastic production. The cellulose that makes up much of the bulk of wood represents the basis for the future development of a wood-based chemical industry. Given dwindling supplies of conventional, petroleum-derived chemical feedstocks, one scientist told the eighth world forestry congress in Indonesia in 1978 that the wood chemical plant of the future would eventually be competitive with petroleum-based synthetics. He predicted that the wood chemical plant would use all parts of the tree in the same way packing plants use all parts of the animal carcass. "Even before the total exhaustion of the world's oil and gas supplies, the costs of these resources will increase to a level at which chemicals from alternative sources such as wood and coal will be able to compete with petrochemicals," the forest futurist predicted.[33]

One advantage of plants converting wood to energy or chemicals would be their relatively modest size, especially in comparison to the vast installations required to convert fossil fuels into useable products. Such plants would have to be local and decentralized in order to keep down the transportation costs of heavy, bulky wood. And the whole enterprise would have the potential of creating more jobs than the capital-intensive petrochemical industry, especially given the forestry measures needed to maintain a supply of wood.

Ross Silversides is one Canadian forester who is especially bullish on the prospects of using the nation's forests in new ways, particularly for energy. In his work with the National Research Council, Silversides identified three phases for biomass energy use. The first, already underway, involves the use of logging and mill residues for energy. The second would entail the actual harvesting of species now regarded as junk, such as poplar, for energy applications using conventional harvesting methods. The third phase would see the development of a distinct biomass energy industry unrelated to current uses of wood.[34] Such an industry would presumably involve the establishment of separate tree plantations, or energy farms. The use of trees to provide energy (or to manufacture chemicals) would, according to Silversides, change the nature of forestry practices. The products needed would be unlike sawlogs or pulpwood, because they would have no particular size or fibre specifications. The primary consideration would be the ability of the forest site to convert solar energy into wood fibre. And Silversides sees a potential advantage of biomass forest harvesting arising from the fact that all wood fibre — dead or diseased trees, tops, branches, all the "green junk" — can be used for these purposes. "Because biomass for energy has no specification, it will make it possible to 'low grade' our forests rather than 'high grade' them," he concludes hopefully.[35]

Such sanguine predictions for the future of Canadian forests might well bear up against the background of continuing needs for forest products: to provide paper products, paper for printing, wood for house construction, furniture, saunas and dozens of other purposes; for energy for home heating and industrial production; for chemicals and carvings. Canadian forest products should continue to find markets in other parts of the world, notably in Europe and the Third World, despite the competition of fast-growing species from southern climates and the onset of the electronic age. In Canada, forests will also no doubt continue to be valued for purposes of recreation and research, as a source of oxygen and wood fibre, as well as for simple enjoyment.

Yet to ensure all this on a renewable basis would require a flexible and variable approach to the handling of the resource. Some forest sites are best suited for mixed hardwood forests of oak, maple, walnut and other species, which provide the fine finishing wood that is so very expensive, even rare, in Canadian lumberyards. Other timberland could provide fast-growing hardwoods for conversion into energy to supplement local and regional needs. And the vast areas of forest land making up so much of the country's mid-northern region are capable of producing the long, strong fibre that in turn provides some of the finest quality wood pulp in the world. Besides all these material considerations, wood is pleasing to the eye and the touch, unlike many plastics. It's almost as if we could have it both ways: forests could be enjoyed by all, but we could also still have all the products made from trees. And so it goes. Or so it should go.

When the country seems to cast about perpetually for new and better industries to create more and more necessary employment, the forest industry appears to stand out as a pillar of economic strength. It is still arguably the most important industry in the country. Certainly it ranks first in providing both foreign trade and jobs. When the industry is at its peak, it puts nearly a million people to work through spinoff effects that stimulate other sectors of the economy. Its jobs are well-dispersed throughout the country and are particularly important in areas far from major cities. There are over three hundred communities in Canada whose only visible means of support is forestry and forest-related economic activity.[36]

So there are many reasons to share Ross Silversides' hopes for an end to the high-grading of the forests, to hope that at last the forest will be treated with a view to the potential it holds. In 1982 Les Reed succeeded in his crusade at Environment Canada to get more federal money pumped into forestry. Yet to get the maximum continuing use from the forest — the mix of fuelwood, hardwood, pulpwood, recreational, environmental and aesthetic values — would require an approach to forestry that took into account the complex variability of forest sites.

ALTHOUGH ITS FOREST PROBLEMS are real enough, among the countries of the world Canada is one of the most richly-endowed with land suited for growing trees, perhaps surpassed in this regard only by the Soviet Union. But as in Canada, the forests of many other nations, especially in the Third World, are facing encroachment from all sides — from landless peasants, from people in desperate need of cooking and heating fuel in an age of expensive energy, from industrial logging operations. And this attack is reducing the number of trees at an alarming rate.

The tropics are particularly prone to this tendency. Much concern about the future health of tropical forests has focused on the astounding destruction of the tropical moist forests. The vast band of rich jungle and rainforest in equatorial countries produces supplies of oxygen vital to the functioning of the bio-sphere. These forest ecosystems, far more varied and complex than those found in Canada, are being decimated by a mixture of logging, agriculture and increasing industrialization of both activities. Forest scientists examining the rate of this deforestation are confronted by a perplexing lack of adequate data, because forest inventories in countries such as Zaïre and Indonesia make Canadian estimates of available wood look sharp and accurate by comparison.* They have not been able to come up with a definite figure on conversion of tropical moist forests, but a 1980 report from the U.S. National Academy of Sciences indicated that long-standing United Nations' estimates of over 100,000 square kilo-meters of valuable forest exhausted annually may be far from accurate. The Academy estimated that the figure was in fact dou-ble that rate. The American scientists calculated a depletion rate of 40 hectares a minute, or 210,000 square kilometers per year.[38]

---

* In 1980 Indonesia was telling the world it had 1.2 million square kilometers of forest cover, a figure over twenty years old that had not been adjusted to take into account logging, shifting cultivation and other forms of forest removal. Zaïre has also been guessing wildly at how much forest it has, using data with an accuracy level of plus or minus 40 per cent.[37]

These forest losses do not occur just due to pressure from logging. The spread of agriculture is the most important cause of forest loss in the Third World, with farmers big and small steadily encroaching on the forest in the same way early Canadian settlers pushed back the frontier of timber. But the situtation in the twentieth-century tropics is far more serious than it was in nineteenth-century Canada. The rapid growth of population in the Third World, combined with inequalities in wealth and power within individual nations, means that the traditional, shifting patterns of cultivation have accelerated in their effects. Peasants forced off the land by powerful landlords either migrate to fast-growing cities or attempt to make a go of it by trying to cultivate forest areas. As cash-crop cultivation expands, as logging accelerates and populations rise, the old patterns of cultivation, which shifted in relative harmony with the ecosystems, disappear and give way to wholesale forest destruction. Aerial photographs of the rainforests of the Ivory Coast in West Africa revealed a reduction of the forest there of 30 per cent between 1956 and 1966.[39]

This growing depletion of tropical wood supplies results from ill-planned or short-term strategies by Third World governments desperate for foreign exchange from cash crops and fearful of social unrest caused by landlessness. In Brazil, a country with the largest tropical moist forest in the world (three times more than each of the next two largest tropical forest nations, Indonesia and Zaïre), the situation is desperate. The government of Brazil initially tried to settle the Amazon basin with poverty-stricken peasants from the northeast part of the country. This program, a massive failure, had as its principal result the annual loss of a million hectares of Amazon forest. The resettled smallholders were granted miserable allotments, which they abandoned in favour of shifting cultivation and slash-and-burn agriculture. The whole venture was an ill-planned scheme by a military government unable and unwilling to confront the causes of poverty in the northeast. In the end, the failure of the pioneer scheme prompted government planners, in a change of direction, to grant massive land concessions to both Brazilian and international companies to raise cattle for export.

Cattle ranching in Brazil ended up accounting for more forest destruction than agricultural colonization, road construction and commercial logging combined. Foreign agribusiness firms such as Goodyear, Volkswagen, Gulf & Western, Brascan-Swift-Armour, United Brands and Mitsui all leapt at the chance to get into Brazilian ranching. Noting that Brazil could have produced more protein by developing a prosperous Amazon fishery, the National Academy of Sciences report concluded, "Brazil seems to have little hesitation about fostering [cattle-raising] on the grounds that there are plenty of untouched forests to support the ranching industry for many years to come."[40]

The startling growth of the North American fast food industry — 20 per cent annually in the mid-1970s — may have a lot to do with this sort of tropical forest depletion. Corporate food chains anxious to tell customers about their 100 per cent pure-beef products can save a few cents on each hamburger by importing cheap, grass-fed tropical beef. In Costa Rica, in Central America, significant amounts of virgin forest were cleared by local cattle entrepreneurs keen on penetrating the profitable U.S. export market. Ecologist Joseph Tosi reported massive soil erosion in the wake of forest clearing, explaining that the land was basically unsuited for pasture, so nature had put forests on it. Though Costa Rican cattle production rose as a result of this export trend, its domestic per capita consumption of beef fell by half within fifteen years.[41] In other words, the country's forests suffered from a Big Mac attack while at the same time the country's people had less beef to eat.

Nearly half of the wood cut in the world is burned as fuel, and although this does not put particular pressure on the tropical moist forests, it does affect savannah woodlands and scrub and brush patches in many areas. Higher prices for fossil fuel have pushed former users of kerosene and similar products towards cheaper alternatives. Shortages of firewood develop, causing higher fuelwood prices. As grazing squeezes drylands in the Third World and people in need of wood for fuel forage for any fibre they can get their hands on, the slow process of desertification accelerates. In Sudan gunfights have erupted between forest rangers and armed crews illegally cutting wood for conversion into charcoal, a product with lively urban markets.[42]

The ecological consequences of tropical forest depletion are alarming. Since trees are vital producers of oxygen and since the burning of wood produces carbon dioxide, the destruction of tropical forests leads to increasing atmospheric levels of CO_2, producing a gradual warming of the atmosphere — the so-called "greenhouse effect". A U.S. State Department publication warned in 1980 that continuing tropical forest losses would contribute to the destabilization of the planet's climate in the twenty-first century.[43] Tropical forest removal, proceeding as it does in a chaotic fashion, often also results in flooding, erosion and siltation in countries where agricultural soil is a crucial resource. Furthermore, it is estimated that half the plant species on earth flourish in tropical moist forests. Many of these species will likely become extinct even before scientists can identify and classify them. "Elimination of a substantial proportion of the planetary spectrum of species will mean a gross reduction of life's diversity on earth," concluded the National Academy of Sciences. "And it will entail a permanent shift in the course of evolution, and an irreversible loss of economic opportunity as well."[44]

In the Third World, where forestry practices are primitive enough to make the Canadian approach look sophisticated by comparison, consumption of wood products is expected to grow rapidly in the future. K.F.S. King of the forestry section of the UN Food and Agriculture Organization has predicted a 500 per cent growth in demand for pulp and paper products by the five members of the Association of Southeast Asian Nations between 1975 and 2000. He has also noted a discrepancy in paper consumption among the nations of the world. In the United States, each person accounts for the consumption of 325 kilos of pulp per year. In the Third World the figure is close to five kilos. One Nigerian may not even consume the equivalent of one kilo of pulp each year — about half of one copy of the Sunday *New York Times*.[45]

Any pessimistic outlook for Canada's forests should be reassessed against this background. It is entirely possible for Third World countries to become self-sufficient in paper products. But the historical record of economies distorted by colonialism, where forests have been exhausted through agriculture and other uses and there has been no forest planning, indicate that this is unlikely to occur, at least in the foreseeable future. A turnaround in Third World forestry practices would hinge on structural changes in the way economies are organized, changes like those needed to turn Canadian forestry around.

DR. MARCEL LORTIE IS ONE forester who has given much thought to how forests could be better managed. For him, the question of jobs is crucial. An author of numerous papers and speeches, the Laval University professor of silviculture often appears at the national gatherings where forest planners regularly mull over the plight of the nation's timberlands. In 1980 Lortie got up before the industry-sponsored Canadian Forest Congress at the Ontario Science Centre in Toronto to give the assembled executives, politicians and academics his thoughts on the relationship between human and forest resources in Canada. Lortie pointed out that while total wood production had risen steadily between 1965 and 1978 (from 107 million to 157 million cubic meters), the number of direct forestry jobs had declined in the same period. The average productivity per job of each forestry worker (in this case the people who actually do the logging) *more than doubled* in a period of less than fifteen years. In other words, far fewer workers have been extracting far more wood from the forest.[46] And at the same time fewer workers are needed to process wood in the modern, automated mills.

Of course, Lortie's figures came as no surprise to company executives and woodlands managers who had been busy mechanizing harvest operations, substituting capital in the form of mobile slashers,* delimbers and feller-bunchers for labour in the woods. Employers had found that capital-intensive logging operations were the answer to problems of high rates of turnover among workers and demands for high wages and better working conditions. But while logging operators had made progress in solving their labour supply problems and making timber extraction a bit easier, Lortie noted that very little was being done to develop those skills necessary to replace the trees

* Slashers are machines that automatically cut treelength logs into shorter lengths, replacing workers who formerly did the job with chain saws.

being cut at an ever-increasing rate. He emphasized that this is where more people were needed and more jobs could be created in the fields of silviculture and forest management. In a country in need of more jobs and more merchantable trees, it would seem a wise course of action to develop the expertise to grow the trees.

At forestry meetings, concerns about foreign competition are frequently raised by people worried that Canada's competitive position as a supplier of fibre is being eroded. In the course of his appeal for more jobs in the forest management field, Lortie reminded his audience of the number of foresters Canada has available in comparison to the most frequently mentioned competitive countries. Norway and Sweden have forest conditions similar to those of eastern Canada's boreal forest. However, in Sweden there is one professional forester for every 19,000 hectares of forest under management; in Norway there is a professionally-trained manager for every 11,000 hectares. In the United States the figure is one forester for every 13,000 hectares of managed forest. But in Canada, there is one forester per 50,000 hectares. And Lortie also noted Les Reed's 1980 calculation that an additional 25,000 silvicultural jobs were necessary for the reforestation of harvested and burned-over timberland, the improvement of existing stands and the development of nurseries.[47] Those jobs, Lortie says, require foresters who appreciate the site-specific nature of a forest, foresters who have been around the woods long enough to appreciate all the aspects of what is such a complex subject. "That's one of our weaknesses, not living with the forest," the former federal forestry chief for Quebec concludes with a shrug. "We just don't know what's happening."[48]

Over the years Lortie has become a bit disillusioned with the status quo in forest management. In 1981 he told a Banff seminar, "Canada's Forest: Transition to Management", that "Forestry is politics." As Lortie put it, "So far we have not managed our forests; we have exploited them. Management begins when we start to invest in growing stock. . . . Human and financial commitments are essential but I am afraid that, as a whole, there is a tendency to go the easy way, to let the forest regenerate by itself even if in the process Canada degrades both its forests and its forest industry. The consequences can be disastrous."[49]

What happens, Lortie said, is that the political decision-

makers are tempted to leave the problems to some future government, which will be expected to perform a miracle after the
forest has already been depleted. "I am sad when I consider
what I have just described to you," Lortie told the seminar. He
added: "There is optimism, though, for in contrast, I see individuals, some labour unions, some forest companies, some provincial governments strongly committed to correct, at least par-
tially, the forest situation in Canada."

In Quebec, where some of the most productive forest land
lies not far from southern population centres, Marcel Lortie has
pinned his hopes for the future on privately-owned forest land.
Woodlots managed by their owners provided 15 per cent of the
province's wood fibre in the early 1960s. In the short space of
twenty years that figure rose to 25 per cent and Lortie expects it
will eventually hit 35 per cent. This production will come from
the intensive management of an area comprising just 15 per cent
of the forest land in Quebec, Lortie predicts.[50]

Lortie likes to use the analogy of Quebec's dairy farmers who
established marketing co-operatives in order to survive and
eventually got into the other end of the business as well by
setting up large, producer-owned manufacturing facilities. He
holds out some hope for a similar development in the wood
industry, where private landowners could manage their woodlots with an eye to the future and at the same time gain some
control over the manufacturing end currently controlled by integrated pulp and paper firms. Lortie bases his thinking on the
fact that the private land includes many of the best, southern
forest sites. There, trees grow more quickly than in the northerly
regions where many pulp companies are now forced to operate.

There is a trend, started in Quebec and slowly taking hold in
New Brunswick, for private woodlot owners to get together to
pool their resources into what have become known as *groupements forestières"*. The land, labour and a little capital from each
member of the pool are put together into a company. The small
business then collectively manages the land of all the members,
who can be paid on a wage basis for whatever harvesting and
forest management work they do on their own woodlots and
those of their fellow members. The economy of scale that the
landowners (who are sometimes part-time farmers) realize
through this co-operative endeavour can enable the business to
purchase machines like skidders and brush cleaners, which

individual woodlot owners can't easily afford. The wood the landowners produce is sold to pulp companies at a price negotiated by forest products marketing boards. Like many small farmers, the woodlot owners are frequently caught in a cost/price squeeze between their costs of production and the price the pulp mill management is willing to pay for logs. But the marketing boards and the *groupements* give them more protection than they would enjoy as individuals. And the collective enterprise enables them to be paid for planting, brush clearing, thinning and other silvicultural measures designed to sustain their own woodlots for future wood production. Government forest management subsidies are also available.

In New Brunswick, one of the largest and oldest wood marketing boards is the North Shore Forestry Syndicate, an organization that sells pulpwood cut by woodlot owners in the northeastern part of the province to several large mills in the area. Several active members of the Syndicate formed the first *groupement* in the province. Renaud Roy, an active backer of this initiative, is a woodlot owner who started working in the bush with his father when he was a teenager. Roy works doing silvicultural thinning and logging in the North Shore region around the Baie de Chaleur.

In many parts of Canada the conifer forest looks healthy and thick from the road because company cutting operations on Crown land are careful to leave strips along the highway to reassure passing motorists with the impression of an abundant forest. In the area where Renaud Roy works it's easy to distinguish private woodlots from Crown land because on private land there is clear evidence of logging right beside the road. Small landowners without powerful logging machines find it easiest to cut wood from as close to the road as possible to avoid long hauling distances and to facilitate loading.

Renaud Roy is well aware of the differences between woodlot owners and the companies like Consolidated-Bathurst and Irving that dominate the New Brunswick forest scene. Although he is experienced at silvicultural work and keen on doing as much as possible, he thinks the provincial government is more interested in helping out big companies with financial support for forest management than it is in helping out small landowners. "The small woodlot owners have a third of the forest land in the province," Roy explains. "But we get nowhere near as much money as the big companies do for silvicultural work on Crown land."[51]

Leo Sisk agrees. The part-time farmer, part-time logger who lives near the town of Black Rock, also in northeastern New Brunswick, says: "A lot of Crown land around here should be left to the farmers instead of giving it to the companies. You can't even go in the woods these days to cut wood unless you have a special permit — even to get a few logs."[52]

But the companies and the government in New Brunswick now say that they are firmly committed to intensive forest management on the clearcut Crown lands. They are proud of their ongoing seeding, planting and tending programs. The Minister of Natural Resources has boasted that New Brunswick has "the most powerful forest management program in Canada... the most intensive forest management program of any province".[53] Leo Sisk and his neighbour, Bedford Whelton, who also farms and logs, are somewhat sceptical about such claims. They think that having the industrial users manage the forest is the wrong way to go about things. They want the local users to run the show and market more pulpwood to the big mills from both private and public land, using the forest products marketing board they have set up in the region. They believe that more money should go to the small operators and farmers to pay for silvicultural work on the forest areas they log.

Similarly, Renaud Roy puts his faith in the small woodlot and the *groupement*, where logging operations can be conducted to promote new growth — unlike company cutting operations on Crown land. "The forest there is being overexploited," he says.[54] A slim, intense-looking Acadian with an easy smile, Renaud Roy acts as informal foreman of a small crew under the auspices of the *groupement*. His corner of the province is dependent on fishing and forestry, and neither promises anything close to secure employment. "But there's a future for small woodlots, though we don't get much for our wood. We have to get together — one machine for the whole gang, one payroll. If we weren't grouped, we might not even be able to work our own land."

One of Renaud Roy's fellow woodlot owners in the *groupement* is Euclide Chiasson, president of the North Shore Forestry Syndicate. Every year Chiasson sits down with negotiators from the paper companies to work out a price for the logs his members have to sell. It's a process made difficult by fluctuating markets and the concern of mill management for cheap fibre. "You can't ask the pulp and paper companies to think of anything else but supplying fibre for the making of paper," says Chiasson, who is well-known on the North Shore as an activist in the *Parti Acadien.* "They're not much interested in the rest — sawmills, recreation, wildlife, water protection."[55]

Chiasson is convinced the companies are far from committed to forestry and that people in the area are disenchanted with the government. Many of the members of the Syndicate base their annual income on the hopes of accumulating enough insurable earnings to collect unemployment insurance for the long periods each year when there is no work available. Everyone is after the magic number of weeks needed to qualify for U.I. benefits. This type of insecurity accounts for a population drain, as it does from so many resource-dependent regions of the country, with people often leaving in search of opportunities elsewhere. Historian A.R.M. Lower pointed out this trend in his 1938 history of the forest business when he looked over the succession of short bursts and long lulls in economic activity characteristic of the Atlantic region. "When export markets for all other commodities have failed," he remarked dryly, "Maritimers have consistently saved the situation by exporting themselves."[56]

For those who feel too attached to their home towns to pack up and leave, this is little comfort. From his home in Petit-Rocher, Euclide Chiasson hopes that people will come to depend more on initiatives like wood marketing boards and *groupements* and less on the government. Chiasson reasons that if forests have to be managed on sixty- or seventy-year cycles, why not let local people, who have a stake in the region six decades down the line, have a go at the job? New Brunswickers like Chiasson and Leo Sisk and Bedford Whelton bring a farmer's perspective to the forest: They see it as a natural resource. After all, they have depended on it for heat and cash income since they were young children. In their communities, most farmyards have two woodpiles, one with four-foot pulpwood for the local mill and another with firewood chopped for the winter. They identify with the forest as a sustaining part of their lives, and feel threatened by changes in the size of the economic units controlling the resource and the technology used to exploit it. They can only wonder why this has to be so.

"I think there are too many experts," Euclide Chiasson points out with some consternation. "The politicians rely on the so-called forest experts — the foresters, the graduates. People like ourselves, ordinary citizens, can't question forest policy because they say right away, 'Ah! That's a technical problem.' Before you talk about technical matters you have to talk about principles and the fundamental questions of control over the resource."[57]

Chiasson's conclusion: "A public forest has to be managed for the entire population." That's exactly what Don MacAlpine thought he was doing on the Black Bay peninsula.

NOT ALL FORESTED AREAS in Canada are close to populated areas where woodlot owners or groups of owners can manage them. Across Canada the forests are most often remote, controlled by provincial governments, licensed to corporations. It would be difficult for individual landowners to manage such areas even if people lived in great numbers there. This is the reason General Howard Kennedy told the Ontario government in 1947 that it had to establish separate operating companies to look after the woods. There had to be an independent organization, subordinate to neither pulp milling company nor provincial government, a body whose sole purpose would be to provide wood in perpetuity. Kennedy had stated baldly, "Only a major reversal of existing policies can supply a remedy" to the deterioration of the resource.[58] His recommended strategy has never been adopted anywhere in Canada, but his concern that good forest management was a matter of chance rather than design still holds true. The independent forest authorities Kennedy had in mind could still be set up, staffed with the most able people available, creating jobs for foresters and forest technicians, loggers, wildlife officials, tourist operators. Control of these bodies could be extended beyond the government and mill representatives Kennedy had in mind.

But in contrast to this hypothetical approach, in most of the principal Canadian forest jurisdictions the thrust of policy initiatives has been to turn the timberland over to forest products companies under long-term licences, along with a government promise to pay for the management of the forests. British Columbia's 1945 Sloan Commission got this ball rolling in spite of the warning veteran provincial legislator Colin Cameron issued to Sloan. Cameron said at the time that having government pick up the tab for forest management — the course industry always advises — is like telling the people to raise the cattle for the companies to milk.[59] This way of doing things perpetuates a situation in which big government and big business find it more profitable, more politically useful and more mutually advantageous to deal with each other at a good distance from the regions where the trees are actually growing and being cut, and the revenues generated. The costs of this course are borne by the forests and the results are the "Not Sufficiently Restocked" lands foresters worry so much about. The costs are also borne by people in forest regions who face the resulting community instability, and ultimately by the rest of us, who depend on the forest for the tax revenues it produces as well as for all its important environmental values.

From Terrace, B.C., Betty Kofoed's appraisal of the history of forestry boils down to the perception that there's a dollar on every tree. The trouble with this is that it ignores the rich, non-monetary aspects of the forest. And those dollars have been far too inequitably distributed among people and among regions. For you really can't talk about why some people have too little money or some areas too few trees without also mentioning the other people who have too much money and who control excessively large tracts of the remaining timberland. "The shareholders put their money to work for them and when they don't get a good return on their invested dollar, heads begin to roll," concludes George Kofoed, who has seen the results in the form of degraded forest land he helped to log. "If you don't want your head to roll you're going to bust your ass and get the shareholder the best possible return on his invested dollar."[60]

As any accountant knows, the return on investment equations rarely includes sixty-year time factors or considerations of social and environmental costs. These are external factors that have no place in what the accountants call "generally accepted auditing standards". At the same time, the notion of local control to ensure perpetuation of the forest is based on sound reasoning from a forestry perspective: Those who know the most about the vast panorama of forest sites would call the shots and make management decisions. It would also seem to be a good idea from the outlook of the people who depend for their livelihood on the wooded hinterlands of the country.

Yet given the workings of the Canadian political economy, that notion seems a remedy unlikely to be prescribed. "Supposing Terrace had taken control over the woods and the amount they produce," speculates George Kofoed, a Terrace native. "Sure we could have said we're going to produce X number of cunits per year, based on our inventories, keeping this town going for five hundred years. But that is in strict violation of the free enterprise system. . . ."

The veteran logger's voice trails off.

Glossary

Annual Allowable Cut (AAC). The idea of cutting down only a calculated amount of forest each year is the backbone to any forestry policy aiming at *sustained yield management.* It is based on the principle of cutting only an amount of wood equal to the quantity replaced each year by new growth. According to the theory, forest operators should not withdraw any of the forest "capital" but use only the annual "interest".

Artificial regeneration refers to a forestry practice of actively planting and nurturing a new generation of trees using seeds or seedlings — as opposed to *natural regeneration,* where forest establishment looks after itself without human intervention, or is attained by planned cutting methods in existing forests.

Chipping is a relatively new practice in the logging end of the forest business. A chipping operation involves a portable machine that converts whole trees and logs to chips right in the forest. The chips are then blown into a large truck for transportation to the mill. This means that whole logs or log lengths don't have to be shipped from the forest to a pulp mill. Also, in a chipping operation, all parts of the tree can be used.

Clearcutting involves the cutting down of all merchantable trees in a given area, excepting only commercially-undesirable trees and species.

Climax forest. This refers to a particular point in the life of a forest, when one or two species dominate and a kind of harmony or equilibrium is achieved. The same species comprise both the upper canopy and the young seedlings on the forest floor. On the other hand, the sequence of forest communities that makes up the process of *ecological succession* culminating in the climax forest can sometimes end before that stage, due to soil or water conditions or fire. This results in a forest never reaching the climax phase, a condition known as a sub-climax forest.

Ecological succession refers to the replacement, in time, of one distinctive plant or animal community by another. In the case of forests, this happens as the treelife becomes older and more "mature".

Ecosystems. This is defined by Barry Commoner as "the great natural, interwoven ecological cycles that comprise the planet's skin, and the minerals that lie beneath it". For the forest, it includes a piece of land and all its biological and environmental elements.

Forester and logger. Foresters, classed as professionals, have completed university courses dealing with the science of forestry, including how trees grow, forest ecology, logging, silviculture and soil science. Loggers are the workers involved in the cutting and hauling of trees.

Full tree logging is the system of tree harvesting whereby the whole tree is cut down and hauled away to a central processing point. An alternative to this is the *tree length system*.

High-grading in forestry, refers to the practice of cutting down and removing merchantable trees of the desired species and leaving the rest. The term itself is most often associated with the mining industry, where it refers to the practice of removing the richest veins and leaving the lower grades of ore in the ground.

Merchantable timber refers to trees that are considered economically usable in relation to the needs of current industrial processes.

Natural regeneration occurs where land that has been cutover or burnt out is left to renew itself without human assistance. It can also be attained by planned cutting methods that leave seed trees or blocks of standing timber.

NSR land — Not Satisfactorily Restocked (with desirable tree species).

Pulpwood is used, not unexpectedly, to produce pulp, a reconstituted form of wood, usually made from wood fibres crushed and moistened into a soft mass. As such, it can be derived from nearly any size tree containing the right type of fibre.

Rotation. A forest rotation is the time period in years it should take for a new stand of timber to become established and grow to the point where it is ready to be cut again. For spruce the period required is about seven years on good sites and ten years or more on swamp sites.

Scarification refers to the technique of churning up the forest floor to expose the mineral soil, where young seedlings can take root. It is often carried out by dragging chains or other rough, heavy objects behind a bulldozer.

Selection cutting means the practice of removing only the mature, overmature, defective and dead trees from a forest site. This gives the young and near-mature trees more light and room to grow and (through natural regeneration) promotes a forest of uneven age.

Shelterwood cutting refers to the removal of a substantial number of trees from a site, leaving enough of the original stand to provide shelter and shade for a succeeding generation. This system promotes the growth of an even-aged forest, and can involve *natural* or *artificial regeneration*.

Shortwood logging system is one in which all wood is cut into short lengths — usually 100 inches — at the stump.

Silviculture is the science of growing and tending forests for the production of wood — more simply put, tree farming.

Slash is the name for the residue left over from logging — the branches, treetops, broken and rotten trees. Forest practice has sometimes been to set fire to this residue, hence slashburning.

Square timber refers to the large "sticks" of squared-off tree trunks that were the main goal of early exploitation, and used mainly for naval purposes. Also referred to as ton timber.

Stumpage is a forestry term for the royalty that the forest owner (the government) collects from the commercial interests cutting trees on the owner's land.

Sustained yield forest management refers to the popular theory whereby forests would be managed so as to ensure supplies of wood in perpetuity, making sure the resource was not only preserved, but also renewable.

Timber. In the parlance of industrial logging, any trees or stands of trees that have potential commercial value are referred to as timber.

Timber limits or **berths** are the particular geographical areas of land for which operators receive licences to cut timber.

Tree length logging is a harvesting system where delimbing and topping take place at the stump. See also *full-tree logging*.

Tree-Farm Licences (TFLs) and **Public Sustained Yield Units (PSYUs)** are forms of tenure introduced in British Columbia in an attempt to regulate forest cutting practices and ensure sustained yield. Timber management on the TFLs was to be carried out by licensees under B.C. Forest Service supervision whereas the Forest Service itself was to administer the PSYUs (later known as Timber Supply Areas).

Endnotes

Preface

[1] A.R.M. Lower, *The North American Assault on the Canadian Forest*, Toronto, 1938.
[2] *The Forest Imperative: The Proceedings of the Canadian Forest Congress*, Toronto, 1980.
[3] Quoted in *Unasylva*, Vol. 9, No. 1, March 1955, p. 44.
[4] For a complete analysis of the economics of ecology, see Barry Commoner, *The Closing Circle*, New York, 1971; especially Chapter 12, "The Economic Meaning of Ecology".
[5] K.W. Kapp, *The Social Costs of Business Enterprise*, Nottingham, 1978 edition, p. 113.
[6] Ken Greaves of the Ontario Forest Industries Association, quoted in *Globe and Mail*, October 14, 1981.

Chapter 1

[1] Interview with George Marek, near Nipigon, Ontario, September 13, 1981.
[2] Environment Canada, *A Forest Sector Strategy for Canada: Discussion Paper*, Ottawa, September 1981.
[3] Interview with Marcel Lortie, Quebec City, October 6, 1981.
[4] Reed, F.L.C., "Forest Management in Canada Compared to Taxes Generated by the Forest Sector," *Pulp and Paper Canada*, May 1979.
[5] Environment Canada, *A Forest Sector Strategy*.
[6] Reed, F.L.C., "The Importance of the Forest Industry in the Canadian Economy", in *The Forest Imperative: The Proceedings of the Canadian Forest Congress*, Toronto, 1980.
[7] Environment Canada, *A Forest Sector Strategy*.
[8] Interview with Marcel Lortie, Quebec City, October 6, 1981.
[9] Interview with George Marek, near Nipigon, Ontario, September 13, 1981.

Chapter 2

[1] Traveller Richard Bonnycastle, 1840, cited in W.H. Graham, *The Tiger of Canada West*, Toronto, 1962, p. 91.
[2] Graham, *The Tiger of Canada West*, p. 91.
[3] *Ibid.*, p. 69.
[4] Leo A. Johnson, *History of the County of Ontario 1615-1875*, Whitby, 1973, pp. 53-54.

[5] Cited in E.D.T. Chambers, "The Forest Resources of Quebec", in A. Shortt and A. Doughty (eds.), *Canada and its Provinces*, Vol. 16, Edinburgh, 1914, p. 533.

[6] A.R.M. Lower, *Great Britain's Woodyard*, Montreal, 1973, p. 45.

[7] F. Ouellet, *Economic and Social History of Quebec, 1760-1850*, Ottawa, 1980, p. 197.

[8] Lower, *Great Britain's Woodyard*, p. 59.

[9] A.R.M. Lower, *Settlement and the Forest Frontier in Eastern Canada*, Toronto, 1936, p. 136.

[10] P.F. Fisher, *History of New Brunswick*, Saint John, 1825, cited in Lower, *Great Britain's Woodyard*, pp. 32-33.

[11] Lower, *The North American Assault*, pp. 101, 116.

[12] Archives de la Chambre de Commerce de Québec, Quebec Board of Trade, *Minute Book, 1832-1842*, report of Nov. 24, 1835, quoted in F. Ouellet, *Economic and Social History of Quebec*, p. 399.

[13] Lower, *Great Britain's Woodyard*, pp. 240-244.

[14] Quoted in D. MacKay, *The Lumberjacks*, Toronto, 1978, p. 24.

[15] Father Bourassa, quoted in *Le Journal de Québec*, May 20, 1847; cited in Ouellet, *Economic and Social History of Quebec*, p. 507.

[16] Chambers, in Shortt and Doughty, *Canada and its Provinces*, p. 535.

[17] "Report of the Commission of Finance", 1900, cited in H.V. Nelles, *The Politics of Development: Forests, Mines and Hydro-Electric Power in Ontario, 1849-1941*, Toronto, 1974, p. 18.

[18] Quoted in Lower, *The North American Assault*, p. 123.

[19] R. Brown, *Ghost Towns of Ontario*, Vol. 1, Langley, B.C., 1978.

[20] J. Langton, "On the Age of Timber Trees and the Prospects of a Continuous Supply of Timber in Canada", *Transactions of the Literary and Historical Society of Quebec*, Vol. 5, 1862, p. 61.

[21] B. Fernow, "Forest Resources and Forestry in Ontario", in Shortt and Doughty, *Canada and its Provinces*, Vol. 18, p. 599.

[22] Lower, *The North American Assault*, pp. 26, 146.

Chapter 3

[1] *Public Archives of Canada (PAC)*, Record Group (RG) 39, Vol. 414, File 12 (1).

[2] A.D. Rodgers, *Bernhard Eduard Fernow: A Story of North American Forestry*, Princeton, 1951, p. 53.

[3] W.J. McGee, quoted in S.P. Hayes, *Conservation and the Gospel of Efficiency*, Cambridge, 1959, p. 124.

[4] Nelles, *The Politics of Development*, pp. 188-194.

[5] Quoted in R.P. Gillis, "The Ottawa Lumber Barons and the Conservation Movement, 1880-1914", *The Journal of Canadian Studies*, February, 1974.

[6] For details, see B. Fernow, *History of Forestry*, Toronto, 1907, pp. 432-433; and Rodgers, *Bernhard Eduard Fernow*, pp. 297-327.

[7] M.A. Grainger, *Woodsmen of the West*, Toronto, 1964, p. 34. The dedication of Grainger's novel — "To my creditors, affectionately" — captures something of the spirit of B.C. logging at the turn of the century.

[8] Department of the Interior, Canada, *Forestry Branch Bulletin*, No. 4, Ottawa, 1909.

[9] British Columbia, *Royal Commission on Timber and Forestry*, 1910, p. D27, cited in R.H. Marris, *Pretty Sleek and Fat: The Genesis of Forest Policy in B.C., 1903-1914*, unpublished M.A. thesis, University of British Columbia, Department of History, 1979.

[10] The analysis of the Fulton Commission and early B.C. forest policy is based on R.H. Marris' thesis (see note 9, above).

[11] Cited in Marris, *Pretty Sleek and Fat*, p. 44.

[12] *Ibid.*, p. 88.

[13] G. Taylor, *Timber: The History of the Forest Industry in British Columbia*, Vancouver, 1975, p. 98.

[14] *Vancouver Sun*, November 2, 1937.

[15] Royal Commission on Canada's Economic Prospects, *The Outlook for Canadian Forest Industries*, Ottawa, 1957, p. 88.

[16] E. Forsey, "The Pulp and Paper Industry", *Canadian Journal of Economics and Political Science*, Vol. 1, 1935, p. 501.

[17] New Brunswick, *Annual Reports of Crown Lands Department and Lands and Mines Department*, New Brunswick Cabinet (Executive Council) Minutes, 1928; both cited in P. deMarsh, *Notes on the Changing Composition of the Wood-Processing Sector in New Brunswick, 1900-1980*, mimeo, 1981.

[18] E.H. Finlayson, *Saturday Night*, May 13, 1933.

[19] P. Dupin, *Anciens Chantiers du St. Maurice*, Trois Rivières, 1953, pp. 33-34.

[20] B. Hodgins *et al.*, "The Ontario and Quebec Experiments in Forest Reserves, 1883-1930", *Journal of Forest History*, January 1982.

[21] Province of Quebec, *Report of the Minister of Lands and Forests, 1924-1925: Report of the Chief of the Forestry Service*, p. 37, quoted in *Ibid.*

[22] The story is recounted by J.P. Bertrand, a veteran lakehead lumberman, in his unpublished manuscript, *Timber Wolves*, 1960, Public Archives of Ontario, Manuscript no. 124.

[23] The timber scandal has been documented in several sources: R. Lambert and P. Pross, *Renewing Nature's Wealth: A Centennial History of the Public Management of Lands, Forests and Wildlife in Ontario, 1763-1967*, Toronto, 1967; P.N. Oliver, "Howard Ferguson, The Timber Scandal and the Leadership of the Ontario Conservative Party", *Ontario History*, September 1970; Nelles, *The Politics of Development*; and Bertrand, *Timber Wolves*.

[24] Quoted in Nelles, *The Politics of Development*, p. 389.

[25] *Ibid.*, p. 397.

[26] *Forestry Quarterly*, March, 1909.

[27] Environment Canada, *A Forest Sector Strategy*, p. 10.

[28] B.E. Fernow, C.D. Howe, J.H. White, *Forest Conditions of Nova Scotia*, Ottawa, 1912; C.D. Howe, J.H. White, *Trent Watershed Survey: A Reconnaissance*, Toronto, 1913.

[29] *PAC*, RG 39, Vol. 414, File 12: letter from Clyde Leavitt to J.E. Rothery, Pejebscot Paper Company, Machias, Maine, January 8, 1920.

[30] Royal Commission on Canada's Economic Prospects, *The Outlook*, p. 92.

[31] *PAC*, RG 39, Vol. 414: draft of an article submitted to the *Financial Post* by Clyde Leavitt, September 20, 1920.

[32] *PAC*, RG 39, Vol. 84: letter from D.R. Cameron, Director of Forestry, Dominion Forest Service, to E. Kennedy, Alcan Aluminum Company, April 2, 1932.

[33] *PAC*, RG 39, Vol. 461, File 49281: speech by J.O. Wilson to the Ottawa Valley Section of the Canadian Society of Forest Engineers, 1947.

[34] *Ibid.*

[35] *PAC*, RG 39, Vol. 461: J.O. Wilson, "Some Forest Problems of Eastern Canada", 1947.

[36] *PAC*, RG 39, Vol. 413, File 3-2-0 #1: Forest Inventory Conference, June, 1929, Memorandum No. 1.

[37] Royal Commission on Canada's Economic Prospects, *The Outlook*, p. 91; and Forsey, "Pulp and Paper Industry".

[38] K.G. Fensom, *Expanding Forestry Horizons: A History of the Canadian Institute of Forestry, 1908-1969*, Montreal, 1972, p. 72.

[39] *PAC*, RG 39, Vol. 461: letter from J.S. Gillies to Hon. T.A. Crerar, February 25,

1937; and memo from R.D. Craig, Dominion Forest Service, to R.A. Gibson, Director of Lands, Parks and Forests Branch, Ministry of Mines and Resources, March 19, 1937.

[40] *Ibid.*, memo from D.R. Cameron, Dominion Forester, to Hon. T.A. Crerar, Minister of Mines and Resources, September 28, 1937.

[41] *PAC*, RG 39, Vol. 1, File 39766: Report of the Director of Forestry, 1934.

[42] G. Godwin, "A Regeneration Study of Logged-Off Lands on Vancouver Island", *Forestry Chronicle*, Vol. 14, 1938.

[43] E.C. Manning, "Sustained Yield from Canadian Forests for the Support of Permanent Forest Industries", *Forestry Chronicle*, March 1941.

[44] *PAC*, RG 39, Vol. 461.

[45] F.L.C. Reed, "Forest Management Expenditures in Canada Compared to Taxes Generated by the Forest Sector", *Pulp and Paper Canada*, May 1979.

[46] *PAC*, RG 39, Vol. 461, File 49281: memo from R.D. Craig, Dominion Forest Service, to R.A. Gibson, Director of Lands, Parks and Forests Branch, Ministry of Mines and Resources, March 21, 1940.

[47] *PAC*, RG 39, Vol. 461: memo from D.R. Cameron, Dominion Forester, to R.A. Gibson, March 25, 1943.

[48] Royal Commission on Canada's Economic Prospects, *The Outlook*, p. 91.

[49] *PAC*, RG 39, Vol. 461: speech of A.H. Williamson to the Canadian Lumberman's Association, February 13, 1945.

[50] Royal Commission on Canada's Economic Prospects, *The Outlook*, p. 61.

[51] *Financial Post*, September 20, 1947.

[52] Royal Commission on Canada's Economic Prospects, *The Outlook*, p. 94.

[53] *Ibid.*, pp. 63-4.

[54] *PAC*, RG 39, Vol. 403: minutes of a meeting at the Petawawa Forest Experiment Station, May 1945.

[55] G.M. Sloan, *Report of the Commission Relating to the Forest Resources of British Columbia*, Victoria, 1945, p. 142.

[56] British Columbia Department of Trade and Industry, *The Growth of Ghost Towns*, brief submitted to the Royal Commission Relating to the Forest Resources of B.C., 1944.

[57] P.H. Pearse, *Timber Rights and Forest Policy in B.C.: Report of the Royal Commission on Forest Resources*, Vol. 2, Victoria, 1976, p. A26.

[58] H. Kennedy, *Report of the Royal Commission on Forestry*, Toronto, 1947, p. 9.

[59] *Ibid.*, p. 192.

[60] *Ibid.*, p. 188.

[61] *Ibid.*, p. 29.

[62] *Ibid.*, p. 187.

[63] Both papers quoted in *Financial Post*, August 23, 1947 and August 30, 1947.

[64] *Financial Post*, September 13, 1947.

[65] Quoted in H.B. Lent, *From Trees to News: The Story of Newsprint*, New York, 1952, p. 22.

Chapter 4

[1] Gordon Gibson interviewed by C.D. Orchard, January 4, 1960, in *Orchard Forest History Collection (Orchard Papers)*, University of British Columbia Library Special Collections.

[2] G. Gibson, *Bull of the Woods*, Vancouver, 1980.

[3] The conversation is part of Gibson's interview with Orchard, *Orchard Papers*.

[4] Environment Canada, *A Forest Sector Strategy*, p. 2.

[5] A. Zimmerman, "Investment in Foresters", *Policy Options*, Vol. 3, No. 1, January/February 1982.

[6] Interview with Bill Pauli, Toronto, Ontario, November 12, 1981.

[7] Gibson, *Bull of the Woods,* p. 213.

[8] *Ibid.,* p. 153.

[9] *Ibid.,* p. 220.

[10] Gibson in *Orchard Papers.*

[11] Gibson, *Bull of the Woods,* p. 222.

[12] Gibson in *Orchard Papers.*

[13] *Ibid.*

[14] Pearse, *Timber Rights and Forest Policy;* see especially Chapter 4, "The Industry".

[15] *Ibid.,* p. 42.

[16] *Ibid.,* Tables 4-2 and 4-3.

[17] *Ibid.,* pp. 42-43.

[18] *Vancouver Province,* March 5, 1980.

[19] F.L.C. Reed and Associates, *Forest Management in Canada* (three volumes), Forest Management Institute Reports FMR-X-102, 103, 104, Canadian Forestry Service, Environment Canada, 1978; F.L.C. Reed and Associates, *Forest Management in Canada and Forest Sector Revenue,* prepared for the Canadian Pulp and Paper Association, 1979; Environment Canada, *A Forest Sector Strategy.*

[20] Reed *et al., Forest Management in Canada,* Vol. 1, Table 26, and pp. 23, 7.

[21] *Ibid.,* Vol. 3, p. 38.

[22] Reed *et al., Forest Management in Canada and Forest Sector Revenue;* and F.L.C. Reed, "Forest Management in Canada Compared to Taxes Generated by the Forest Sector", *Pulp and Paper Canada,* May 1979.

[23] Reed *et al., Forest Management in Canada,* Vol. 1, p. 54.

[24] Interview with F.L.C. Reed, Hull, Quebec, November 17, 1981.

[25] *Ibid.*

[26] *Ibid.*

[27] Interview with Gerry Burch, Vancouver, B.C., February 12, 1982.

[28] *Ibid.*

[29] *Vancouver Sun,* June 16, 1978.

[30] Interview with Terry Slaney, Parksville, B.C., March 5, 1982.

[31] Interview with Gerry Burch, Vancouver, B.C., February 12, 1982.

[32] *Ibid.;* and interview with F.L.C. Reed, Hull, Quebec, November 17, 1981. Reed expresses similar confidence in future wood supply assured by the allowable cut effect.

[33] Interview with Bill Young, Victoria, B.C., March 8, 1982.

[34] *Ibid.*

[35] British Columbia Forest Service, *Annual Reports,* various years.

[36] *Ibid.*

[37] Interview with Bill Young, Victoria, B.C., March 8, 1982.

[38] Interview with Bob Ploss, Slocan Park, B.C., February 5, 1982.

[39] *Ibid.*

[40] Reed *et al., Forest Management in Canada,* Vol. 3, Table 5.

[41] Interview with Bob Ploss, Slocan Park, B.C., February 5, 1982.

[42] *Ibid.*

[43] Interview with Gerry Burch, Vancouver, B.C., February 12, 1982; and interview with F.L.C. Reed, Hull, Quebec, November 17, 1981.

[44] Royal Bank of Canada, "The Forest and the Trees", *Monthly Letter,* Vol. 60, No. 7, July, 1979.

[45] John Walters, "Summation Address to the National Forest Regeneration Conference, Quebec City, October, 1977", in *Proceedings of the National Forest Regeneration Conference,* Canadian Forestry Association, 1977, p. 214.

[46] *Ibid.,* pp. 213, 216, 223.

[47] *Ibid.*, p. 216.

[48] Interview with Ken Hearnden, Normandale, Ontario, August 14, 1981.

[49] Interview with F.L.C. Reed, Hull, Quebec, November 17, 1981.

[50] Forest Management Agreement, No. 500500, signed August 11, 1980, between the Ontario Ministry of Natural Resources and the E.B. Eddy Company under The Crown Timber Act, as amended, and the Public Lands Act.

[51] Interview with Ken Hearnden, Normandale, Ontario, August 14, 1981.

[52] *Ibid.*

[53] *Ibid.*

[54] Interview with Bill Pauli, Toronto, Ontario, November 12, 1981.

[55] Interview with Ken Hearnden, Normandale, Ontario, August 14, 1981.

[56] Background on Terrace area logging from B.R. Kofoed and G. Kofoed, *The Social, Economic and Environmental Effects of Logging in the Terrace Area*, mimeo, Terrace, B.C., 1979.

[57] Interview with Betty Kofoed, Terrace, B.C., February 27, 1982.

[58] Interview with George Kofoed, Terrace, B.C., February 27, 1982.

[59] *Ibid.*

[60] *Ibid.*

[61] Interview with Jack Walters, Maple Ridge, B.C., February 15, 1982.

[62] Interview with Ross Silversides, Ottawa, Ontario, July 20, 1981.

Chapter 5

[1] A. Koroleff, "The Role of Forest Utilization in Forest Management", *Pulp and Paper Magazine of Canada*, March 1941.

[2] Quoted in *Canadian Lumberman*, February 15, 1918; cited in Ian Radforth, *The Mechanization of the Pulpwood Logging Industry in Northern Ontario, 1950-1970*, paper presented to the Canadian Historical Association, mimeo, June 1982.

[3] J.A. McNally, "Mechanization in the Woods: From the 1930s to the 1970s", *Pulp and Paper Canada*, September 1978.

[4] PAC, RG 39, Vol. 461, File 49281: speech by J.O. Wilson to the Ottawa Valley Section of the Canadian Society of Forest Engineers, 1947.

[5] *Pulp and Paper Magazine of Canada*, January 1941.

[6] PAC, RG 39, Vol. 403, File 47272.

[7] E. Lucia, "Joe Cox and His Revolutionary Saw Chain", *Journal of Forest History*, July, 1981.

[8] *Ibid.*

[9] Interview with Jake Hildebrand, Vermilion Bay, Ontario, June 1, 1981.

[10] Interview with Terry Slaney, Parksville, B.C., March 5, 1982.

[11] J.P. Curran, *The Process of Mechanization in the Forest Industry of Newfoundland: An Analysis of Technological Change and Worker Resistance to Change*, unpublished M.A. thesis, Memorial University, Nfld., 1971.

[12] T.M. Pond, "Report of the Cutting Tool Committee", *Woodlands Section Report*, No. 1274, October 1952.

[13] Interview with Ross Silversides, Maitland, Ontario, June 23, 1982.

[14] "Technological Change and its Consequences on Woods Operations", *Pulp and Paper Canada*, April 1963.

[15] *Ibid.*

[16] *Pulp and Paper Canada*, March 1968.

[17] Interview with Ross Silversides, Ottawa, Ontario, July 20, 1981.

[18] R. Silversides, "Achievements and Failures in Logging Mechanization — Why?", *Pulp and Paper Canada*, February 1972.

[19] Interview with Ross Silversides, Maitland, Ontario, June 23, 1982.

[20] R. Silversides, "Achievements and Failures".

[21] Pulp and Paper Research Institute of Canada, *Woodlands Report No. 28,* (Prototype Evaluation: Koehring Shortwood Harvester), October 1970.
[22] R. Silversides, "Progress and Problems in the Mechanization of Forest Work in Relation to Modern Silvicultural Techniques", *The Proceedings of the Seventh World Forestry Congress,* Buenos Aires, 1972, p. 962.
[23] Forest Engineering Research Institute of Canada, *Technical Report No. 7,* September 1976; and interview with Mike, a feller-forwarder operator for Great Lakes Forest Products Company, August 7, 1981. Mike's surname was not audible due to the "73-86 dBa" in the cab of the machine: sound measured by FERIC *Technical Report No. 7.*
[24] Interview with Don Harris, Great Lakes Forest Products camp supervisor, August 7, 1981.
[25] Interview with Bedford Whelton and Leo Sisk, Black Rock, N.B., May 27, 1982.
[26] R.V. Stuart, interviewed by C.D. Orchard, *Orchard Papers,* Interview No. 26.
[27] *Pulp and Paper Magazine of Canada,* March 1941.
[28] These concerns are still widely debated among forest researchers who, in the absence of long-term, scientifically-based research on Canadian conditions, can still only speculate as to the effects of logging on future forest productivity. See *The Impact of Intensive Harvesting on Forest Nutrient Cycling,* the proceedings of a conference held at the State University of New York (Syracuse) School of Forestry, 1979 and note particularly I.K. Morrison and N.W. Foster, "Biomass and Element Removal by Complete Tree Harvesting of Medium Rotation Forest Stands". See also V.R. Timmer and H. Savinsky, *Impact of Intensive Harvesting on Forest Nutritional Budgets in the Nipigon Area,* University of Toronto, Faculty of Forestry, 1981. Also, I.K. Morrison, "Full Tree Harvesting: Disadvantages from a Forest's Viewpoint", in *Pulp and Paper Canada,* October 1980.
[29] *PAC,* RG 39, Vol. 510, File 30-2-3: I.C.M. Place, "The Impact of Mechanization on Silviculture in Eastern Canada", mimeo, 1964.
[30] *Ibid.*
[31] G. Frisque *et al.,* "Reproduction and Trial Projected Yields Ten Years after Cutting 36 Pulpwood Stands in Eastern Canada", *FERIC Technical Report,* No. TR-23, April 1978.
[32] *Ibid.,* p. 4.
[33] *Ibid.,* pp. iii-iv.
[34] G. Weetman, "The Need to Study Silvicultural Effects of Mechanized Logging Systems in Eastern Canada", *Forestry Chronicle,* June 1965. At the time he made these observations about industry's priorities, Weetman was employed by the Pulp and Paper Research Institute of Canada, the research arm of the Canadian pulp and paper industry.
[35] Wilmot MacDonald, quoted in D. MacKay, *The Lumberjacks.*
[36] See Reasons *et al., Assault on the Worker: Occupational Health and Safety in Canada,* Toronto, 1981, Table 2-3; Labour Canada, Occupational Safety and Health Branch, *Fatalities in Canadian Industry, 1969-1978,* Ottawa, 1980.
[37] British Columbia Workers' Compensation Board, *Annual Reports,* various years, 1940-1980.
[38] Interview, (anonymous), Great Lakes Forest Products, August 7, 1981.
[39] D. Lanskail, "Union Attitude and Employees' Carelessness Hamper Cause of Industrial Health and Safety", *CLV Reports: Health and Safety Forum,* November 17, 1980.
[40] Interview with George Kofoed, Terrace, B.C., February 27, 1982.
[41] E. Ekstrom, "Increased Safety in Forestry: Fixed Wages — Fewer Accidents", *Working Environment,* (Annual), Sweden, 1981.
[42] P.V. Pelnar *et al.,* "Vibration Disease in Forestry Workers in Canada"; Brubaker *et al.,* "Vibration White Finger among Forestry Chain Saw Workers in Canada";

G. Theriault *et al.*, "Étude de la Prévalence du Phénomène de Raynaud chez les Travailleurs Forestières de la Province de Québec"; all in *Abstracts of the Third International Symposium on Hand-Arm Vibration*, Ottawa, May, 1981; see also A.J. Brammer, *Chain Saw Vibration: Its Measurement, Hazard and Control*, National Research Council, Ottawa, 1978; G.P. Laroche, "Traumatic Vasospastic Disease in Chain Saw Operators", *Canadian Medical Association Journal*, December 18, 1976.

[43] J.C. Paterson, "Canadian Compensation Law and Vibration-Induced White Finger: A Preliminary Description", paper presented to the Third International Symposium on Hand-Arm Vibration, Ottawa, May, 1981.

[44] J. Gregg, "Chain Saw Vibration: Loggers Face Daily Pain from White Finger", *International Woodworkers of America Region 1 Annual*, 1979.

[45] Interview with William Taylor, Ottawa, Ontario, May 5, 1982.

[46] Data obtained from John Nicolaiff, Environment Canada, interview, June 15, 1982.

[47] D. Noble, *America By Design: Science, Technology and the Rise of Corporate Capitalism*, Oxford, 1977, p. xvii.

Chapter 6

[1] D.J. Stuart, "Where are We in the Multiple Use Picture?", *Pulp and Paper Canada*, September 1970.

[2] The CPPA ads cited appeared in the *Globe and Mail*, October and November 1978.

[3] G.H. Lash, *A Walk in the Forest*, Montreal, 1976, p. 5.

[4] *Ibid.*, p. 31.

[5] Interview with Hamish Kimmins, Vancouver, B.C., March 12, 1982.

[6] J.P. Kimmins, "The Renewability of Natural Resources — Implications for Forest Management", *Journal of Forestry*, May, 1973; "The Ecology of Forestry — The Ecological Role of Man, the Forester, in Forest Ecosystems", *Forestry Chronicle*, December 1972; "Forest Ecology — The Biological Basis for the Management of Renewable Forest Resources", *Forestry Chronicle*, February 1973; "Sustained Yield, Timber Mining, and the Concept of Ecological Rotation — A British Columbian View", *Forestry Chronicle*, February 1974; "Evaluation of the Consequences for Future Tree Productivity of the Loss of Nutrients in Whole-Tree Harvesting", *Forest Ecology and Management*, No. 1, 1977.

[7] J.P. Kimmins, "The Ecology of Forestry".

[8] *Ibid.*

[9] *Ibid.*

[10] J.P. Kimmins, "The Renewability of Natural Resources".

[11] Interview with Herb Hammond, Vallican, B.C., February 9, 1982.

[12] *Ibid.*

[13] *Ibid.*

[14] J. Toovey, "Incentives for More Intensive Forest Management — Industrial Viewpoint from B.C.", *Pulp and Paper Canada*, July 1979.

[15] F.L.C. Reed, *Will There Be Enough Trees in Canada?*, Address to the American Paper Institute, Homestead, Virginia, October 1981.

[16] Kimmins, "Evaluation of the Consequences".

[17] *B.C. Lumberman*, September, 1980.

[18] V.R. Timmer and H. Savinsky, *Impact of Intensive Harvesting on Forest Nutritional Budgets in the Nipigon Area*, Faculty of Forestry, University of Toronto, 1981; interview with Vic Timmer, Toronto, September 24, 1981.

[19] J.P. Kimmins, *et al.*, *FORCYTE — An Ecologically-based Computer Simulation Model to Evaluate the Effect of Intensive Forest Management on the Productivity, Eco-*

nomics and Energy Balance of Forest Biomass Production, Faculty of Forestry, University of British Columbia, 1981.
20 *Ibid.*
21 *Ibid.*
22 A. Koroleff *et al., Stability as a Factor in Efficient Forest Management*, Pulp and Paper Research Institute of Canada, Montreal, 1951; see especially pp. 257-267.
23 *Ibid.,* p. 260.
24 *Ibid.,* p. 262.
25 W.M. Robertson, "Silviculture — Cost and Production", in Koroleff *et al., Stability as a Factor.*
26 Anonymous forester in *Forestry Chronicle*, 1935; cited in Fensom, *Expanding Forestry Horizons,* p. 83.
27 Task Force for Evaluation of Budworm Control Alternatives, *Report,* Fredericton, 1976, pp. 8-9.
28 Province of New Brunswick, *Report of the Forest Resources Study,* Fredericton, 1974, p. 60.
29 *Ibid.,* p. 61.
30 *Forestry Quarterly,* March 1909.
31 New Brunswick Forest Development Commission, *Report,* Fredericton, 1957, p. 57; cited in P.G. deMarsh, *Notes on the History of New Brunswick's Forest Resource,* mimeo, 1981, p. 29.
32 J.D. Tothill, "An Estimate of the Damage Done in New Brunswick by the Spruce Budworm", *Proceedings of the Acadian Entomological Society,* 1921, pp. 45-48; and "Notes on the Outbreaks of Spruce Budworm, Forest Tent Caterpillar and Larch Sawfly in New Brunswick", in *Proceedings of the Acadian Entomological Society,* 1922, pp. 172-182; cited in P.G. deMarsh, *Notes on the History,* p. 32.
33 J.M. Swaine and F.C. Craighead, "Studies on the Spruce Budworm", *Bulletin,* No. 37, Dept. of Agriculture, Ottawa, 1924; cited in P.G. deMarsh, *Notes on the History,* p. 31.
34 J.J. deGryse and M. Westveld, cited in A. Koroleff, *Stability as a Factor,* pp. 250-251.
35 A. Koroleff, *Stability as a Factor,* p. 253.
36 Interview with Ken Hearnden, Normandale, Ontario, August 14, 1982.
37 R. Carson interview aired on *The Journal,* CBC, June 16, 1982.
38 Tothill, "Notes on the Outbreaks".
39 For details of this and other New Brunswick scandals of the time, see A.T. Doyle, *Front Benches and Back Rooms,* Toronto, 1976, especially Chapter 2.
40 Task Force for Evaluation of Budworm Control Alternatives, *Report,* pp. 120-121.
41 *Ibid.,* p. 62.
42 H. Thurston *et al.,* "The Enemy Above", in *Harrowsmith,* April/May, 1982.
43 Quoted in *ibid.*
44 F. Stevens and W. Schabas, "Budworm Fighters Seek New Weapons", *Pulp and Paper Canada,* October 1978.
45 *Halifax Chronicle-Herald,* February 8, 1982.
46 *Ibid.,* November 19, 1981.
47 J.A. Gray, *The Trees Beyond the Shore: The Forests and Forest Industries in Newfoundland and Labrador,* Economic Council of Canada, Ottawa, 1981, p. 13.
48 *PAC,* RG 39, Vol. 403, File 47272.
49 Correspondence from G. Baskerville, Assistant Deputy Minister, New Brunswick Department of Natural Resources, to P. Leblanc, President of the New Brunswick Federation of Woodlot Owners, April 23, 1982.
50 Quoted in Thurston *et al.,* "The Enemy Above".
51 Correspondence from G. Baskerville to P. Leblanc, May 11, 1982.

[52] Interview with Dave Curtis, May 31, 1982.

[53] Concerned Parents Group, *Press Release*, March 6, 1981.

[54] G. Baskerville, quoted in the *St. Croix Courier*, St. Stephen, N.B., January 6, 1982.

[55] Interview with Aurele Mallet, Bathurst, N.B., May 30, 1982.

Chapter 7

[1] Quoted in P. George, "Southern Moresby: Just Another Wilderness Area?", in *Telkwa Foundation Newsletter*, Vol. 2, No. 2, January 1979.

[2] *Ibid.*

[3] South Moresby Wilderness Planning Team, *Ecological Reserve Proposals: Windy Bay Watershed/Dodge Point, Queen Charlotte Islands*, December 1981, p. 21.

[4] *Ibid.*, pp. 27-28.

[5] International Woodworkers of America Regional Council No. 1, *1979 Annual*, pp. 121-122.

[6] R. Overstall, "Rennell Sound: The End of Multiple Use?", *Telkwa Foundation Newsletter*, Vol. 2, No. 5, April 1979.

[7] Quoted in T. Donnelly and C. Martin, "Fall Rains at Rennell Sound", documentary broadcast on *Northwest Morning*, CBC, December 12, 1979; reprinted in *Telkwa Foundation Newsletter*, Vol. 3, No. 1, January/February 1980.

[8] R. Overstall, "Rennell Sound".

[9] *B.C. Business Week*, April 4, 1979.

[10] B. Wright, "Effect of Stream Driving on Fish, Wildlife and Recreation", *Pulp and Paper Canada*, November 1962.

[11] D. Estrin and J. Swaigen, *Environment on Trial: A Handbook of Ontario Environmental Law* (revised edition), Toronto, 1978, pp. 181-182.

[12] L. D'Amore, "The Canadian Forest: For Profit, For People or Both", *Business Quarterly*, April 1973.

[13] R.D. Ayling and B. Graham, "A Survey of Herbicide Use in Canadian Forestry", *Forestry Chronicle*, December 1978.

[14] *St. Croix Courier*, St. Stephen, N.B., July 23, 1980.

[15] Canadian Forestry Association, *Annual Report*, 1909, p. 77; cited in Nelles, *The Politics of Development*, p. 186.

[16] For a comparison of the two movements, see S.P. Hays, "The Environmental Movement", *Journal of Forest History*, October 1981.

[17] S. McNeil, "The Trouble with Clearcutting", *The Carpenter* (Official Publication of the International Brotherhood of Carpenters and Joiners), January 1973.

[18] Stewart, "Where Are We in the Multiple Use Picture?".

[19] *Globe and Mail*, October 14, 1981.

[20] K.D. Greaves, *Speech to the Municipal Advisory Committee of Northwestern Ontario*, June 6, 1981.

[21] *Globe and Mail*, October 14, 1981.

[22] Ontario Ministry of Industry and Tourism, *Northwestern Ontario: A Strategy for Development*, Toronto, 1978.

[23] *Globe and Mail*, June 4, 1981.

[24] Lakehead Social Planning Council, *The Forest Industry in Northwestern Ontario: A Socio-Economic Study from a Social Planning Perspective*, Thunder Bay, July 1981.

[25] Canadian Environmental Law Research Foundation (Willms *et al.*), *The Administrative Basis of Land Use and Environmental Decision-Making North of Latitude 50°: A Guidebook and Selected Observations*, Thunder Bay, March 1980, p. 202.

[26] Interview with Bill Addison, Thunder Bay, Ontario, August 23, 1982.

[27] *Northern Daily News*, Kirkland Lake, Ontario, April 29, 1982.

[28] Interview with Ken Hearnden, Normandale, Ontario, August 14, 1981.

[29] *Ibid.*

[30] A. Abugov, *A Review of the Socio-Economic and Demographic Data Relevant to Assessing Child Welfare Needs in Northern Ontario,* prepared for the Administrative Staff of Northern Children's Aid Societies and the Ontario Association of Children's Aid Societies, September 1980.

[31] *Ibid.*

[32] Lakehead Social Planning Council, *The Forest Industry in Northwestern Ontario,* p. 48.

[33] Interview with Don Smith, Lakehead Social Planning Council, June 14, 1982.

[34] CPPA, *The Forest Environment,* report of a seminar on forestry and the environment, 1972.

[35] Interview with Gerry Burch, Vancouver, B.C., February 12, 1982.

[36] K. Bernsohn, *Cutting Up The North,* Vancouver, 1981, p. 139.

[37] Interview with Richard Overstall, Smithers, B.C., February 24, 1982.

[38] See especially: Smithers Forest Advisory Committee, *The AAC in the Smithers PSYU,* April 19, 1977; and Smithers Forest Advisory Committee, *Brief to Tom Waterland,* February 2, 1979.

[39] Letter from A.C. MacPherson, District Forester, to Smithers Forest Advisory Committee, May 12, 1978.

[40] Smithers Forest Advisory Committee, *The AAC in the Smithers PSYU.*

[41] Letter from A.C. MacPherson to Smithers Forest Advisory Committee, June 30, 1978.

[42] Smithers Forest Advisory Committee, *Brief to Tom Waterland.*

[43] Interview with Bill Young, Victoria, B.C., March 8, 1982.

[44] Interview with Gerry Burch, Vancouver, B.C., February 12, 1982.

[45] Interview with Richard Overstall, Smithers, B.C., February 24, 1982.

[46] M. Trew, "Forestry Management", *B.C. Outdoors,* December/January 1982.

[47] Interview with Michael Trew, Victoria, B.C., March 9, 1982.

[48] Interview with Gerry Burch, February 12, 1982.

[49] Interview with Michael Trew, Victoria, B.C., March 9, 1982.

[50] *Financial Post,* May 31, 1980.

[51] Interview with Susie Hammond, Vallican, B.C., February 9, 1982.

[52] Interview with Herb Hammond, Vallican, B.C., February 9, 1982.

[53] *Nelson Daily News,* June 2, 1976.

[54] *Vancouver Province,* September 7, 1980; *Nelson Daily News,* January 22, 1981.

[55] Slocan Valley Community Forest Management Project, *Final Report,* 1974, p. 4-1.

[56] *Ibid.,* p. 3-7.

[57] Interview with Corky Evans, Winlaw, B.C., February 4, 1982.

[58] *Ibid.*

[59] *Nelson Daily News,* April 25, 1980.

[60] E.S. Fellows, *The Moulding of Public Opinion on Forest Management: What Public, Whose Opinion?,* Faculty of Forestry and Landscape Architecture, Weyerhauser Lecture Series, University of Toronto, November 1975.

[61] R. Carson, *Silent Spring,* New York, 1966 edition, p. 23.

Chapter 8

[1] Letter from W.T. Foster, Deputy Minister of the Ontario Ministry of Natural Resources, to A.S. Fleming, vice-president of Domtar Ltd., April 22, 1981; interview with David Bak and Lief Gran, Thunder Bay, Ontario, June 12, 1982; testimony of Edward Markus, Director, Timber Sales Branch, Ontario Ministry of Natural Resources, to the Ontario Public Service Grievance Settlement Board, August 30, 1982.

[2] Memo from W.T. Foster to G.A. McCormack, Assistant Deputy Minister of Natural Resources for Northern Ontario, June 5, 1981.

[3] Testimony of Don MacAlpine to the Ontario Public Service Grievance Settlement Board, August 31, 1982.

[4] Interview with David Bak and Lief Gran, Thunder Bay, June 12, 1982.

[5] See, for instance, Bertrand, *Timber Wolves.*

[6] Ontario Commission on Election Contributions and Expenses, *Statement of Campaign Receipts and Expenses*, Form CR-1, Hon. Leo Bernier, Kenora Electoral District, December 5, 1977 and September 8, 1981.

[7] Interview with A.S. Fleming, vice-president of Domtar Ltd., broadcast on *The Fifth Estate*, CBC, October 29, 1981.

[8] Testimony of Don MacAlpine, August 31, 1982.

[9] Interview with Don MacAlpine, Nipigon, Ontario, June 10, 1982.

[10] Testimony of Don MacAlpine, August 31, 1982.

[11] Interview with Glen Swant, Toronto, Ontario, August 30, 1982.

[12] K.A. Armson, *Forest Management in Ontario*, Ministry of Natural Resources, Toronto, 1976, p. 130.

[13] *Ibid.*, p. 140.

[14] *Ibid.*, pp. 142, 139.

[15] Interview with Don MacAlpine, Nipigon, Ontario, June 10, 1982.

[16] Testimony of Don MacAlpine, August 31, 1982.

[17] For details on the historical development of European forestry, see B.E. Fernow, *History of Forestry*, Toronto, 1911.

[18] Interview with George Marek, Thunder Bay, Ontario, August 5, 1981; and near Nipigon, Ontario, September 13, 1981.

[19] Interview with Herb Hammond, Vallican, B.C., February 9, 1982.

[20] Interview with Helen Marek, Beardmore, Ontario, June 9, 1982.

[21] Interview with George Marek, near Nipigon, Ontario, September 13, 1981.

[22] Interview with Vic Timmer, Toronto, Ontario, September 24, 1981.

[23] Interview with George Marek, Thunder Bay, Ontario, August 5, 1981; and near Nipigon, Ontario, September 13, 1981.

[24] J. Walters, *Summation Address*, p. 213.

[25] Interview with George Marek, Thunder Bay, Ontario, August 5, 1981.

[26] *Globe and Mail*, November 27, 1982.

[27] Interview with George Marek, Thunder Bay, Ontario, August 5, 1981.

[28] M. Lortie, "Human Resource Development in the Canadian Forest Industry", *Proceedings of the Canadian Forest Congress*, Toronto, 1980.

[29] See D.W. Einspahr and M.L. Harder, "Acid Rain: Its Effects on the Forest Industry", *TAPPI*, April 1981; P.J. Rennie, "Acid Rain and the Forest: A Serious But Elusive Threat", *Canadian Pulp and Paper Industry*, August 1980; and M. Livingstone, "The Industrial Plague", *Canadian Forest Industries*, June 1982.

[30] Interview with Keith Burcher, Omnifuel Gasification Systems Ltd., Toronto, Ontario, July 23, 1981.

[31] Interview with Jacques Lecours, Bioshell Inc., Hearst, Ontario, July 7, 1981.

[32] *Canadian Renewable Energy News*, Vol. 4, No. 2, April 1981, supplement on industrial wood energy.

[33] I.S. Goldstein, *Chemicals from Wood*, paper presented to the Eighth World Forestry Congress, Jakarta, Indonesia, 1978.

[34] C.R. Silversides, *Industrial Forestry in a Changing Canada*, University of Alberta Forest Industry Lecture Series No. 1, 1977.

[35] C.R. Silversides, "Forest Biomass for Energy and Forest Industries", *Pulp and Paper Canada*, September 1981.

[36] Environment Canada, "A Forest Sector Strategy for Canada", September 1981.

[37] National Academy of Sciences, *Conversion of Tropical Moist Forests*, Washington, 1980, p. 173.

[38] *Ibid.*, p. 175.
[39] J.P. Lanly, "Régression de la Forêt en Côte d'Ivoire", *Bois et Forêts des Tropiques*, September/October 1969; cited in E. Eckholm, *Planting for the Future: Forestry for Human Needs*, Worldwatch Paper No. 26, February 1979, p.18.
[40] National Academy of Sciences, *Conversion of Tropical Moist Forests*, p. 125. This report provides a detailed examination of the Brazilian situation, pp. 118-130.
[41] *Tico Times*, November 3, 1978, cited in Eckholm, *Planting for the Future*, p. 17.
[42] Eckholm, *Planting for the Future*, p. 20.
[43] U.S. Interagency Task Force on Tropical Forests, *The World's Tropical Forests: A Policy, Strategy and Program for the U.S.*, Washington, Department of State, 1980, p. 2.
[44] National Academy of Sciences, *Conversion of Tropical Moist Forests*.
[45] K.F.S. King, "The Political Economy of Pulp and Paper", *Unisylva*, No. 117; National Academy of Sciences, *The Conversion of Tropical Moist Forests*, p. 38.
[46] Lortie, "Human Resource Development in the Canadian Forest Industry".
[47] *Ibid.*
[48] Interview with Marcel Lortie, Quebec City, Quebec, October 6, 1981.
[49] M. Lortie, *Some Institutional Constraints to Intensive Forest Management in Canada*, paper presented to the conference, "Canada's Forests: Transition to Management", Banff, Alberta, 1981.
[50] Interview with Marcel Lortie, Quebec City, Quebec, September 9, 1982.
[51] Interview with Renaud Roy, Bathurst, N.B., May 26, 1982.
[52] Interview with Leo Sisk, Black Rock, N.B., May 27, 1982.
[53] Hon. Bud Bird, New Brunswick Minister of Natural Resources, *Press Release*, October 8, 1981.
[54] Interview with Renaud Roy, Bathurst, N.B., May 26, 1982.
[55] Interview with Euclide Chiasson, Bathurst, N.B., May 30, 1982.
[56] A.R.M. Lower, *The North American Assault*, pp. 77-78.
[57] Interview with Euclide Chiasson, Bathurst, N.B., May 30, 1982.
[58] H. Kennedy, *Report of the Royal Commission on Forestry*, p. 184.
[59] C. Cameron, *Brief to the Royal Commission on the Forest Resources of B.C.*, Public Archives of B.C., RG 529, September 9, 1944.
[60] Interview with George Kofoed, Terrace, B.C., February 27, 1982.

Photo Credits

A new series:

Ecology and Resources

Chemical Nightmare: The Unnecessary Legacy of Toxic Wastes
    by John Jackson, Phil Weller and the Waterloo Public Interest
    Research Group
Electric Empire: The Inside Story of Ontario Hydro
    by Paul MacKay and OPIRG
Cut and Run: The Assault on Canada's Forests
    by Jamie Swift

With these three titles, Between The Lines initiates a series of books
that explore the economic and environmental consequences of
Canada's resource-based strategy of growth.

The **Ecology and Resources** series draws connections between
pollution, economic stagnation and rapidly depleting resources. It
examines the forces that generate waste in our throwaway society's
mad rush for profits and growth, and argues that we need a new
social vision; that we can no longer afford the "business-as-usual"
approach to economic growth.

The series examines the main actors — like the huge utility Ontario
Hydro and the timber companies that are sacrificing our environment
and future resources to short-term gain. It exposes the tunnel vision
that is destroying the ecological basis of life through chemical
pollutants, acid rain, toxic wastes and radiation poisoning.

Chemical Nightmare is a devastating critique of the failure of current
waste management strategies — a critique based on the authors'
knowledge of techniques and technologies already available that
could eliminate the problem of environmental destruction by
poisonous wastes.

Electric Empire documents how Ontario Hydro's uncontrolled and
unnecessary expansion program has created a $15 billion public debt,
stripped the Ontario Treasury of funding for social services, and
caused incalculable environmental damage.